"Dr. Gustavo Parajón was caring, compassionate, and brilliant. He was a peace-maker, a miracle healer, and an educator. He transformed people's lives for the better."

Dr. Lidya Ruth Zamora, Director of the School of Nursing and former President of the Polytechnic University, Managua, Nicaragua

"We exclaim in paraphrase, what has been said of the martyr Monsignor Oscar Arnulfo Romero: With Dr. Gustavo Adolfo Parajón Dominguez, God passed through Nicaragua."

Rev. Carlos I. Sanchez, Pastor of First Baptist Church in San Salvador, El Salvador

"Gustavo Parajón, a true Christian peacemaker, dedicated his life to putting his faith into action with intelligence and compassion."

President Jimmy Carter

"Gustavo was a mentor to all those of us connected with Amos Trust and Greenbelt Festival—we learnt from him. He taught us how listen to poorer communities with dignity and respect. His love of the Bible, and exposition of it, reflected a generous, non-violent, loving God whom Gustavo himself revealed with his kind, open spirit and warm humour. Memories of time spent with him are filled with laughter and joy."

Garth Hewitt
Singer/songwriter
Founder of Amos Trust
Anglican Priest and Canon of St. George's Cathedral, Jerusalem

"Gus Parajón was a soft spoken, short man, with a polio limp, but he had the presence, vision and courage of a Gandhi. He inspired many of us who knew him in Nicaragua to accompany him in his work with the gasoline boys, Provadenic, CEPAD, and later AMOS."

Harry Strachan, INCAE professor, Strachan Foundation

"One of the ways God has shown up in my life, bearing gifts, is in the people I've been brought to cross paths with. Gustavo Parajón was one of those. He radiated a thoughtful kindness. Without pretense or any kind of showiness he seemed to tune in automatically to the essence of whoever and whatever he had to deal with. Though I didn't know him well, I got to enjoy his company on several occasions, in Nicaragua and in the UK. This book is a fascinating and fast-reading chronicle of the life of a man who, more than anyone I've met, seemed to exemplify what it means to bring the teachings of Jesus Christ into the world."

Bruce Cockburn, singer/songwriter

"Whenever I travelled with Dr. Gustavo Parajón, in both Nicaragua and the UK—which I was privileged to do over a period of 24 years of friendship and work—I saw the same thing. He found the most unassuming person in the room and engaged with them. Then he would tell the rest of us what he had learned from them and how we could all respond to it. He just loved being part of a community—of family, friends, or strangers—and gently bringing us together to achieve something remarkable. This book shows how much was achieved as a result. It's a fascinating read; a true record of an amazing life, very well lived (and full of fun and laughter)."

Sue Plater, former Chair, Greenbelt Festivals

"While other members of Nicaragua's National Reconciliation Commission, afraid of being captured, remained safely in the capital city, Gustavo Parajón went into his country's conflict zones, explaining, "I was afraid of not doing what God asked of me." God asked a lot of this extraordinary physician, pastor, teacher, visionary, and peacemaker, who believed that the Bible was his strongest weapon and the Holy Spirit his greatest protection. He faced the worst that humanity and nature can dish out—dictatorship, persecution, war, earthquake, hurricane, tsunami—always with courage, compassion, and calm. I'm grateful for this detailed chronicle that preserves and spreads his remarkable legacy."

Joyce Hollyday, author, pastor, and co-founder of Witness for Peace in Nicaragua

"Gustavo Parajón exemplified the famous Micah text perhaps more than anyone I ever knew—to "do justice, love kindness, and walk humbly with your God." This doctor who could heal a nation, this pastor who could lovingly shape all who came near him, and this prophet who always, eloquently, and consistently spoke the truth to power; was one of the greatest unsung heroes of faith and justice on a global scale while transforming countless local communities. This wonderful book beautifully sings the most lovely songs and stories of this man who would always turn everything back to Christ who was his abiding hero. Please everyone, this book is a must read if you want to know what it really means to follow Jesus in times just like we are in right now! "

Jim Wallis, Inaugural Chair and Director of the Center for Faith and Justice at Georgetown University

"Dr. Gustavo Parajón inspired my life though his sincere humility, his vast medical knowledge translated into service for the poor, his determined commitment to empower marginalized communities from its same potentiality, to struggle for peace facing opposite political powers and to seek constantly in the Bible the will of God in the midst of his life and ministry."

Rev. Dr. José Norat-Rodríguez, Area Director for Iberoamerica and the Caribbean (1992–2015), American Baptist International Ministries.

"If Baptists had saints, Gustavo Parajón would be among that elect. And like all genuine saints, he would complain loudly at being so named. In this biography, Dan Buttry and Dámaris Albuquerque provide a vivid account of Parajón's array of visionary and organizational skills, along with his underlying spirituality. He is proof perfect that saintliness is not an honor but an anointment: Drawing forth the godliness (and exorcising the demons) in all life's intersections."

Ken Sehested, founding director of the Baptist Peace Fellowship of North America and writer at prayerandpolitiks.org

"I urge you to read this book and be inspired by the amazing way Gustavo put his faith and love into action in the middle of danger, violence, and widespread despair. What a joy and a privilege it was to be able to work with him and watch him shine light into such darkness year after year!"

Don Mosley, founding member of Jubilee Partners, a Christian community which has hosted thousands of refugees from war zones around the world and made dozens of peacemaking trips to Nicaragua.

Healing the World

Gustavo Parajón,
public health and
peacemaking pioneer

Daniel Buttry
Dámaris Albuquerque

To learn more about this book and its author, please visit AMOSHealth.org.

Cover design and illustration by Rick Nease
www.RickNeaseArt.com

Map of Nicaragua by Peter Fitzgerald, minor amendments by Joelf. Own work based on the map of administrative divisions by Vrysxy, CC BY-SA 4.0. commons.wikimedia.org/w/index.php?curid=22746862

Scripture quotations marked (NIV) are taken from the Holy Bible, New International Version®, NIV®. Copyright © 1973, 1978, 1984, 2011 by Biblica, Inc.™ Used by permission of Zondervan. All rights reserved worldwide. www.zondervan.com. The "NIV" and "New International Version" are trademarks registered in the United States Patent and Trademark Office by Biblica, Inc.™

Scripture quotations marked NRSV are from the New Revised Standard Version Bible, copyright © 1989 National Council of the Churches of Christ in the United States of America. Used by permission. All rights reserved worldwide.

Published by
Read the Spirit, an imprint of
Front Edge Publishing
42807 Ford Road, No. 234
Canton, MI
48187

Front Edge Publishing books are available for discount bulk purchases for events, corporate use and small groups. Special editions, including books with corporate logos, personalized covers and customized interiors are available for purchase. For more information, contact Front Edge Publishing at info@FrontEdgePublishing.com

This book is dedicated to:

Joan Parajón
Gustavo's compañera,
loving wife and partner
in service to Christ

and

Gilberto Aguirre
Gustavo's compañero,
dear friend and colleague
in service to Christ

Contents

Daniel Buttry with Gustavo Parajón at the Global Baptist
Peace Conference in Rome, Italy February 2009.

Author's Foreword

By Daniel Buttry

Gustavo Parajón, Stan Slade, and I were on a panel at a World Mission Conference for International Ministries (IM) at the beautiful American Baptist Assembly conference center along the shores of Green Lake, Wisconsin. Central America was aflame with wars, including those in Nicaragua and El Salvador. Gustavo Parajón and Stan Slade were IM missionaries in those two respective countries. I was director of the Peace Program for National Ministries, the American Baptist Home Mission Society. Together we were telling conference participants about what was going on with the wars in Central America and what Baptists were doing and could do about them.

After we each made our presentations, the time came for audience members to ask questions. The first questioner bolted to his feet, and with a loud voice and wagging finger demanded, "Are you telling us that our president is not telling us the truth about Central America?!" From his aggressive tone, it was evident that this man believed Ronald Reagan over and against his denomination's missionaries. Stan and I, the younger ones of the panel, tensed up ready for the battle we knew was coming. Gustavo, in the middle of our panel, gently placed his hands on our forearms: "I'll take this one."

"Brother, I didn't get your name," Gustavo calmly said. You could feel the tension and aggression immediately ease. That one simple sentence said so much: "Brother, I didn't get your name." It reminded the questioner and all of us that we were first and foremost God's children, brothers and sisters of one another. "Brother, I didn't get your name." It yearned for a relationship sufficient to hold a frank and difficult discussion. "Brother, I didn't get your name." It called us to put our politics in the context of our common faith.

That was my introduction to Gustavo Parajón. His actions had already impacted my life in a way I didn't know until I was working on this book. I was a Christian peacemaker, working first as an activist pastor, then as a national level program executive. But with that one simple sentence—"Brother, I didn't get your name"—Gustavo Parajón took me to the graduate school of deep peacemaking.

I would learn that this sentence held the secret for his peacemaking efforts that occurred in the heart of a bitter and brutal war. Where humanity was being denied in the violence visited on human bodies and the stories told about "those terrible people" on the other side, Gustavo was always seeking relationship. More than that, he was creating family where there was horrific enmity. From the level of top officials in the government and in the insurgents to the grassroots rural communities where people had fought on both sides of the conflict, the way Gustavo treated people created the safe place for new possibilities to first be imagined and then built.

After that panel with Stan and Gustavo, I went on to engage in peacemaking around the world. At three key junctures, I shared in international conferences where I invited Gustavo to speak and share his vision and work for peace, always deeply rooted in the stories he told from the Bible. In each of those conferences, God unfolded a new dimension of my peacemaking call. Though not directly midwifed by him, Gustavo was helping to set the overall context. He had a way of stepping into what seemed impossible, following God's call to bring peace and healing to our torn and ailing world.

Later, I became a colleague of his as I joined the missionary staff of International Ministries. I learned more of the public health and pastoral dimensions of his ministry in Nicaragua. I also learned of the impact he made in the lives of individuals who had been shaped by him, even as I had been by that one riveting moment I shared with him on a conference panel.

When I was asked to write this book by the Parajón family and the leaders of CEPAD and AMOS, I was humbled but also immensely excited. What I knew about Gustavo had already inspired and shaped me, so I was eager to tell that story. However, as I interviewed people and researched his life, I realized I only knew a small sliver of the story of this amazing man of God. He never blew his own trumpet, rather, he always lifted up Christ and people in need. As I listened to story after story, I realized the task of writing Gustavo's biography was both more daunting and more thrilling than I ever anticipated.

So Dámaris Albuquerque and I invite you into the journey we have experienced of discovering so much more about a man we thought we knew. We did know him, Dámaris far more than I. Yet we discovered we still had more to learn. We invite you into that blessed journey of discovery of the work and personality of one of God's special servants. Whether you knew him in person or not, we invite you now to learn more about this special brother named Gustavo Parajón.

Gilberto Aguirre (left) and Dámaris Albuquerque (right) with Gustavo Parajón.

Author's Foreword

By Dámaris Albuquerque-Espinoza

In Nicaragua, where the name of Gustavo Parajón is heard, everyone thinks of him as a promoter of service, peace, and reconciliation, and as a pastor and medical doctor. Very few would think of him as a planner, a teacher, as technologically savvy, and as an administrator. Most people would agree on his being humble but firm, and on his deep love for the Bible.

I had the huge privilege of working for and with him for more than twenty years. I assisted him through his different roles: director of PROVADENIC, president of CEPAD's board of directors, pastor of First Baptist Church, president of PRESTANIC, president of AMOS Health and Hope, and many more. But I also knew him as a loving husband and father, who always had time for his family when they called him at the office. He had a lot of stamina for working day by day in a packed agenda that he managed. He went through back-to-back meetings, giving the attention needed to all the topics as they changed from meeting to meeting.

With him I learned about treating each situation as a medical file, where he and I described the situation, the desired outcome, the action plan, and updating that file with the different happenings and actions done. He said that those were like the tests done in order to reach a diagnosis and treatment.

Many people came to his office asking for personal advice, and they came out strengthened by the Word of God that was delivered by him. He never gave any advice before helping the person look for the solution first. He led meetings by asking questions of what the nature of the problem was and what one would think was the solution.

He also paid attention to details. He always asked the name of the person and asked about their family. And he always remembered those names. When I was pregnant for the first time, he took the time to medically explain to me what was going on inside my body and what to expect during the pregnancy and birth. When my son, Selim, was born, he gave me as a gift a book by one of the renowned American doctors of the time so I could further my education on parenting.

I feel honored to participate in this book because I owe him and my husband, Gilberto Aguirre, my professional growth. But most of all, he helped me clarify what should motivate my daily life, which is the obedience to Jesus to carry His mission of service to others. This book is also a tribute to my husband, who worked alongside Dr. Parajón during the period of 1972–2000. He had the same driving inspiration and suffered the same risks and criticisms for doing what was right. It is my wish that this book inspires others to follow Jesus in a meaningful way.

Introduction:

Who Was This Man?

The man with a limp from a childhood bout of polio launched a massive campaign to eliminate the disease from his country. Who was this man?

In the ruins of a massive earthquake that shattered his city, he gathered church leaders under a mango tree to initiate an organization that would have a deep and lasting impact on the poor of Nicaragua. Who was this man?

He said "No" to the dictator who wanted him to tell the U.S. Congress that there were no human rights abuses in Nicaragua. "I cannot lie," he told the dictator. Who was this man?

He refused requests from that dictator and from the later revolutionary government to head their national health department because he believed he could best help the most needy outside of a government position. Who was this man?

His phone call to U.S. religious peacemakers ignited a huge nonviolent resistance campaign against the U.S. war efforts in Nicaragua. Who was this man?

As a reconciliation effort during a war turned into a riot, he formed a ring of church leaders to protect the political leaders and led them through the hostile crowd to safety. Who was this man?

When a dozen armed insurgents burst into a meeting threatening to kill everyone, he calmed everyone down by reading from the Bible. Who was this man?

He went unarmed into front-line regions to meet with insurgent leaders to explore ways to peace. Who was this man?

The global rock star Bono of U2 put on a disguise so he could slip into a British Christian rock and justice festival to hear this man speak. Who was this man?

He envisioned using ordinary people to become health promoters and vaccine providers in poor communities beyond regular health systems, setting up the structures and trainers to provide that care. Who was this man?

He was awarded the Francisco Morazán Medallion from the Central American Parliament in a special ceremony held at his church, First Baptist of Managua, an unprecedented action in this predominantly Catholic region of the world. Who was this man?

He was nominated for the Nobel Peace Prize by former U.S. President Jimmy Carter. Who was this man?

A London media personality interviewing him before a live audience was unable to get much about his personal life, only about the situation and work in Nicaragua. He turned to the audience and said, "It's difficult to interview the most humble man in the world." Who was this man?

He was Gustavo Adolfo Parajón Domínguez. He was GAPD to many with whom he worked, reflecting how he signed his letters and messages. Some colleagues humorously turned GAPD into Gran Águila Permanentemente Dominante (Great Eagle Permanently Dominant). He was Dr. Parajón. He was Gustavo. He was Gus. He was Papi. He was Abuelito (Grandpa). He saw himself as a child of God, a follower of Jesus, and a servant of God.

This book seeks to unpack some of the many dimensions of this humble man who accomplished great things. He was a doctor and public health worker. He was a pastor and choir member. He was a leader in bringing Christians together. He was a relief and development worker. He was a peacemaker and mediator. He was a mentor who trained and empowered countless people. He was a sought-after speaker around the world. He was a husband, father, and grandfather. His impact in the lives of people around him, in his nation, and in the world is a treasure we will examine from many aspects. Though he died in 2011, his legacy continues. May this book serve the strengthening and furtherance of that legacy of faith and love.

Gustavo Adolfo Parajón Domínguez

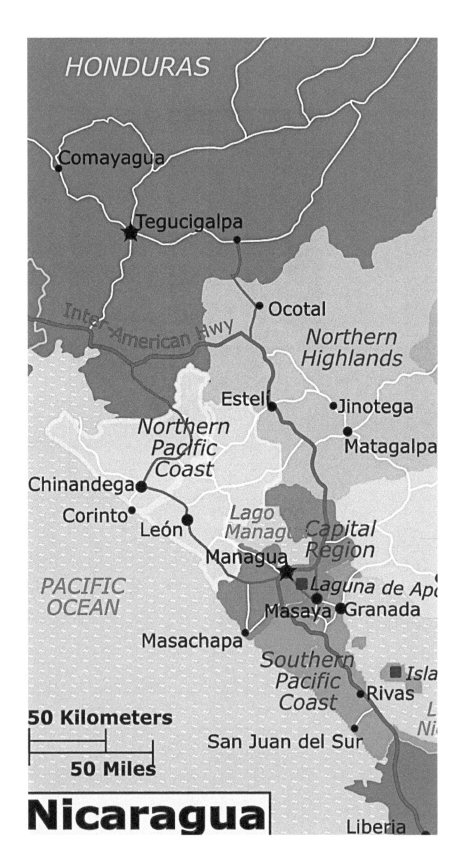

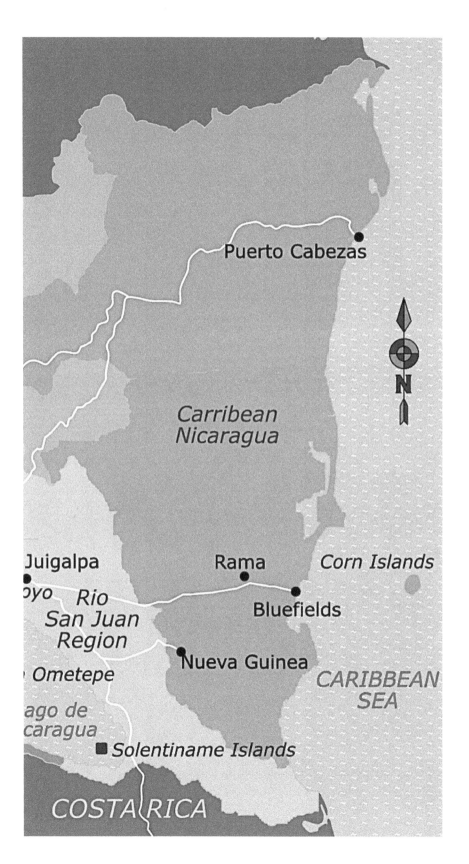

Joan and Gustavo at Denison University.

A Parajón-Domínguez family portrait.

The Parajón-Domínguez family, Gustavo the youngest.

Gustavo and Joan after their wedding.

Beatriz Domínguez with little Gustavo, 1936.

Roots:

The Making of a Man of God

Childhood

Gustavo Adolfo Parajón Domínguez was born November 22, 1935 in Managua, Nicaragua. He was born the year after Anastasio Samoza Garcia had assassinated General Augusto César Sandino, the popular leader of the resistance to the invasion by United States Marines. The U.S. had trained and financed Somoza's National Guard forces. As young Gustavo entered into the world, hundreds of Nicaraguans were being executed by Somoza's soldiers. The dynamics of the United States, the Somoza family, the National Guard, and the resistance inspired by Sandino would shape and be woven into the life of this young one.

But a more central influence were Gustavo's parents, Arturo Parajón and Beatriz Domínguez de Parajón. They were deeply committed Baptist Christians at a time when being a Protestant or evangelical in the Catholic dominated countries of Latin America put one at the margins. (The term "evangelical" generally means "Protestant" in most of the world, rather than the more narrow theologically conservative stream of Protestantism, as in the U.S.) One had to be clear about what one believed if you were to be a Protestant because there was a social cost to that commitment, which don Arturo suffered personally when he was disowned by his father when he converted. However, it was their compassion for which they were most known. Beatriz was sensitive to the needs of others. Arturo would be willing to help anyone in need, even in the middle of the night. As a result, though they were in a religious minority, they were highly respected by all who knew them.

Gustavo grew up in the setting of the Baptist Church. When Arturo returned from the Baptist seminary in Saltillo, Mexico with his wife, Beatriz, in 1922, they began working alongside the pastor of the First Baptist Church of Managua, the Primera Iglesia Bautista de Managua. When the pastor, the Rev. David Wilson, passed away in 1925, Arturo was appointed to serve as the church's pastor. Some years later while Gustavo was just a toddler, Arturo spearheaded the incorporation of the small group of Baptists in Nicaragua to form the Convention of Baptist Churches of Nicaragua (now known as the Baptist Convention of Nicaragua) with seven member churches. Arturo was elected president. He also directed the production of the Baptist monthly magazine *La Antorcha*. Arturo wrote frequently about issues important to the Baptist faith at a time when Protestants were under attack by the dominant Catholic Church.

The congregation met on the grounds of the Colegio Bautista, the Baptist School. Nicaragua didn't have good public schools, and those that existed were run by Catholic nuns and priests who were not welcoming of students from other faiths. In such a context, this Baptist school with its religious tolerance drew Catholic and even Muslim, Buddhist, and Jewish students, many from the international business and diplomatic community in Managua. The school also drew Nicaraguan students from the rural areas, who boarded in the girls' or boys' dorms. The director of the colegio was Dr. Lloyd Wyse, serving in Nicaragua as an American Baptist missionary. The Parajón and Wyse families lived side by side, also on the colegio grounds. Beatriz Parajón taught penmanship at the school and taught and led music for the Sunday school of First Baptist. Lloyd Wyse was a deacon in the church. The two families were bonded together in many aspects of their family life and work, a caring network that would play a great role in young Gustavo's life.

When Gustavo was 4 ½, he contracted polio, a common scourge in Nicaragua and across the world at that time. For a while, the young boy couldn't walk. At church, an older boy, Carlos Escobar, had the job of lifting Gustavo into his seat and then lifting him out of it. Carlos acted like a big brother to him, though later Gustavo had to ask him to stop using the diminutive name Gustavito for his younger buddy. The Parajón family lived in California during two periods of time in the 1940s to get better treatment for Gustavo's polio and for don Arturo to be able to attend Berkeley Baptist Divinity School. Gustavo eventually recovered from the polio but was left with a significant limp for the rest of his life. He never once complained of being tired or of not being able to walk or stand for long periods of time. The bout with polio helped shape his lifelong calling in medicine and public health.

Arturo Parajón shaped young Gustavo in many ways, but five stand out in the context of his life's work. Arturo took many trips to the countryside to evangelize and care for the needs of people. In these rural communities, a concern for the poor was ignited in Gustavo's heart. As Gustavo later wrote, "Many people came to my father for advice and guidance, not only spiritual, but also concerning many other matters, among which health was at the top of the list."[1] The high mortality rate of children under 5 impressed this child deeply. Combined with his own experience of polio, these encounters gave birth to his passion for vaccination against childhood diseases.

Arturo and Beatriz had an open house, always providing hospitality to friends, church members, and visitors. People who came for a visit and a meal were treated as family. Gustavo grew up with this kind of a home and continued it when he and his wife, Joan, established their own home.

Arturo also was a mentor. He would "gather strays," young men who needed spiritual guidance as they laid the foundations for life and career. This pattern of gathering groups of young people to be discipled and nurtured became a major part of how Gustavo operated. Almost every experience became a teaching moment and an opportunity for growth.

Arturo knew when and how to stand his ground. The Somoza family was very suspicious of anybody who worked with the poor because their wealth was derived from the systems of oppression and corruption they maintained. Arturo was often engaged in ministry to the poor, particularly out in the rural areas, which put him on the wrong side of the Somoza government. Arturo was arrested a couple times out of suspicion, once as he was returning from one of the trips to the countryside. Arturo always stood his ground as a minister called to share the compassion of Christ. Gustavo absorbed this faith-filled fearlessness he saw in his father.

Arturo was known for his kind generosity. Denis Cuéllar, who later married Gustavo's daughter Marta, recalls an early interaction with the Parajón family told by his mother. Her brother died, and the family had no money for a coffin for the funeral. Arturo heard about it somehow. Denis' mother never forgot seeing Arturo coming to their house on a bicycle with a coffin tied across the back. With his father as a model, Gustavo carried on similar generosity to those with deep needs whom he encountered.

Trauma in his family shaped Gustavo even before he was born. He carried a vivid memory shared about an earthquake on March 31, 1931. Because of mischief, his parents did not allow his brothers to go with their paternal grandmother, Bersabé Parajón, to the market. While she was shopping, a massive earthquake struck the city. The family never saw her again. She was killed at the market, and her remains were never found. She was likely buried in a common grave as were thousands of the dead who were hastily buried in mass graves to prevent outbreaks of disease. The story lived on in the family, including the guilt of the brothers for

---

1 International Ministries "Pen Sketch," 1974.

not being there for their grandmother, so much so that for Gustavo it was almost as if it was his own memory.

Gustavo had three older brothers. Another family trauma that shaped the family involved the first child. Little Samuel died at the age of 13 months from German measles, so Gustavo never knew him. Beatriz was devastated by her little one's death and felt so distant during her time of grief from the comfort of her family back in Mexico. Arturo and Guillermo were next, with quite a gap between them and Gustavo. By the time Gustavo was a teenager, his older brothers had moved to the U.S., joining the U.S. army as soon as they graduated from high school.

At a young age, Gustavo made a commitment that would direct him for the rest of his life, a commitment to the living Christ. As he put it: "There came a moment in my life when I was face to face with Him, and I had to make a choice: Christ and His Love or the glorification of myself and my desires. I chose to accept Him as Master and Lord of my life."[2] The commitment propelled everything that would follow in his life.

Then there were the Three Amigos: Rolando Gutiérrez-Cortés, Roger Velásquez-Valle, and Gustavo. Sometimes they were called the Three Stooges of the Baptist churches. They called each other "brother." Then, later, as they had families, their kids called each other cousins. Gustavo was always the diplomatic one of the three, honing peacemaking skills with his more energetic and volatile friends. On Easter they had a competition to see who would call first to say, "The Lord is Risen!"

Gustavo introduced Rolando to Edna Lee-Ramos, the woman who would be his wife. Edna and Gustavo both had Mexican roots, as Gustavo's mother was from Saltillo, Mexico. Gustavo showed Rolando a letter from Edna, and Rolando fell in love with her because of the beautiful handwriting, like the script of a love story!

Another friend was George Pixley, the son of the Dr. John Pixley, who was the head of the Baptist Hospital. Gustavo, George, and Philip Wyse would often travel together into various Managua neighborhoods to engage in evangelism, singing, and sharing the Gospel. Sometimes there would be boyish energetic horsing around, but with his bad leg Gustavo couldn't join in fully. Not to be deterred, he would use his mind and his voice to keep in the thick of the action.

Orphan and Opportunity

In 1951, doña Beatriz died from breast cancer. She had been very sick, and when she died, it was a shock to her surviving husband and the three boys. The wake was held at the church, which met at the colegio's primary school building.

---

2 International Ministries "Pen Sketch," 1974.

The whole congregation gathered to vigil through the night with a heavy pall of sadness resting over everyone.

Don Arturo and Gustavo were left alone in one way, but they became the center of loving attention in another. The women in the church poured out compassion on them in practical ways, by bringing food and helping with household duties. Gustavo was forever fond of the older women in the church who had helped him and his father in this terrible time. He affectionately referred to them as "the girls," though everyone knew they were older women. He saw them as pillars of the church for their incredible service, not just to him but to others in times of need.

In 1954, Arturo died of cancer at the age of 55, leaving Gustavo an orphan. Having lost both his parents in their 50s, Gustavo never thought he would live beyond that, a feeling that haunted him for most of his life. He never shared his feelings about these traumatic losses at such a young age. Rather he emphasized the support and comfort he received from his faith and from the folks at First Baptist Church, often calling the church a "healing community."

Shortly after Pastor Arturo's death, Gustavo's older friend Carlos Escobar invited Gustavo to accompany him to Sabana Grande for the worship service of the First Baptist Church mission. The mission congregation gathered in their best clothes in mourning for don Arturo. During the service, with everyone feeling the pain of their grief, Carlos noticed that the brothers and sisters were comforted by holding hands with young Gustavo. The one who supposedly came to be consoled ended up comforting everyone else, a preview of the grace and comforting strength that would be evidenced throughout Gustavo's life.

Gustavo had one more year left at the colegio, so the Wyse family took him in. Before the cancer took Arturo, Lloyd Wyse promised him that Gustavo would finish his education. Gustavo had a sharp intellect and love of learning, so it was more a matter of providing the opportunity. Marion and Lloyd Wyse had five children, a daughter and four boys, some around Gustavo's age. Gustavo fit in right from the beginning with this family he knew so well. The kindness of the women of the church and the cooks at the school continued, filling the Wyse household with food. The dinner table was also a class, as Marion Wyse taught English during the meals, a language in which Gustavo became fluent.

Gustavo loved spicy food, a result of his Mexican mother's cooking. When he moved in with the Wyse family, some relatives would send him pickled hot peppers, something the Wyses wouldn't dare touch! Gustavo would grin as he devoured the peppers in front of his adopted family.

In his recovery from polio, the young Gustavo learned how to swim. Swimming strengthened his muscles and became an activity he loved throughout his life. While living with the Wyses, he would get up around 5 a.m. and head down to the volcanic crater lake near the Presidential Palace, the Laguna Tiscapa. The Wyse boys thought he was daring to do this, because if Lloyd Wyse found out, Gustavo would get in trouble. But Gustavo continued to slip out, not in a rebellious spirit, but with a fearlessness that became a trademark as he passed through danger.

Lloyd Wyse had graduated from Denison University, an American Baptist-related school in Granville, Ohio. He contacted the leadership of Denison and arranged for a number of Nicaraguan students to attend on scholarship. The first group of three students included Gustavo Parajón, Philip Wyse, and their friend Alejandro Martínez.

College and a Partner for Life

When Gustavo began at Denison University, he majored in chemistry. Besides his rigorous academic schedule, he had to make time for work. He was enrolled in a "grant-in-aid" program that required him to be employed on campus. He began working in the boys' dining room, cleaning the used trays.

David Wyse, who was ahead of Gustavo and Philip at Denison, had a job working as an assistant to the wife of the university chaplain, Harry Kruener. Martha Kruener had contracted polio as an adult and became seriously disabled, bound to a wheelchair. She slept in a rocking bed because she could not breathe otherwise. When David left, Gustavo took over the job. Like David had done, Gustavo cared for her not only in her home but wheeled her around the campus. He was very devoted to Mrs. Kruener, likely with great empathy from his own experience with polio's devastation on the body, but also from the compassion that had long been nurtured within him.

Chaplain Kruener, on the other hand, received little respect from Gustavo. During Gustavo's last year in high school, a Costa Rican group connected with the Latin American Mission came to hold an evangelistic campaign in Managua. They used the Baptist school yard for their services. Gustavo was swept up in the passion for Bible reading and prayer with a fundamentalist quality. Back in his Three Amigos childhood, they would respond to friendly critiques saying, "Do not call me a fundamentalist!" But he certainly seemed that way as a Denison freshman, perhaps also colored by the experience of marginalization of Protestants amid the Catholic dominance in Nicaragua. In December of his freshman year, he wrote Marion Wyse a long letter in which he said of Kruener's messages, "Not once have I heard Christ preached." Gustavo wrote with dismay about the lighting and extinguishing of candles in the service, something that seemed far too Catholic for his Nicaraguan Baptist sensibilities. Things obviously changed along the way, for he grew into someone who never lost the passion of his core faith with deep Bible study and prayer, but also expanded his embrace of others to the point where he could be creatively engaged in shared ecumenical work.

The Spanish department would host a dinner once a week for the Spanish-speaking students. Someone came up with the idea, likely Gustavo, of singing Spanish songs after the meal. Gustavo would lead the singing, insisting, "We have to sing these songs." One of the popular songs was the silly children's song "La Cucaracha" about the cockroach. As a folk song, it could be adapted and changed. In the 1910 Mexican Revolution the song became revolutionary, speaking of need (the cockroach had no legs) and triumph (the cockroach eventually takes over the house).

Gustavo attended a Bible study at First Baptist Church of Granville, a few blocks from the university. Another student, Joan Morgan, was also in the study group, and they became good friends. Joan could speak many words in Spanish, something that assuaged Gustavo's feelings of loneliness and homesickness. He would often speak to her in Spanish.

Originally from Oak Park, Illinois, just outside of Chicago, Joan came to Denison to study music. Joan and Gustavo began to spend a lot of time together, sometimes traveling to churches in neighboring towns. Gustavo would preach and Joan would sing. One evening, Gustavo asked Joan if she would like to live in Nicaragua. Joan was shocked with the question but answered: "Yes, I would!!" Gustavo then said: "Because if not, we cannot continue seeing each other. The Lord has called me to return to Nicaragua, and I can't date someone who doesn't want to go."

Joan graduated in 1958, a year ahead of Gustavo. After graduation, she moved to Boston for a year. Joan and Gustavo wrote letters extensively while they were separated, and in the process they decided to get married. After Gustavo proposed, Joan's parents were worried that their daughter would be marrying a foreigner and would be taken to a strange country. Gustavo collected all his diplomas and awards to show them and assure the future in-laws of his good intentions and worthiness.

June 8, 1959 was a momentous and very full day. In the morning, Gustavo graduated from Denison University. In the afternoon, he and Joan were married at the First Baptist Church in Granville, the place where they had first met. Joan's family was there. Lloyd and Marion Wyse stood in as Gustavo's parents. At first, they were worried that Joan would lure Gustavo into a materialistic lifestyle and not return to Nicaragua. They also worried that eligible Nicaraguan women would be jealous of Joan for stealing Gustavo. But once they met Joan, they realized what a special person she was and gladly blessed the marriage.

Medical School and Building a Network

From 1959 to 1963, Gustavo attended the Western Reserve Medical School in Cleveland, which later became Case Western. He completed his medical studies then undertook his internship. Following that, he did his residency in internal medicine at Metropolitan General Hospital in downtown Cleveland, where he worked for four years. He became the head resident. One of the students he oversaw was George Jackson. Over the years, George would become a key partner in the work in Nicaragua as well as a family friend.

Also working in the hospital was an older receptionist who was in charge of transferring calls. For some reason, she was never very nice to Gustavo and could be quite uncooperative. In his characteristic peacemaking manner, Gustavo decided to buy her a box of chocolates and give them to her personally. When he approached her to give her the chocolates, she started crying and apologized for her unfriendly attitude toward him. He made a good friend and ally within the hospital. Gustavo used to tell this story to illustrate how important it was to make human connections with people, even though they had been rude or offensive.

Gustavo and Joan became members at First Baptist Church of Cleveland. They had a good experience being part of that community and living in Cleveland. The friendships at First Baptist would grow into a groundbreaking mission partnership. The folks from the church and medical school would join in Gustavo's first public health initiatives and continued for decades to be deeply engaged in the various projects he launched. Sparked by the Parajóns, more than five hundred members of First Baptist Cleveland have traveled to Nicaragua on various mission trips over forty years.

Meanwhile, Joan became a member of the Cleveland Orchestra Chorus and Chamber Chorus under direction of the famous Robert Shaw. This was a life-changing experience for Joan. For five years she strengthened her musical skills in ways that would flourish in the decades ahead. As a member of the chorus, she traveled to Puerto Rico in 1962 and 1963 to sing Pablo Casal's oratorio "El Pesebre" ("The Manger") under his direction, along with Bach's "St. Matthew Passion" and Beethoven's Symphony No. 9. Mr. Casals said "El Pesebre" was his offering for peace in the world. They repeated it again in the Dominican Republic and for the General Assembly of the United Nations in New York.

Gustavo's parents had been musical, and upon their return from Mexico, founded and directed the choir at First Baptist Church in Managua. But the choir had fizzled out. Gustavo told Joan, "When we get back to Nicaragua, you could put a choir together and direct it." Joan protested, "I don't know if I can do that!" In what would become one of his signature words of encouragement Gustavo replied, "Yes, you can!" Joan's musical ministry in Nicaragua would prove to be groundbreaking.

When Gustavo began his residency, life became more difficult for the young family. He was away from home a lot because of his work at the hospital. Also, they had their first children, Marta Elena born in 1964 and David Gustavo in 1966.

Initially, Gustavo wanted to return immediately to Nicaragua, but respected advisers convinced him that he needed to expand his medical knowledge into the field of public health. So the family moved to Massachusetts while Gustavo studied and earned his master's in public health at Harvard Medical School. They lived in the apartments for international students. While Gustavo studied, Joan would take little Marta and David on walks around the city and to local parks to feed the ducks and geese.

Music continued to be Joan's passion even though she had to deal with the limitations of being the mother for a young family. Joan sang in the Chorus Pro Musica in Boston and continued to think about starting a choir in Nicaragua. Gustavo encouraged her in that dream, telling her not to worry. He said he would help her with this project.

Gustavo, David & Marta (center) with Sixto Ulloa (right) and Octavio Cortés (left).

Gustavo and Joan.

Joan, Gustavo, and children in Jeep driven from U.S. to Nicaragua.

Gustavo with David and Marta visiting
Nicaragua in summer of 1967.

Dr. Gustavo gifting a Bible to PROVADENIC health promoters upon their graduation.

Dr. Gustavo looking over a training manual for PROVADENIC health promoters.

The Three Amigos (from left): Gustavo Parajón,
Rolando Gutiérrez-Cortés, and Roger Velásquez-Valle.

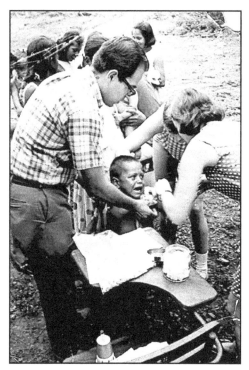
Dr. Parajón in the children's vaccination campaign.

Inauguration of PROVADENIC Community Clinic in Fila Grande, Matagalpa.

2

A Doctor for the People

1967 and 1968 were very volatile years around the world. The U.S. was heavily involved in the war in Vietnam. The Civil Rights Movement was forcing new legislation to protect the rights of African Americans who had been denied for so long because of structural racism. In 1968, the assassinations of the Rev. Dr. Martin Luther King Jr. and Bobby Kennedy left everyone shaken. The 1968 student revolutions in France and Mexico and the Prague Spring in Czechoslovakia were highlights of global unrest.

Nicaragua was not in the front pages of the world's news but was also going through serious upheaval. In January 1967, a demonstration by the opposition Conservative Party was brutally repressed by the National Guard. Many people were killed, wounded, and arrested. That February, Anastasio Somoza Debayle was reelected as president in an election that was a foregone conclusion. Underneath the seemingly entrenched Somoza regime was a new political dynamic. In 1961, the Frente Sandinista de Liberación Nacional (FSLN, often called the Sandinistas) was formed. Their resistance started slowly, but they became a persistent expression of opposition to Somoza's dictatorship.

Nicaragua was one of the poorest countries in the Western Hemisphere. The average daily income was less than $2 per day. Most rural homes had dirt floors and tin roofs. In 1967, 117 Nicaraguan babies died per 1,000 live births. Nicaragua had one of the highest rates of childhood mortality by the age of 5 in the Western Hemisphere. The main causes of death for these children were infectious diseases: gastroenteritis, respiratory tract infections, measles, whooping cough, and tetanus.

Polio was a persistent scourge. All these problems were complicated by extensive malnutrition.

The Baptists in Nicaragua were among the marginalized Protestants in a heavily Catholic country. Their work and life were dynamic, however. In 1967, a Baptist university was founded, the Polytechnic University of Nicaragua (UPOLI), an initiative of several Baptist intellectuals and professionals, including Gustavo. Into this context, Gustavo Parajón returned to Nicaragua with his family.

Guns for Peace Vaccination Campaign

Dr. Parajón's own suffering as a child must have been a motivating force for his service. He knew intimately what a disease such as polio could do in a tiny body, and he didn't want people to suffer as he had. So, in 1967, he took a summer break from his residency in Cleveland to take a team back to Nicaragua to vaccinate children against polio and other major illnesses.

A major medical technological breakthrough happened when Dr. Robert Hingston invented the jet injector. The injector looked somewhat like a gun, where the barrel was put against a person's arm. A piston under compression would fire a small stream of liquid, including the vaccine, into the recipient's arm, penetrating the skin and getting into the underlying tissue. No needles or syringes were used. The liquid could contain vaccinations for multiple illnesses: smallpox, tuberculosis, diphtheria, and leprosy, as well as polio. Hundreds of people could be inoculated in one hour. Gustavo called the injectors "peace guns."

Gustavo pulled together a group from his church, First Baptist in Cleveland, including doctors and high school students, to help with logistics. Joan and the two kids came for the summer. He also recruited medical personnel from the Cleveland Medical Hospital, where he served as chief resident. George Jackson was a medical student. He'd never been outside the U.S. except to cross the border into Canada. His field was obstetrics and gynecology, not the focus of the trip, but Jackson saw this as a great opportunity to see the world. He would return to Nicaragua almost a dozen times to help in public health efforts.

Their first stop was Colonia General Somoza, near Chinandega, a bit north of the city of León. The Colonia was a community of people settled by the ruling Somoza family. It was supposed to be a noble project showing the dictator's care for his people to tamp down rising calls for land reform, but in reality, the worst land held by the rich was given to poor people to engage in subsistence farming. The Colonia had a polio epidemic, so Gustavo led the team there.

The team set up a clinic in the school building. Team members slung hammocks and set up cots. The non-medical folk worked on preparing the food for everyone and coordinating lines for the vaccinations. The medical personnel took up the "peace guns" and vaccinated everyone they could. They would often set up vaccinations around church services. After a service, all the children would line up, getting the shots in both arms.

The team traveled along the coast and up into the mountains. Jackson had practiced medicine amid the poverty of East Cleveland, but the poverty he saw in rural Nicaragua was a totally different order of intensity. Through this trip and subsequent trips coordinated by Gustavo, over one million children were vaccinated for polio, smallpox, and other diseases. The experience of this initial trip would be worked out in a more comprehensive way to address the public health needs of the poorest of the poor in one of the poorest nations in the hemisphere.

The jet injectors powered massive global vaccination campaigns like the one Dr. Parajón launched in Nicaragua. By the 1990s, concern grew for transmission of blood ailments through contact with the injector, so their use was phased out. However, in their time they were the main tool for profound public health breakthroughs as a result of mass vaccination.

Becoming a Missionary and Return to Nicaragua

Gustavo and Joan applied to be missionaries to Nicaragua through the American Baptist Home Mission Society. At that time, mission partnerships with Central American Baptist bodies were handled by the American Baptist Home Mission Society. Their application was approved, and in May 1964 they were appointed missionaries of the American Baptists. However, Gustavo had to continue his medical studies, so the pay and pension related to the missionary appointment became effective only after he was finished with his studies and had moved to Nicaragua to work at the Baptist Hospital.

In 1968, the family moved to Nicaragua in an epic journey. They shared the trip with Alejandro (Alex) Martinez, one of Gustavo's friends from the colegio who had gone with him to Denison. Martinez and his wife had three children. The families piled into two Jeeps. There were no seatbelts, so the kids were bouncing around as the Jeeps navigated the bumpy roads. For a month they traveled from Ohio to Nicaragua, stopping along the way to visit family and friends. In Saltillo, Mexico they visited the family of Gustavo's mother.

Earthquakes were a theme of the trip. When they arrived in the Mexican city of Tonalá, a recent earthquake had destroyed the main bridge. The Jeeps were loaded onto a train that took them around the damaged area while the families traveled in the passenger car. The unexpected train trip gave them many additional gas-saving kilometers for the journey. The two families also experienced a minor earthquake while staying in a hotel along the way. The hotel swayed, and cracks appeared in the walls and swimming pool. They pressed on.

In El Salvador, they visited Gustavo's dear friend Roger Velásquez-Valle, who was working as the pastor of the First Baptist Church in San Salvador. During the trip, Gustavo decided to stop speaking to his children in English, but to use Spanish so as to speed their language capacity in their new home culture.

Once in Managua, the family moved into the home of Amandita Mejía, a Baptist woman who had a large house. The house was located near the Baptist school, the church, and hospital where Gustavo planned to work, a perfect location to start the new chapter of their lives. After a year the Parajóns were able to get their own house, a little further up into the hills, where it was cooler.

On an occasional weekend, Gustavo and Joan would take the children to the beach. Sometimes they would even skip church, but if they did, Gustavo made sure to go through the Sunday school lesson there on the beach. First the Bible story, then play in the water!

Gustavo began his work at the Baptist Hospital in Managua, which was one of the best in the country. The hospital had been founded by American Baptist missionary Dr. John Pixley, whose son George was a friend of Gustavo's. George Pixley went on to become one of the great liberation theologians in Latin America while also serving as a missionary educator. Gustavo began as the hospital's associate director and staff internist, and also taught in the school of nursing, positions he held from 1968 to 1972.

Many poor people heard about Dr. Parajón, including those from the Baptist church. He wouldn't charge any fees for the consultations, so his office was always full of people seeking his help for both medical and spiritual matters. Patients noticed that along with the medical prescription, there was always a Bible verse written at the bottom of the sheet. Lydia Ruth Zamora was a nursing student at the Baptist Hospital in 1969. She said of Dr. Parajón, "I witnessed many instances in which he approached patients in a very warm and caring attitude, very different from other doctors in the hospital. He respected people, no matter their social background. He made them feel important."[3]

Dr. Parajón was also an excellent diagnostician. People would bring information about their conditions to him along with X-rays and other tests, and he would connect them to the specialists who could help them the best. Fran Korten, an American woman living in Managua, believes that Dr. Parajón saved her husband's life. Dave Korten became severely ill in 1970 and went to the Baptist Hospital. The attending doctor diagnosed him as having malaria and began treatment. Gustavo came by to visit and realized Dave had hepatitis instead. He immediately ordered a change of treatment, and Dave recovered.

Sixto Ulloa used to call Gustavo "the divine doctor." Dr. Zamora revised that assessment: "Of course, we know that only God is divine! But I think he said it because Dr. Parajón was wise in his diagnoses. Once, he made a diagnosis on a

---

3 Interview of Lydia Ruth Zamora by Dámaris Albuquerque.

nursing classmate that the doctors of the Baptist Hospital had not been able to. So for me, he was a miracle health doctor or a miracle healer doctor."

The good doctor was also a good teacher, according to medical students who worked with him. He would never miss a teaching opportunity, not just lecturing, but asking questions to help the students think and analyze for themselves. With his connections from the U.S., he could bring some of the most updated information about various conditions and treatments.

However, Dr. Parajón's vision went far beyond the Baptist Hospital. His experience with his father in the countryside and his own leadership in the vaccination campaigns gave him a huge heart for those who were most vulnerable and far from medical care. He said, "If we are ever to move ahead medically in this country, public health work in the rural areas is the key." Many poor people came to the Baptist Hospital, along with some of the social elites who wanted excellent care, but Parajón was unsatisfied. He wanted to bring health care to those beyond the scope of the hospital.

PROVADENIC Launched

Gustavo's dream of reaching the poorest people in the rural areas spurred him to build on the success of the vaccination program. In 1967, he pulled together folks from the First Baptist Church of Cleveland, the First Baptist Church of Managua, and the Baptist Convention of Nicaragua to found PROVADENIC. PROVADENIC stands for PROyecto de VAcunación y DEsarrollo de NICaragua, or in English, the Vaccination and Development Project of Nicaragua. This was the first community-based primary health care program (CBPHC) in Nicaragua. PROVADENIC was established to work in rural areas training local health promoters to diagnose and treat common illnesses. They also taught suturing, giving vaccinations, and midwifery.

Dr. Parajón believed doctors in developing countries should be primarily educators for health. Curing people of diseases was important, but preventing those diseases would make a far greater impact in the lives of ordinary people. He said, "A doctor in Nicaragua should not be a doctor, but a teacher to share our knowledge and empower others to serve." For Parajón, the key was training people from rural villages to be health promoters and bringing other, more extensive services out to the villages where there were no doctors or nurses.

Dr. Parajón was ahead of his time by envisioning that local people could be trained to provide some basic health care in their own communities. Others were engaged in similar visionary initiatives, such as Dr. Raj and Dr. Mabelle Arole in India and the "barefoot doctors" in China. Dr. Parajón adapted Dr. Carroll Berhorst's work with health promoters in Guatemala to the Nicaraguan context. He didn't just work on the theory; he worked on the ground in the communities.

He even welcomed people who were illiterate to be health promoters if they were selected by their communities. Besides teaching health, he taught leadership strategies, such as setting goals for one's work. He had health promoters write goals on newsprint such as "I want to make ten home visits every month" and "I want to build fifteen latrines in the village." The quality of leadership exhibited in the health promoters and health committees impressed many of the more educated workers who came from North America.

The community-based primary health care system did not replace the government health services. Instead, PROVADENIC served as an extension of the low-resourced health care service of the government's Ministry of Health. They were able to reach communities that would never have had care otherwise. The health promoters were able to prevent and treat the most common illnesses. They could promote health in their communities, including organizing community members to work on problems such as water and sanitation that had a huge impact on people's quality of health.

As he built the organization, Dr. Parajón always tried to keep a sense of the group. Each week had the same schedule. Monday through Thursday, medical teams went into the various communities. Friday was reserved for meetings to build team spirit and a sense of belonging. Some of the PROVADENIC staff didn't have families or their families were far away, so relationships were front and center. Parajón always included a devotional time with Bible study and singing. For him, the foundation of their work was seeing health care as Christian ministry because Jesus went about healing people.

He created an organizational culture of caring modeled on his own life and how he treated people. Many people spoke about how he would stop what he was doing when someone asked him a question. He would focus on the person so that they felt they were the most important person to him at that moment. This included staff, students, and patients. It included wealthy people and the poorest of the poor. He saw each as precious to God and precious to the doctor as well.

PROVADENIC began to expand. The Instituto Agrario de Nicaragua (IAN) had established communities for farming in different parts of the country. Gustavo knew the leadership at IAN, and they asked if he could provide health care to those communities. IAN would provide the vehicles and PROVADENIC would provide the staff. PROVADENIC workers and volunteers would go to the IAN colonies to hold weekly or biweekly clinics. The Nicaraguan Ministry of Health committed to provide the medicine and vaccines.

Baptist connections and leadership led to a special connection with the region of Nueva Guinea. The president of IAN was Dr. Rodolfo Mejía-Ubilla, a member of First Baptist Church in Managua. In the 60s, there was a volcanic eruption in León in western Nicaragua, which forced many people to be uprooted. IAN gave large tracts of land in Nueva Guinea to those displaced people who wanted to resettle there. The land was a thick jungle, but the people who had been relocated from the area around the volcano began to build homes and farms there. The new communities drew other people to Nueva Guinea from around the country, many of them Baptists and from other Protestant denominations.

PROVADENIC served these new communities. They were so remote in the late 60s that Dr. Parajón had to travel there by small missionary airplanes. The deep connections developed in Nueva Guinea would play a key role in the peace work of the 1980s and 1990s.

When Dr. Parajón and all his staff went into a village, they did not come with an established program. Rather, they began by gathering community leaders and listening to them. Parajón elicited from the community what their priority needs were. Then he had the communities form their own committee, including a president, a vice president, a secretary, and health promoters, who would also be selected by the people in the community.

They took the community leadership seriously enough that they crossed the Protestant/Catholic divide. Though PROVADENIC was a Baptist organization, they found some local leaders who were Catholics, such as the nuns in Acahualinca, one of the poorest neighborhoods in Managua. A clinic was set up there and the nuns worked perfectly with the PROVADENIC staff and volunteers. Sometimes the Catholic Delegates of the Word were involved as well. These connections to grassroots Catholic leaders would become invaluable in shaping reconciliation work during and after the war years.

Carlos Escobar, who served with PROVADENIC as a dental health promoter, told about the love people had for Dr. Parajón. "Once I asked him if he would like to go with me to Colonia General Somoza (renamed Colonia Germán Pomares after the revolution), a village in Chinandega. He said yes; he wrote it in his calendar. I then told the community about his visit, and I thought that the same number of people that always came to the consultations would arrive, and that was not so! A lot came, the men with long sleeves and white shoes, and the women, all so elegant, waiting for the doctor. They loved him very much in the communities."

Carlos Arosman Barahona was selected as a health promoter in his small town of San Gregorio in the province of Nueva Segovia. A meeting was held at the Baptist church. The pastor said the person chosen would travel the 350 kilometers to Managua to study medicine and come back to help the community that suffered from multiple diseases. Carlos was barely 17 years old, but he was respected for his good behavior and faithfulness in church. He packed his few belongings in a suitcase and headed for the capital.

When he arrived in Managua, he gathered with all the other newly chosen health promoters. Dr. Parajón met with them and quickly made them feel at ease.

Though he was Harvard educated, he was humble and approachable. The training lasted ten weeks. After five weeks of training, the heath promoters returned to their communities. PROVADENIC supplied them with medicines as they sought to meet the medical needs of those around them. Then the health promoters would return for another five weeks, this time bringing their experiences and questions to provide a sharper focus for the next stage of learning.

Once, Carlos Arosman Barahona traveled some 27 kilometers into the mountains to study a cruel disease that the population called "mountain leprosy." The disease disfigured people's faces and limbs. There was no known cure, so the people simply suffered. Carlos raised the case with Dr. Parajón. The correct name of the disease was Leishmaniasis, an illness transmitted by sand flies. There were no medicines to deal with this disease in Nicaragua, so Parajón found out where to get the medicine in the U.S. Soon the medicine was taken to the remote areas to cure those who had suffered so much from this disease.

Dr. Parajón found a new and unexpected source for health workers. Harry Strachan was a missionary kid raised in Costa Rica. His father was friends with Gustavo's father, Arturo. Harry eventually went to Harvard Law School and then got a doctorate in business. He returned to Nicaragua as the president and professor of INCAE, Instituto Centroamericano de Administración de Empresas, a training center for organizational and business management.[4] Harry and Deirdre Strachan moved into the house next door to the Parajóns. The showers of the two houses were next to each other, so one couldn't miss hearing when the other was in use! Joan and Deirdre became best friends.

However, for PROVADENIC, the important development was a cluster of women, the wives of men involved with INCAE. One of those wives was Fran Korten, who came to Nicaragua with her husband, Dave, so he could be the Harvard representative at INCAE. She was a bright new Ph.D. in social psychology from Stanford, caring for two young children and pregnant with her third. Fran had hired someone local to help with the house and family, so she had extra time on her hands, a condition common to other INCAE wives. Gustavo had a conversation with Deirdre about these talented women with time on their hands, so they gathered Fran, Deirdre, and a number of others. Only one or two were nurses, the rest willing volunteers.

Gustavo gave the training on simple medicine. The idea was to go into areas of Nicaragua that were beyond the reach of the government clinics, to go to the remote rural areas that had no medical care at all. The women would provide some basic care such as washing wounds, providing bandages, and giving vaccines. The doctor told them that the best medicine was soap: Providing soap, latrines, and

---

4 INCAE's main regional offices are now near Alajuela, Costa Rica while maintaining a national office in Managua, Nicaragua.

clean water was the foundation of good public health. Gustavo also showed them when and how to refer someone to get the next level of care.

Gustavo would send a Jeep early in the morning, around 5 or 6 a.m., to pick up the women. They would drive maybe four hours, often on rutted, muddy, bumpy roads. Gustavo had formed committees in each community, and the committee would be there to greet them. The women called themselves the "quack corps"; they wondered what the villagers called them!

The group would hold a clinic in a rudimentary schoolhouse or some other community building. They set up curtains to give patients privacy. The villagers were already waiting for them. Most of the patients were women and children. Most of the women were pregnant. They would give vaccinations to the children and help people with fevers and diarrhea, common maladies that could become catastrophic if not treated properly. The team would break for food from the villagers, the common rice and beans called gallo pinto, and occasionally iguana meat.

As Fran and Deirdre worked with the pregnant women, they had conversations about their families and their desires about children. Many of the women had more than six children. One woman, when asked if she would like more children, just laughed. Fran asked Gustavo if they could talk more with the women and explore family planning. The doctor said, "Fine, do it!" They began offering pills and Depo-Provera shots.

The demand for assistance in family planning from the rural women outstripped the supply they could provide. Fran and Dierdre realized they had a management problem, so they continued to explore the problem with support from the INCAE community, including Fran's husband, Dave. Eventually this led to the development of a family planning program for all of Central America. Dave and Fran later edited a book of case studies in family planning management.

As PROVADENIC grew, they added more services, such as dental care. Carlos Escobar worked as a dental technician in Río Blanco. He would come into a village and find that people had walked there from long distances. He would start with five or ten patients the first day, then find an even larger crowd waiting for him in the morning. He said, "This was the work in the communities. We did extractions because people had, you can say, rotten teeth, all the gums with infection and then that forced us to take care of as much as we could."[5]

In a remote community called Baká in Río Blanco, Carlos spent an exhausting day with some thirty patients. As he was trying to close at 5 p.m., the local health promoter don Antonio asked him to see one more patient. Carlos replied, "What? How can you ask me that at this hour?" Then he heard an amazing story from the patient: "Two days ago I left my community and spent last night at a relative's house. When I was about to leave this morning for the clinic, the cat was in the

---

5 Interview of Carlos Escobar by Dámaris Albuquerque.

way, and it would not let me pass." The cat was a mountain lion! No wonder she was late! Her cheek was severely swollen. Her moving story transformed Carlos' impatience to pity. He cared for her, feeling great joy to be able to help in such a situation.

Once Carlos removed six rotted teeth from a woman. When the patients left, Carlos would tell them not to eat anything for a while, which is what he told this woman as she departed. Later, when the team was leaving the community, they stopped by a nearby house to purchase some curd to eat. Carlos found the same patient from whom he had extracted the six teeth, eating tortilla with curd! He asked her, "Why are you eating? It will make you sick!" She quickly replied, "No, it is very soft food."

When a team went to the communities, they had to leave very early because of the long travel time. So they would sterilize all the equipment the day before travel. They took additional sterilizing liquid for the community clinics to keep everything clean as they were working. The teams were proud that they never got a complaint that someone was infected by dirty equipment as they were treated. As Gustavo said, soap is the main tool for public health.

Health promoters sometimes faced severe physical challenges to get to the most remote spots. Some had to hike forty-five minutes in rough terrain just to get from one house to the next. They had to cross mountains and sometimes rivers. Some workers literally had to swim across rivers to carry out their responsibilities. The commitment of the health promoters to their work was tremendous, causing some patients to say they "saw the face of Christ" in them.

Gustavo would form groups of Baptist young people and short-term mission people from other countries. They would go to a particular district and live on a farm or in a community center. They slept in cots, girls on one side, boys on the other. They would work with the community leaders to do a needs assessment, dealing with issues such as water, latrines, births, and deaths. The team would hold clinics on some days, dig latrines on other days, and on still other days run literacy programs. This hands-on engagement revolutionized the lives and vision of the young people involved.

George Jackson returned from Cleveland many times. Once, he and Gustavo were in a remote community when an old man was brought to them in extreme pain. He couldn't urinate. They had no catheters in their equipment. They did have IV catheters with needles in plastic sheaths. So they improvised with the IV equipment to get up to the inflamed bladder. They were able to get a bit of urine dripping out, but the man was still in a severe crisis. They loaded him into a truck to cross the river to get to Colonia Somoza. George was driving because Gus didn't like to drive. They looked at the swollen river in flood stage. They agreed to go, but Gustavo said to go slow so as not to create waves that would swamp the engine.

George wanted to go fast, but agreed to take it easy. George swore as they got stuck in the water. They both got out and waded to the people on the other side. An ox cart was found and ropes looped around their truck. The ox pulled the truck and patient safely to dry land, and they were able to get the suffering man to the hospital for the care he needed.

Another special friend was Dr. William "Bill" S. Cumming, an internist with a private practice in Cleveland. He was also a member at First Baptist Church of Cleveland and had a heart for serving others in the name of Christ. Bill began organizing and leading teams of young people from the FBC Cleveland who traveled each summer to Nicaragua to work in public health education. They built clinics and latrines in the PROVADENIC communities. Bill had also sung in the Cleveland Orchestra Chorus with Joan, so he had close ties to the whole Parajón family. He came down to Nicaragua more than forty times, almost every year from the founding of PROVADENIC until his death in 2010. After Bill's death and at his request, his ashes were scattered at First Baptist Managua, AMOS (which succeeded PROVADENIC—see Chapter 11), and one of the AMOS communities, showing how deeply his heart was in Nicaragua and the ministry there.

Over the course of forty years, PROVADENIC served more than sixty communities, providing access to health care in remote rural areas and bringing about significant decreases in both child and maternal mortality. In 1983 and 1984, the World Health Organization praised Nicaragua for the greatest achievement in health care of any developing country, termed "third world" at the time. In communities served by PROVADENIC, the infant mortality rate dropped from 25% to 1%. Beyond statistics were the relationships. People felt valued as human beings in the way they were cared for and in how people from their own community participated in the health work. The model of working with community leaders would pay a different sort of dividend when the health of the entire country was torn apart by war. Dr. Parajón's methodology of bringing people together from Catholic and evangelical churches and from different political perspectives to serve on the health committee prepared the way for the work of reconciliation needed in the years ahead.

A Youth-Run Gas Station

Parajón served as president of the Social Assistance Commission of the Baptist Convention of Nicaragua. The purpose of the commission was to serve others in the name of the Lord through very concrete physical actions to meet those needs. One of their projects was the Student Chevron Gas Station.

However, the real beginning of the project was Gustavo helping to lead the youth group at First Baptist. He quickly involved them in service projects such as tutoring with a literacy program and digging latrines in rural communities with

PROVADENIC. What impressed them was not that he was a medical doctor trained at a prestigious U.S. university. Rather it was that this doctor would eat and sleep with everyone else on the mission trip. Nobody knew of an educated person acting like that, so he quickly earned their admiration and respect.

Then the doctor started asking questions about their lives, particularly the lack of jobs for poor students so they could continue their studies. They brainstormed various ideas, including selling pigs and charcoal as well as running a gas station. They organized teams to study each possibility.

Gustavo recruited his neighbor Harry Strachan from INCAE to serve as a business mentor to the young men. Harry invited the middle and high school students over to his home for a time to analyze their findings together. Later these young men were amazed that one of the top business people in the region would take such time with them to teach them how to do financial analysis and develop business plans. They formed a service cooperative and decided to go with the idea of running a gas station.

Harry introduced them to his business acquaintance Hugh Renfro, the general manager for Chevron in Nicaragua. He liked the novelty of the idea. A brand new station in downtown Managua was assigned to the cooperative. Renfro first spread them around a number of existing gas stations so the students could get a sense of the business. Then, in early 1971, the cooperative gas station was launched, run by a dozen eager students.

Gustavo had the Social Assistance Commission purchase the station with the help of a $5,000 grant from the Baptists in Ohio. Right away, the young folks made leaflets that they passed out in the surrounding neighborhoods to inform people of the new ownership, stirring up interest and new customers. Business began to pick up. Octavio Cortés was one of those students. He remembers, "Once on the field, we discovered customer behavior, the good and the not-so-good. We wised up on how to deal with credit, when credit cards did not exist; and learned that there were financial problems when sales did not hit the target to cover expenses, or when bad debts increased. We acquired skills listening to customers' complaints and how to address them; and developed character when we had to comply with work shifts, either day or night or during holidays, all year round. We learned the basics in analyzing situations and solving problems, many of them our own. We gained experience on how to relate to each other in the group, and realized that running a business was different than doing voluntary work. Together with the good learning, there were also many mistakes and undesirable behavior among some members who had to part. The station became, in fact, a hands-on business school for all participants."[6]

---

6 Interview of Octavio Cortés by Dámaris Albuquerque.

Gustavo was unflappable, whether the gas station was running in the red or in the black, while Harry agonized over turning it into a profit-making enterprise. When they finally were in the black, Harry was stunned that the first action of the young people was to hire another needy young person. Care for one another rather than profit was their driving value.

Gustavo and Harry would both often stop by to offer assistance and encouragement after their own days at the hospital and INCAE. Gustavo would talk with the students and sometimes pray. He would help them with some of the office work. Someone once approached Gustavo with an offer to buy out the station and run it with the students as employees, "to straighten things out." Gustavo refused, keeping the vision of not merely making a profit but of growing future leaders with a broad set of skills. He also wanted to stay true to his philosophy about people participating in the processes that affect their lives, which was at the heart of the cooperative model with these young people.

Some twenty years later, when those involved in the gas station project gathered, Strachan was delighted to see how all of them had become key leaders in church, business, and society. That gas station was their proving ground for leadership development, handling financial affairs, and personal accountability. One commented that the gas station was like having an internship prior to going through formal studies.

Literacy Campaign

Vernon Jantzi was a Mennonite worker who moved to Nicaragua from Costa Rica to bring an adult literacy program to the country. Eulalia Cook and Justo and Luisa Gonzalez established the Alfalit International literacy program based in Costa Rica. They utilized the world-famous Frank Laubach literacy methodology with a profound addition that was right in line with Gustavo Parajón's health care vision of training volunteers. Each student would become a teacher, or as they said, "Each one teach one."

Jantzi found the Baptist community very eager partners in the work, and many of the Nicaraguan Baptists became close friends. American Baptist missionary Hugh Smith joined the Alfalit board, and the initial training sessions were held in the Baptist school in Masaya. But Alfalit was also ecumenical, involving folks such as the Pentecostals and Nazarenes. The network of these relationships would prove vital in the creative response to the crises that were ahead.

As Gustavo worked in training the health promoters, he had difficulties conveying instructions to people who couldn't read. He realized that effective public health work would need to be partnered with literacy efforts. So he joined Alfalit.

Gustavo had a strategic concern to engage young people in bringing about change. He saw them as more open to new ideas, with lots of energy and not bound to traditions as much as their elders. He sought to bring them into programs such as PROVADENIC and later CEPAD. He invited Jantzi to connect with these young people. "I want you to work with these kids, connect them to the rural communities," Gustavo said. So many of the kids had come to the cities for education and jobs, but their parents and grandparents were back in the rural villages. Many of the young ones eagerly joined in the literacy work and thrived. They learned leadership while respecting and working with the community elders. Later they would be the emerging leaders who would move into other projects.

When Jantzi went back to Costa Rica to engage in more regional work, he took along the focus he gained from Gustavo of looking to equip young people to be the change agents. Gustavo, as a Baptist, modeled for the Mennonite Jantzi how to work in collaboration with government officials to carry out a project such as literacy. Jantzi later said that his own work with the Costa Rican government was directly affected by what he learned from Parajón.[7]

Eventually, Gustavo was appointed director of Alfalit International's literacy work in Latin America, which covered twelve countries. That was just another role he added to his already full plate. But Dr. Parajón had no idea of the tragedy and opportunity that was to open up shortly and demand even more of him.

---

7 Interview of Vernon Jantzi by Daniel Buttry.

3

Earthquake!

Massive Earthquake Shatters Managua

'Twas two nights before Christmas, and the Parajón family was asleep like so many of the citizens of Managua. They had a Christmas tree all decorated in their living room. That evening, Gustavo and Joan had gone with the youth choir of First Baptist to Getsemaní Baptist. They performed their Christmas concert with great joy, sharing between the brothers and sisters of the two churches. Everyone went to bed with a warm feeling.

Twenty minutes after midnight, the Christmas peace was shattered as the earth shook violently. Gustavo jolted up, ran to grab 6-year-old David and took him outside. David woke up on his father's shoulder as he was being carried through the house into their yard. As Joan tried to get out, she slipped on water that had sloshed out of the toilet from the severe shaking. With relief, the three made it outside, worried about Marta, who was staying with a friend not far away.

The Parajón home didn't collapse, but it was a mess. The walls were cracked. The refrigerator had popped open, spilling milk and food all over the floor. Books had fallen off the bookshelves. Their Christmas tree toppled. Gustavo explained to David what the earthquake was, though David remembered the smaller quake they had been through in Mexico on their way to Nicaragua.

Gustavo first went to the friend's house where Marta was staying. He found that they were all right, shaken like everyone else, but unhurt. Just as he brought Marta home, a second tremor rumbled through the earth. Marta struggled to stay on her feet. Their gate cracked and fell. Trees waved up and down as the ground seemed like the sea. Gustavo said, "We should find out if our friends are okay." They dragged the mattresses outside for Joan and the children to sleep in the yard, if they could manage to get back to sleep.

Not too far away, Fran Korten, the PROVADENIC volunteer, was jarred awake by the first shock. She rushed to the other bedroom to see her youngest child, Alicia, 2 years old, standing in her crib excitedly saying, "More bumpity bump!" When the next shock struck, the terrified child cried, "No more bumpity bump!" In the Korten home, the water pipes burst, the bookcases collapsed, many household items were smashed, but their house stood.

Gustavo left again to check on other friends, joining up with Sixto Ulloa, sharing a Jeep. Sixto had been a volunteer at a PROVADENIC clinic, but the National Guard branded him a communist. To go out in the streets without suspicion, he put on the green scrubs of a doctor, complete with a stethoscope around his neck. The damage up in the hills was less than down in the city. Down in the city it didn't look so good. Fires lit up the darkness. Periodically explosive fireballs showed where gas stations had been; they later learned that the Chevron station run by the young men was damaged, but not destroyed.

While Gustavo and Sixto were checking in with friends, a third massive tremor hit. The vicious ripples of the earth were visible, rocking the Jeep to and fro. Finding their friends and associates in the area all safe, they drove back to the Parajón home. Picking up Joan and the children, they drove down into the city, where they encountered hellish scenes. The drive was a nightmare. Most of the streets were obstructed with fallen trees and other debris. Their way was littered with wood and stone from collapsed walls. They thanked God for the four-wheel drive Toyota that got them through the mess. People were wailing beside buildings with the roofs collapsed to ground level. There was no electricity, and the darkness was pierced by fires burning amid the chaos. They found the Baptist seminary in good shape, so they left the children in the care of friends there while Gustavo, Joan, and Sixto went to help where they could.

Gustavo was dropped off at the Baptist Hospital into a scene of confusion. The electricity was out. Some folks had flashlights. The hospital was partially destroyed, but still standing. Eventually, it would be torn down. The floors were covered with shattered glass and fluids from the broken medical vials and bottles. Gustavo's office was destroyed. There was no water and no phones.

Then the people began to stream in. Many beds in the hospital were destroyed. There were no usable stretchers. People were carrying injured family members and neighbors upon doors. Everyone seemed as if they had been submerged in a giant chamber of dust. The dust was everywhere, on everything and everybody. Dr. Parajón felt so helpless that there was absolutely nothing they could do. In the first twenty minutes he told thirteen families that their loved ones had died. People started flowing over into the yard, and they were tended to there as best as possible.

After about two hours, a nurse heard from the hospital in Masaya that they were okay and standing by to help. Examining people with a triage mentality, the doctor began sending folks who were serious but survivable to Masaya with any transportation that could be found.

Meanwhile, Joan and Sixto went on to look for an Alfalit volunteer, Roberto Breckenridge, who was living very close to downtown Managua. They found Roberto sitting outside a ruined building. He told a story of miraculous survival. He woke up with the first quake and tried to get out of his apartment, but a wall had collapsed, blocking the door. He screamed for help. A Costa Rican tourist had just come in by bus and was walking through the center of Managua. He heard Roberto's scream and kicked the door in. Just as Roberto climbed out, the building collapsed.

As the sun rose over the shattered city, people were desperately looking for family and friends. Gustavo and Joan looked for members from the church. They found that the mother of Lilliam Quezada, one of the young women who sang in the youth choir at the church, had been crushed by a wall in her bedroom. The Parajóns accompanied Lilliam and the Quezada family to the Nejapa Cemetery, where the mother was buried that same morning. There was no time for wakes and funerals. Bodies needed to be buried quickly to prevent disease from erupting. Perhaps Gustavo took time for this burial because of the pain in his own family of not knowing where his grandmother was buried from the 1931 earthquake.

A major geological fault line runs close to the city, so when an earthquake occurs, Managua is often at the epicenter. Over 10,000 people lost their lives just before Christmas 1972, most dying as they slept in their homes. Eight hundred blocks of houses were leveled and 500,000 people were left homeless. The Catholic cathedral in the center of Managua was left a roofless shell. There were no construction codes in Managua, and slap-dash construction spelled doom for so many that night when the earth shook.

In the Aftermath

As word got out about the scale of the earthquake, international aid began to pour in. A planeload of Cuban medical personnel and supplies was one of the first flights to arrive. The Somoza regime did not have good relations with Cuba, so this might have been problematic. However, immediately after the earthquake, all the immigration and customs personnel at the airport fled to find and look after their families. The Cubans arrived to find the airport empty, so they simply headed into the city to help wherever they could.

More planes arrived with aid, and then they would take some of the seriously injured people out for treatment in neighboring countries. One such person was Gustavo and Joan's next-door neighbor, Deirdre Strachan, who volunteered with PROVADENIC. She was in her ninth month of pregnancy and had begun labor when the earthquake struck. Harry asked Gustavo, "Do you have a book on how to deliver a baby?" Knowing how badly damaged and overwhelmed the hospital was, Gustavo told him to get Deirdre out of the country on one of the departing aid planes, many of which were returning home empty. The doctor knew disease was sure to come with a vengeance in the wake of such a catastrophe; definitely not a time or place to bring a baby into the world. So Harry and Deirdre headed to the airport with their 2-year-old child. They boarded a plane after the relief supplies had been unloaded, along with people lying on stretchers. As the plane landed in Costa Rica, Deirdre was in heavy labor. They rushed to a hospital in San José that had been founded by Harry's grandmother, and there the child was safely born.

Aid came in by land and air. A convoy of four or five vehicles loaded with medicines and food drove up from Costa Rica, sent by Caravanas de Buena Voluntad. This program was led by Dr. Arturo Cabezas, director of the Biblical Clinic in San José. Dr. Cabezas was a friend and colleague of Dr. Parajón. They had worked together with Alfalit, a network that came through many times in crises. This was the first concrete help to arrive at the Baptist Hospital. In the days that followed, a steady stream of vehicles poured in from Costa Rica.

Around Managua's neighborhoods, people rummaged through the ruins of their houses, trying to salvage whatever possessions they could. Many people piled their belongings in the middle of the street, making travel even more difficult. Thousands fled the city, trying to find refuge in nearby towns and cities that hadn't been so damaged. Many people whose homes had been destroyed or damaged took refuge on the grounds of the Baptist school.

Communication was severely hampered as the phone lines were down and electricity out throughout the region. Joan operated a ham radio that became a communication lifeline. The Parajóns had a little generator to power up the radio. An antenna had been installed in the backyard, something little David loved to climb for the view. Under her call letters YN1-JMP, Joan sent one of the first messages from the earthquake zone telling the world about the calamity. Joan had connections with friends John Kiener in Cleveland and Al Suhr in Florida. She spent as many as twelve hours a day on the radio for three months after the earthquake. She passed John and Al messages from the people in Nicaragua to be relayed to family and friends across the U.S. about how their loved ones were faring.

Some tents were donated to the Parajóns, arriving in some of the first trucks. They slept in tents pitched in their yard for a month. Other families camped with them, mostly people from the church who had been displaced. Everyone slept outside with the tents butted up next to each other. They got up in the morning together. The Parajóns and all gathered with them would eat and bathe in the house. David would nap inside, but Marta was terrified to be indoors. Aftershocks continued, leaving everyone shaky and on edge. In such a disaster it was vital for everyone to pull together, and they did.

The young men from the Chevron gas station were available, confident, and eager. They had vehicles gassed up and ready for use in rescue efforts. Darwin López was sleeping in a car at the gas station when the earthquake struck. He joined in helping rescue trapped women, children, and older people from the rubble. Later, when he went back home, he found a massive stone in the middle of his bed. He would have been seriously injured or killed if he hadn't slept at the gas station. Gustavo utilized the young men from the gas station team as communicators to connect with folks throughout the city. Sometimes he sent them simply to find out what was happening in other parts of Managua. They found eight church families whose homes were burning and helped them get to the Baptist school. This cadre of young men helped in many of the organizing tasks, turning their new skills towards this new crisis. Trucks with aid had to be quickly unloaded, and the young men brought their energy to that vital chore.

The Birth of CEPAD

Prior to 1970, the evangelical and Protestant churches in Nicaragua tended to stay in their separate denominational silos. In the heavily Catholic country, the denominations competed for the small numbers of people willing to live at the religious margins. But Alfalit had begun to weave church leaders together across denominational lines by meeting a common need with a shared ministry. Also, PROVADENIC, though it was Baptist, had organized community leaders from various denominations as well as Catholics. Besides, as a Baptist, Dr. Parajón was accepted both by the traditional denominations and the more independent and Pentecostal churches. Dr. Parajón was also the personal physician of missionaries from various denominations who utilized the excellent resources of the Baptist Hospital. Thus, he had a personal web of relationships that cut across many denominational lines, quite a list to respond to the vast needs before them.

Gustavo called together evangelical leaders who were interested in working together to help in this catastrophe for a meeting on December 27. Darwin López was able to go to Radio Nacional because it was the first station that Somoza was able to get back on the air after the earthquake. López announced that a meeting would be held on the grounds of the Colegio Bautista, the Baptist School.

The first meeting of CEPAD was held under a mango tree. About twenty people from eight denominations gathered, along with some mission organizations.

The denominations were the Central American Convention of Churches, the Mennonite Church, the International Baptist Mission, the Assemblies of God, Church of God, the Church of Christ, the Baptist Convention of Nicaragua, and the United Brethren in Christ. They were joined by representatives from Alfalit, the Baptist Hospital and the Baptist Theological Seminary.

Everyone was afraid to go into the building over safety concerns, so Parajón and the pastors met in the shade. By 9 a.m., they had committed to form the organization. The initial name was the Evangelical Committee to Aid the Victims, later changed to the Emergency Committee for Relief and Development (CEPAD as the Spanish acronym). A representative was present from Church World Service (CWS), a major ecumenical relief organization in the United States, providing an immediate significant link to a funding and supply partner.

Lidya Ruth Zamora was one of those who had taken refuge in the colegio compound. She had returned from school in the U.S. to visit with her family during Christmas break, arriving the evening of the earthquake. Gustavo recruited her to help by taking notes of the meeting, the first of her many expanding leadership roles in Baptist circles dealing with education and human need.

Gilberto Aguirre was a science teacher at the colegio. He was usually referred to by his nickname "El Profe." On the day of the meeting under the mango tree, he was trying to salvage scientific equipment in the damaged classroom. He was planning to leave with his family to teach at the Baptist school in El Salvador, but Gustavo demanded that he stay. Parajón quickly put him to work. Gilberto was profoundly moved by all those gathered to serve even though everyone faced the same dire situation. Such compassion and dedication excited him and inspired him to stay. El Profe and Gustavo became close friends and inseparable partners, eventually with Gustavo as president of CEPAD and Gilberto as executive director from 1980 to 2001.

The new group had a little money to begin their work together. Through her radio, Joan had reached the Ohio Baptist Convention with the news of the earthquake. Less than two hours later, the Parajóns learned that the convention had made a wire transfer of $5,000 for immediate assistance. Harry Strachan was willing to cash the check from the Baptists from INCAE funds, getting the resources into the hands of Gustavo and the other gathered church leaders. They called on other denominations and organizations to lend a hand.

Recovery Continued

CEPAD mobilized with stunning speed. Jerry Aaker had served as a missionary with the Lutheran Church in America, including helping during a major earthquake in Peru. He and his wife, Judy, were in Minneapolis praying about their next ministry call. Dwight Swartzendruber, the Latin American director for

CWS, called them and asked them to go to Nicaragua. Judy and Jerry looked at each other: "There's where we're going next!" A week after the meeting under the mango tree, Jerry flew into Managua.

As Jerry arrived, all he had was the name Gustavo Parajón. Gustavo sent Cathy Strachan to pick him up. She took Jerry to the destroyed building of the Baptist School, where another meeting of CEPAD was being held. Many of the young men from the gas station were part of the first staff for the new organization.

After the meeting, Gustavo invited Jerry to drive around the city with him and see what they could see. At the airport relief supplies were coming in, some to be distributed by churches, as CEPAD wasn't fully organized yet. The supplies were in a warehouse, but most weren't moving from there. It was a problem that needed to be urgently addressed.

President Somoza had designated his son, known as Anastasio "the Kid" or "El Chigüin," to oversee the relief supplies coming in. Reports had begun to surface about Somoza and his son diverting money and supplies for themselves. Gustavo had received a specific report from Joan's work on the radio about 220,000 pounds of supplies coming from Medical Assistance Program International out of Chicago. They had not received any of the aid. Joan got the plane number, the company flight number, and the airway bill number.

Dr. Parajón and Jerry Aaker went to General Somoza to protest, and the dictator sent them to his son. The Kid was designated by his father to receive and administer all information about supplies coming through the airport. They had found cans of meat sent for assistance already being sold at the Oriental Market in Managua, so obviously the aid was being siphoned off. Parajón and Aaker insisted that the need was so great that they must have the food. Dr. Parajón was respected by Somoza's wife, Hope Somoza, so he approached her and appealed for the release of supplies. She joined in insisting the supplies be released to the churches. Eventually about 80,000 pounds was released, a bit more than a third of what had been sent. The rest disappeared into the Somoza family's black market operations. People knew what was going on. So many were living in tents and struggling to get anything to eat. To know the government was taking money from the church aid sent to help them fueled a deep, angry frustration. This blatant corruption in the middle of a national disaster significantly added to the discontent that began to take shape in violent resistance to the Somoza dictatorship.

After the tour of Managua, Gustavo and Jerry brainstormed about how to formally organize CEPAD. They quickly formed a provisional committee to decide how to structure the group. Jerry shared his previous experience with Lutherans and CWS in Peru and Vietnam. He insisted that it would be vital for the organization to be fully Nicaraguan from the beginning. Nicaraguans needed to take the responsibility to set up an administrative structure and program structure as well as find a director. Gustavo quickly did that.

They had to move fast as resources were pouring in. Besides setting up the organization, they had to act quickly to develop a plan to rationally distribute and use the supplies that were arriving.

People came as well. About ten days after the earthquake, Dr. George Jackson came with another team from First Baptist Cleveland. "Where do you start?" Jackson asked. Fires were still burning around the city. The Baptist Hospital had set up tents for the patients outside the ruined building. Jackson and his team got to work at the hospital.

Nancy Wheaton from the Cleveland church came with a team driving a Ford pickup and a GMC truck. It wasn't so simple to just drive down. They had to replace the Ohio plates in Mexico with Mexican plates. Then, at the border, Honduras armed guards thoroughly inspected the trucks for fear that they might be bringing in arms for Nicaraguan rebels. When they finally got into Nicaragua, the rain was pouring down. One of the trucks hit a donkey. A man at the scene, who was drunk, had a phone, so the team called Gustavo. He sent Sixto to lead them the rest of the way in. While the seven labored at the relief work, they spent their nights jammed into one hotel room as there was so little space available. It didn't matter; they were helping their friends in a severe crisis.

Vernon Jantzi from Alfalit had been living in Costa Rica during the earthquake. He returned to Nicaragua in February. The Taca plane hopped in a circle through the Central American capitals. When they landed in Guatemala City, Jantzi's 7-year-old son, Terry, complained that his side hurt. Jantzi had had appendicitis, and what Terry complained about seemed just like his own earlier experience. Managua was the next stop, and the plane landed in the rain. They went to the Mennonite house, where people were still sleeping on the floors. Terry's condition deteriorated and he became wracked with vomiting. Jantzi called Gustavo, who immediately said, "Meet me at the hospital." Jantzi found the hospital partially in ruins, but Dr. Parajón operated on the boy immediately. After the successful surgery, the only bed available was an X-ray table. Terry stayed there until he was discharged two days later.

In the first ten weeks of CEPAD's life, the organizers set up a program to serve food to children, pregnant women, and needy adults. Almost 220 maternal and child kitchens were established, serving 35,000 hot breakfasts each day. The kitchens were scattered throughout Managua's neighborhoods, but also in Granada, Masaya, Tipitapa, León, Matagalpa, and Rivas. Such a massive rapid mobilization was possible because 1,700 volunteers stepped forward, mostly women from the women's societies of the churches in CEPAD's denominations. Gustavo loved these women's organizations and was able to mobilize them quickly. The volunteers got up at 3:00 or 4:00 a.m. to cook breakfast for the one to two hundred children served by each kitchen, as well as the adults. For some children, this was the only nutritious food they would get that day.

Someone asked if the food was for the evangelicals. "The food is for the hungry," was the quick reply. That set the principle that CEPAD would not be an organization seeking to meet only the needs of evangelicals. Rather, they would seek to meet the needs of anybody regardless of religious affiliation or commitment. They were to be expressions to people in need of the love of Jesus, pure and simple.

At their March 31, 1973 General Assembly, the members of CEPAD set their main purpose. CEPAD would be organized for "... the promotion of the well-being of Nicaraguans in the following fields: integral development of individuals and communities; health in the physical, mental, and spiritual spheres; adult basic education; adequate housing." This purpose was anchored in their belief that "the church has a ministry to humanity in the name of Christ that reaches into the spiritual, physical and emotional needs of persons."[8]

Years later, when El Salvador, Costa Rica, and Haiti had their terrible earthquakes, Nicaraguans remembered what it was like and sent aid. CEPAD shared the experience they had gained with people in many other disaster areas. They would need that experience again and again in Nicaragua as hurricanes, earthquakes, and wars tore through people and communities.

---

8 Contact, Christian Medical Commission, World Council of Churches, October 1979, pp. 3-4.

Dr. Parajón speaking to a community group.

Loading supplies for CEPAD relief work.

Boarding for an emergency airlift.

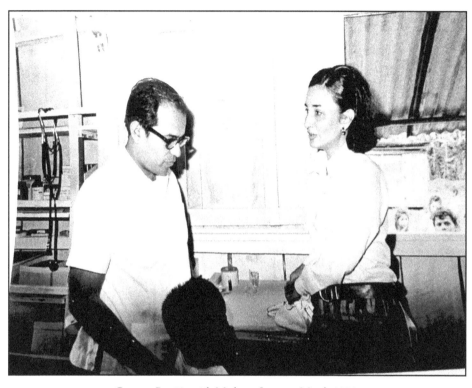

Gustavo Parajón with Madame Somoza, March 1971.

4

Dictatorship and Revolution

Working Among the Poor

With the support of new international partners and a historic moment of need, CEPAD began to develop. It took them about six months to a year to get well established. Early in their organizational journey, there was unity among the denominations involved. Eventually, more than seventy Protestant groups joined the organization. Gustavo was the president of the board. He never worked as staff for CEPAD, continuing rather as director for PROVADENIC, located next door to the CEPAD offices. The first executive director of CEPAD was Professor Gustavo Wilson. He was followed by Benjamin Cortés until 1980.

CEPAD expanded and refined the various areas where they could help poor communities. They developed seeds for planting, developed more productive crops, and replanted forests. They developed projects to offer small-scale technology to rebuild homes. They worked on sanitary water and waste systems. However, key to CEPAD's way of operating was that training always came first, before projects. The training was specifically designed to empower local leadership in the work of building up their own communities. Furthermore, the foundation to the training was laid in Bible studies. For this organization, made up of churches across Nicaragua, the Bible studies weren't just add-ons, but were central to shaping their philosophy of development and community engagement.

PROVADENIC also continued to grow. Most of the women from INCAE left in the years following the earthquake as their families moved on to Costa Rica, where INCAE's central campus had relocated. Other INCAE folks moved on for opportunities in academia in the U.S. But the training and development of local health promoters had hit its stride, as well as volunteer mission teams coming in to supplement the Nicaraguan staff.

Gustavo related well to international volunteers and staff in both PROVADENIC and CEPAD. International workers came from the Christian Reformed World Relief Committee, along with Jerry Aaker representing CWS and Lutheran World Relief. Sometimes volunteers worked out well, though sometimes they didn't. Whatever the situation, Gustavo was always encouraging to the volunteers and staff. The Nicaraguans led both organizations. International folks were not allowed to direct, but took on roles as supporters and advisors. Judy Aaker especially appreciated that Gustavo was easy to talk to. He spoke perfect English, but his Spanish was also understandable and clear to outsiders with modest Spanish skills.

Central to the work of CEPAD and PROVADENIC was the understanding that everyone is created in God's image and likeness. For Parajón, this was foundational for everything they did. People were to be valued not for how much they possessed or what titles they had, but because of their inherent dignity as God's creatures. He valued human intelligence even if people had not been given access to education. This value shaped the way Dr. Parajón and all those in CEPAD and PROVADENIC approached people in local communities.

Carlos Mejía Ruiz experienced that valuing of people firsthand. Sixto hired Carlos in 1973 as a teenager to be a messenger or office boy. Once Sixto told him to take a document to the next office, which was Dr. Parajón's. Parajón invited him to sit down. He remembered Carlos and welcomed him to be working at CEPAD. They would often see each other. Carlos remembered, "We became more confident. He was the only one who called me Chale. Everyone else called me Carlos or Carlitos. He was very special." Once Dr. Parajón asked him, "Chale, are you studying?" The young man wasn't, but Parajón encouraged him to pursue his further learning.

Taking their cues from Gustavo, the leaders of CEPAD and PROVADENIC assumed the local folks were intelligent and could contribute to developing and shaping the answers for their own concerns. People could be subjects in transforming their own realities. This is why leadership development was woven into all they did. Parajón later said, "You know that always giving aid, like in an earthquake, can become very paternalistic. We are used to 'give me, give me' and nothing 'I give' to help me. So, we wanted there to be that change, and the communities could become self-sufficient, discovering the capacities that God has given us all to work together to overcome these needs." Local folks would be trained to run committees, to be health promoters, to become teachers, to become agricultural promoters, and to lead peace and reconciliation committees. Grassroots leadership was not just a nice-sounding concept, but the organizational lifeblood. Those leaders could look to Dr. Parajón as a role model for leadership exercised as servanthood rather than for self-aggrandizement. He could easily have had a career making him wealthy in the U.S., but chose not only to practice medicine in his homeland, but to spend time in the rural areas sleeping on floors and dealing with mosquitos. People noticed and aspired to serve like he did.

Based on this value of people as made by God, communication became central, beginning with listening to people express their own needs and ideas. Trips to rural communities began not with presenting their program or resources, but listening to the hearts and aches of the people in those communities. Parajón also insisted that staff not use technical jargon, instead urging his team to communicate in terms people could understand.

He also saw people as whole persons, with their physical, material, social, psychological, and spiritual needs and realities interwoven. Many of the agencies involved in supporting Nicaraguan projects focused on material aid, but Parajón challenged them toward a more holistic approach. Although he was involved and often created organizations to deal with different concerns, such as health, literacy, housing, agriculture, financial credit, peace, and reconciliation, they were all interconnected, sometimes as projects of one organization and sometimes through close collaboration of staff, churches, and local committees.

Parajón was the chair of the board of CEPAD for almost thirty years, from 1972 to 2000, some of the most turbulent years in Nicaraguan history. Many felt he was the only person who could serve in that capacity as strains began to develop between the Moravians, Anglicans, Methodists, and Baptists on the one hand and the Pentecostals, Apostolic, and independent churches on the other. Part of his secret was that he knew the Bible more thoroughly than most pastors. He used Scripture studies as the basis of their work together. Everyone learned from him and therefore placed their trust and confidence in him.

One Bible passage Gustavo often used was 2 Kings 4:1-7, in which Elisha helped a poor widow. Gustavo would invite people to elicit all the lessons they could get from such a passage. In this story, one sees Elisha involve the woman in solving her own problem, empowering her to meet her needs. He saw her as a subject to change her own reality. The woman's own honesty to meet her debt was noteworthy and honorable, along with acknowledging what she had and what she needed. There was faith that God's grace would meet their needs. There was solidarity between the woman and her neighbors. This ancient story spoke directly to the Nicaraguan context of poverty and how organizations like CEPAD and PROVADENIC and later PRESTANIC could participate in bringing relief and health to poor communities.

Though most organizations would have general meetings on an annual basis, CEPAD held their General Assembly once a month to keep the relationships strong and vital. The meeting was more for building and keeping unity than for handling the business. Gustavo would lead an in-depth Bible study for about an hour to start the meetings. Then the business would follow, sometimes lasting only fifteen minutes! It was definitely not a model used much elsewhere, but for the Protestants in Nicaragua it worked.

Conflicts inevitably arose. Some would complain that others were being favored over them. Gustavo would quickly nip the conflict in the bud, though never becoming either accusatory or defensive. He would simply say, "Hermano, where did you hear that? Tell me more." *Hermano*—"the other" was always brother or sister to him. His gentle language and tone would sap the hostility in the conflict and turn people toward collaborative problem-solving.

Parajón could also be gently challenging to international experts arriving with paternalistic attitudes to help the poor Nicaraguans. Evenor Jerez was working with CEPAD when an external consultant was doing an evaluation of CEPAD's impact. In presenting their report, the term "remarkable results" was used. Dr. Parajón asked, "What does 'remarkable' mean?" His gentle question punctured the implied superiority on the part of the consultant. The consultant later commented: "Dr. Parajón made me feel stupid. Of course, that was not his intention, but he wanted us to know that he knew the meaning of the words we used. That was his way of educating us."[9]

Over the years CEPAD developed an amazing document to direct their work as human rights advocates. This is the "Decalogue (Ten Commandments) of the CEPAD Promoter of Human Rights":

1. You will always keep in mind that the love to God and your neighbor is what motivates you to be in solidarity with others.

2. You will defend the cause of the just, regardless of their political or religious beliefs.

3. You will seek the truth above everything and will present every case in such a way that it will be credible to others.

4. You will act in the most diligent way possible, remembering that the lives and physical and mental integrity of many are in your hands.

5. You will think and act with prudence, maturity, and discipline, at all times.

6. You will be as perceptive as possible; that will help you to obtain the necessary proofs so that your research and documentation will be very serious.

7. You will treat every case you research with the utmost discretion.

---

9 From interview of Evenor Jerez by Dámaris Albuquerque.

8. You will promote in your community the development of a spirit of solidarity among its members.

9. You will keep in your heart the ardent desire for justice to prevail in the society you live in.

10. You will make it your responsibility to promote the necessary knowledge to defend and exercise human rights in your community.

Sadly, there would be many opportunities to exercise these commitments in the years to come.

When Hurricane Fifi hit Honduras in 1974, CEPAD was the first agency to be on-site to provide relief. Even though CEPAD was still a very young organization, they felt obligated to share with their brothers and sisters across the border. They had developed the skills, the infrastructure, and the connections to mobilize resources and assistance quickly. After a couple years, Jerry Aaker worked himself out of a job at CEPAD, replaced by Nicaraguan leadership. Jerry spent more time representing CWS across Central America. He saw disasters up close, both Fifi in Honduras and then the earthquake in Guatemala in 1976. Each time, Gustavo, Gilberto, and CEPAD were there to help mobilize and support evangelicals in the crises. Aaker noticed, however, it was not possible to simply translate CEPAD's structure and principles to other countries. Many of the churches would come together, work for a while, then break apart because of disagreements. The success of CEPAD in Nicaragua showed the special impact of Gustavo's leadership in keeping everyone pulling together.

In 1978, the World Health Organization sponsored a global conference on public health in Alma-Ata in Kazakhstan, in what was then the Soviet Union. Representatives gathered from 130 countries, from governments and nongovernmental organizations. Dr. Gustavo Parajón was among them, representing PROVADENIC and the Christian Medical Commission of the World Council of Churches. (See more about the Alma-Ata Conference in Chapter 10.)

Dr. Parajón was one of the public health practitioners who were dialogically developing a new paradigm for how public health would be carried out. The prevailing model was hospital-centered, with medical professionals providing the services. The new paradigm was decentralized, bringing primary health care to those in the most needy and marginalized communities. Furthermore, the providers were envisioned as ordinary people who were trained in some of the basic areas of illness, prevention, and treatment that involved the vast majority of health problems in poor communities.

One in five children under 5 were dying preventable deaths, succumbing to illnesses such as diarrhea. Poverty and lack of access to health care were the prime factors in these high death rates. Children did not have enough food, leading to malnutrition and lowered immune systems. Even problems such as tuberculosis and later HIV/AIDS could be significantly reduced by equipping local folks with the tools and knowledge to educate, monitor, and care for their neighbors. Training community health workers was the model at work in PROVADENIC. The drastic drop in infant mortality rates where PROVADENIC worked showed the dynamic impact of this new paradigm for public health.

Saying "No" to the Dictator

Anastasio Somoza Debayle became president of Nicaragua in 1967 after his father was assassinated and his brother died. The West Point graduate was brutal in suppressing dissent. He came into power just as the Parajóns returned to Nicaragua. Everything that Parajón was involved in was counter to Somoza's concerns, even literacy. Somoza said, "I don't want an educated population; I want oxen."

Gustavo vividly remembered coming into his own office to meet the director of a government feeding program for Somoza's Ministry of Health. They knew each other because Parajón always coordinated the work PROVADENIC did in the rural clinics with the government, including the earlier vaccination campaign, "Pistols for Peace." The woman from the government asked how it would be possible to set up a feeding program: "We have spent five years thinking about how to carry out a similar program and you have succeeded in an earthquake?" The doctor told her, "Because of Christian women willing to serve." Gustavo saw the tremendous capacity for service, especially in the Nicaraguan Christian women. He felt they gave tremendous testimony in the name of the Lord. They served all the people of Nicaragua, not just those in the capital city, where the government tended to operate. Dr. Parajón was asked to serve as Somoza's minister of health, but he turned the offer down. He felt he could do more to help the poorest of the poor, especially in the rural areas, by continuing the work of PROVADENIC. He also simply did not want to serve under Somoza himself, though he was willing to serve on a local board chaired by the dictator's wife.

The corruption of the Somoza regime was very stark, as had been evident in relief supplies coming for CEPAD being siphoned off by Somoza's son for private family profit. The sanctuary of First Baptist Church in Managua sustained damage in the earthquake. Members wondered if it was so structurally damaged that it needed to be demolished. Or was the building condemned so that the company that Somoza had created to demolish all these buildings could make a lot of money? Some architects who knew the site thought the flaws of the church building were actually superficial. The basic structure of the building was still strong, and the sanctuary could have been restored. This type of corruption was so endemic that it sowed the seeds of discontent that helped to overthrow Somoza.

In December 1974, the Sandinistas launched their first major action, seizing the home of a former government minister during a party. The minister and a few others were killed. To release the hostages, the Sandinista National Liberation Front (FSLN as the Spanish acronym) had their declaration read over the radio and were given safe passage to Cuba. From that point the revolution was on and in the open. It simmered until 1978, with small-scale attacks and government reprisals, including mass killings of civilians. Then it burst into a major revolt.

As the revolution simmered, Carlos Mejía Ruiz, the CEPAD communications runner, often ran errands through the streets of Managua. Carlos remembers that CEPAD was very interested in when there were outbreaks in the neighborhoods from boys who were against the government. The youth sometimes threw contact bombs, set up barricades, and ambushed the National Guardsmen. CEPAD was concerned about what was happening in those neighborhoods, but even more about what was to come. The leaders of CEPAD already knew that small incidents would spur more serious repression from the regime's forces. CEPAD helped the churches provide guidance to young people so that they did not get sucked into the violence. When there were shootings at night, the next day the National Guard would arrive ready to arrest, torture, and kill any young people they could catch. Many young people had to flee but had nowhere to go. CEPAD helped steer those young people into safer areas.

One youth from the Church of the Nazarene named Lenín Peña Sánchez was a university student. He was interested in the revolution, but tried to flee to Costa Rica. He was arrested in San Carlos near the San Juan River. A CEPAD commission made up of Dr. Parajón, Professor Aguirre, and the Rev. Nicanor Mairena, superintendent of the Church of the Nazarene, went to San Carlos to see if they could get Lenín out of jail, but to no avail. Dr. Parajón sent many letters to Somoza, carried by Carlos to Somoza's bunker, pleading his case.

In late 1975, there was an amnesty, and Lenín Peña was released. However, on his way to Managua, the young man was seized again. This time he was quickly killed. His body was taken back to San Carlos, and reportedly the National Guard threw Lenín's body into a well on the military base there. CEPAD protested the extrajudicial execution of this young person from one of their churches, again to no avail.

CEPAD was working in communities, both in towns and rural areas, all across the country. They held pastoral meetings called Interdenominational Retreats of Evangelical Pastors of Nicaragua (RIPEN). The retreats were special moments for the pastors to get together and support each other, as well as support the work they shared. However, as Gustavo met with the pastors from various regions of Nicaragua, they heard reports that there was an imminent bubbling threat of war in order to get Somoza out.

At a CEPAD Assembly in 1977, they received the shocking report about how Somoza's National Guard in northern Nicaragua had executed twenty-one people from an Assemblies of God church. Defenseless Christian brothers and sisters had been murdered and later buried. The Rev. Rodolfo Fonseca, pastor of the Church of God and a member of the CEPAD Assembly, brought this information before the body. The Assembly investigated further and made the decision that a delegation had to meet with Somoza about what happened.

Gustavo Parajón led the delegation, along with Brother Jerónimo Pérez from the Assemblies of God and Brother Eugenio Zamora from the Baptist Convention, to protest and demand an explanation. Knowing how things were deteriorating under the dictatorship, Gustavo thought that perhaps it was the last day that he was going to see the freedom of the sun. Many friends were praying for them. The delegation gathered the details, including three names of National Guardsmen involved in the atrocity. They visited Somoza in his bunker, La Loma, in the center of Managua. The dictator said he wasn't happy to hear this. He was very civil and wrote down the names of the offending officers. He said it couldn't have happened, but he would investigate. Nothing was done.

As the revolution picked up steam in 1978, U.S. President Jimmy Carter refused to send further military aid to Nicaragua because of the human rights violations of the Somoza regime. Somoza heard that Carter was a Baptist, so he thought he might listen to Nicaraguan Baptists. He wanted to send a Baptist delegation to testify to the U.S. Congress that there were no human rights violations in Nicaragua. He met with three Baptist leaders. Parajón later said, "I was shaking in my boots!" but he knew he just couldn't do it. He said to the dictator, "I'm sorry, but no, I can't go. I would have to tell the truth." The other two Baptist leaders went and gave testimony before Congress. One leader later regretted what he had done, calling it a "youthful indiscretion." Even so, Parajón would recognize and honor this person every time he could rather than criticize him for what he had done.

Ministry in a Time of Revolution

In 1978, Estelí, a city about two and a half hours north of Managua, had become a center for the insurrection. The city suffered much destruction, especially at the hands of the National Guard. Several young people from First Baptist traveled there on a bus, joining a crew from CEPAD in other vehicles full of supplies for the suffering populace. As they entered the city, they stopped at a Catholic school where displaced people had gathered. Before they could enter the school compound, they were stopped by the commander of the Estelí National Guard, a tall man with a notorious bad temper who was nicknamed "Cherry." Cherry demanded that everyone get out of the vehicles and show their identification documents. When Dr. Parajón took out his wallet, Cherry aggressively reached to snatch it, but the doctor wouldn't let him. Parajón spoke to the commander in a firm voice, "What documents do you want? I will show them to you, but do not touch my wallet." The stunned young people watched the cowed Cherry wait respectfully for the doctor to show him the documents.

As the revolution intensified, Dr. Parajón and Lidya Ruth Zamora traveled to various churches and homes of church members throughout the country. Zamora was the president of the Christian Service Commission (CSC) of the Baptist Convention of Nicaragua. They brought food for families and money for repairs for members' homes and church sanctuaries. Early in 1979, they traveled back to Estelí. The Baptist Church in Estelí had been partially destroyed by bombs from Somoza's planes. The hospital had also been partially destroyed. They met with the hospital director, Dr. Alejandro Dávila Bolaños, to hear firsthand about what had happened. They delivered food and supplies for the patients of the hospital from the CSC. Not too long after their visit, they were saddened to learn that Dr. Dávila had been killed by Somoza's National Guard, another in the growing list of human rights violations.

As before, displaced people ended up living at the Parajón house. Some came from a Managua neighborhood that had been bombed by Somoza's air force. Sandinistas—called "Marxist communist rebels" by the government—entered some of the neighborhoods of Managua. Joined by some of the civilians, they set up barricades of rocks and bricks. The air force bombed the neighborhoods, even though most civilians were still living in their homes. Helicopters dropped explosives in barrels that could destroy a whole house. Many civilians fled the fighting by foot. Some were taken in by elderly relatives. Some who knew the Parajóns made their way to their home. Joan gathered big pots and pans for cooking rice and beans for all the new mouths to feed. She gathered big pitchers for water and orange juice and large urns for the coffee. Their home was like a church fellowship hall, but for a sorrowful gathering. Joan and Gustavo were once again hosting those who had no place to go.

Somoza's air force continued to bomb urban areas, and Dr. Parajón and many of the PROVADENIC staff ministered to the victims. At one point, the National Guard went on door-to-door searches through neighborhoods of Managua, seizing young men either for arrest or to conscript them into Somoza's army. Sometimes, even in those situations, human decency won out. Parajón often told a story about one of the young men in his church who was found at home by a National Guardsman. The soldier looked at him and then chose to do nothing; he simply left.

Somoza's National Guard surrounded the universities. The soldiers fired tear gas into the rooms, forcing classes to be canceled. Many students stopped going because of the danger and fear they might be killed or forced to join the Guard.

One key leader for CEPAD began her work in 1978 amid the revolution, starting at an entry-level position in a local office. Dámaris Albuquerque's father had pulled her out of the university because of the rising violence, but the violence hit Masaya as well. The Sandinistas tried to take Masaya, and Somoza responded by bombing parts of the city. Meanwhile, people struggled on. Dámaris was involved with the youth group of the First Baptist Church in Masaya. Her pastor invited Dámaris to apply to be secretary for the local CEPAD office, and she got the job. "Office" makes it sound like more than it was. The staff was Dámaris and the local director, the pastor of the Assemblies of God church in Masaya. They occupied the front room of the Baptist church parsonage. They had to buy all the office supplies. The pastors of the various denominations would gather for meetings, the first exposure young Dámaris had to church leaders outside the Baptists.

Many people were losing their jobs or being injured in the attacks. CEPAD provided vital food and medicine for these needy folks. For many displaced people, CEPAD was a lifeline. As the revolution reached its climax in June and July, CEPAD had to close the Masaya office as the city center had become too dangerous. CEPAD paid the salaries of their workers even when the rising violence forced them to shut down some operations.

On July 19, 1979, a new government was declared as General Somoza, his family, and many National Guard leaders fled the country. The Sandinistas took control, with the young insurgent Daniel Ortega as leader of the junta. The FSLN was now ruling a nation that had been devastated by war and impoverished by decades of massive corruption. They had a monumental task before them.

Aid continued to come in for CEPAD to deliver within this new context. Sixto Ulloa had earlier made contact with the Sandinistas letting them know the work of CEPAD. CEPAD was willing to help rebuild the country, but was not willing to join in the revolutionary violence. On July 19, as the Sandinistas triumphantly arrived in Managua, Gustavo and Sixto were at the airport to receive a planeload of aid. Because of the relationship Sixto had established with the Sandinistas, they had no problem getting the shipment. The work of CEPAD was able to continue, quickly helping those with desperate needs because of the war's devastation.

In areas where CEPAD's work had been suspended, they were able to restart their operations. The pastor who headed up the work in Masaya left, and in early 1980 Dámaris Albuquerque was selected by the board to be the coordinator of the Masaya office. Dr. Parajón had gotten to know her since his days at the Baptist Hospital as a doctor and through some of the staff meetings in Managua. In 1981 he asked her to become his personal secretary at PROVADENIC, and she agreed.

As the Sandinistas came into power, most Nicaraguans were happy to see Somoza gone, but they wanted to figure out who these new leaders were. Some feared their country would turn into another Cuba, a model demonized by the

Somoza regime. The evangelical Christians were especially concerned. They wondered if they would have the freedom to meet and conduct their religious services. The suspicion went both ways as some of the Sandinistas didn't understand evangelicals and feared conservative extremism. They thought the evangelical focus on "saving souls" was linked to supporting the imperialist aims of the U.S. government.

Dr. Parajón and Gilberto Aguirre were called to a government office. Everyone was dressed in military uniforms. The new Sandinista officials asked, "What is CEPAD?" Though Sixto had established a relationship with some of the Sandinistas, as more of the top leadership arrived and took over the government, more relationship-building was needed quickly. A doctrinaire Marxist said, "Religion is the opiate of the people!" El Profe replied by dumping annual reports of CEPAD on the table and said, with fire in his voice, "Please read these reports and tell me religion is the opiate!" Gustavo kicked his friend under the table!

The meetings continued, and trust and respect began to build. Initially, some of the new Sandinista officials blasted the evangelical church leaders and their work as "cultural imperialism," but Parajón, Aguirre, and other CEPAD folks patiently persisted in showing their actual work to the new government. Respect for the church leaders grew, a relationship that in the years ahead would produce much good fruit.

The Sandinistas opened a religious affairs office in the government. Only the Protestants connected with these officials as the conservative Catholic archbishop kept his distance. Commandante René Núñez was installed as the new director for Religious Affairs. Dámaris became the point person relating to the office for CEPAD and PROVADENIC. She found Núñez firm, but accessible. Gustavo invited the commandante to the CEPAD annual meeting so he could see things firsthand and build relationships both ways.

CEPAD sponsored another Interdenominational Retreats of Evangelical Pastors of Nicaragua (RIPEN). Church leaders visited Nicaragua from Yugoslavia, Bulgaria, and Cuba, and they were invited to the retreat. The Nicaraguan evangelical pastors entered into a dialogue with these Christians from communist countries so they could learn from each other and discuss the new situation in Nicaragua.

The euphoria at the overthrow of Somoza was extensive in the country. But some distrusted these revolutionaries, with their Marxist philosophy. The pastor at First Baptist Church in Managua was Juan Pablo Tamayo. He had fled Cuba after Castro's revolution. He was afraid the same thing would happen in Nicaragua as had happened in Cuba. The popularity of the revolution also diminished for people with property as the Sandinistas started working on agrarian reform. Property was confiscated, and new cooperatives were set up for rural people to work the land together. Some of those property owners fled to the U.S and other countries, eventually becoming a key source of counterrevolutionary fervor. Another source for discontent, especially for farmers and middle business people, was the central economy model the Sandinistas tried to impose.

To build the working relationship between CEPAD and the new government, Gustavo invited Omar Cabezas, head of the Human Rights Attorney's office, to the CEPAD assembly in September 1979. Members of CEPAD churches were able to question and converse with him. Cabezas spoke about a time when he was wounded close to the Honduran border. He went to a remote village on the Río Coco. There he was seen by the health provider for PROVADENIC, and his wound was dressed. Cabezas was deeply moved to find that the Baptist churches were concerned about the health of poor people in such a remote area. Seeing that care firsthand made a difference to the perceptions about evangelicals for this Sandinista.

When the revolution achieved its victory, Sixto Ulloa shifted his work at CEPAD to be the head of public relations. He became the person who represented CEPAD before the new government. He shifted Carlos from running errands to handling the details related to people's immigration status. They handled the paperwork for missionaries and volunteers who poured in from Europe and the U.S. to help CEPAD rebuild communities out of the ruins of revolution.

Though Gustavo Parajón was one of the great peacemakers of our time, he was not a pure pacifist. In a discussion with a South African Christian leader, they explored nonviolent direct action in their two contexts. Both were committed to nonviolent action themselves, but they both agreed that there would have been no change in their countries unless the African National Congress in South Africa and the FSLN in Nicaragua had not taken up arms. Working for justice in our muddled, violent world is never simple and straightforward.

Gustavo and Jimmy Carter at left with Rosalyn Carter walking toward them.

Gustavo Parajón, center next to Daniel Ortega, in 1981 meeting
with pastors, CEPAD staff, and donors at INCAE.

Family of slain PROVADENIC health promoter Néstor Antonio
Castilblanco at funeral at First Baptist Managua.

The destruction of war.

5

Counterrevolution:

The Contra War

The Sandinista revolution was hardly given any room to try to build the new society they envisioned. Because they were a leftist group, they were immediately targeted by the most powerful country on earth. The government of the same land from which so many volunteers came to work in projects with CEPAD and PROVADENIC began to fund the remnants of Somoza's National Guard, based mainly in Honduras. The basic needs of the poor did not just continue but intensified as war devastated so many communities and even the health infrastructure. Dr. Gustavo Parajón stepped into a new calling even as he continued serving the poor in Nicaragua as he had in the past. He became one of the powerful prophetic voices calling out and acting for justice and peace.

In Nicaragua, there was a great fear of a U.S. military invasion, stoked by harsh statements coming from the Reagan administration. The government built trenches along highways and near schools. Having had horrifying experiences with Somoza's air force, the encounters still fresh in their minds, they constructed bomb shelters. Meanwhile, the U.S. had placed an embargo on Nicaragua, severely affecting the economy. Long queues developed in front of any store that had food or clothing. Remnants of Somoza's National Guard were gathered together, reorganized, funded, and supplied by the U.S. Soon, these groups, informally called the Contras, were launching attacks in Nicaragua from their bases in Honduras.

In the face of the growing war, the government set up an office for censorship. They went through everything said by churches. All of Gustavo's sermons and radio messages had to be transcribed and sent to the government office to clear what he said. Every day, he was involved in broadcasting a message on the radio. At times, the clearance arrived just an hour before they went on air.

Draft Exemptions

One of the early issues between the Sandinista government and CEPAD was the drafting of men for military service. Some of the denominations in CEPAD were pacifist, such as the Mennonites and Brethren in Christ. Others believed that pastors and seminary students should be exempt. The Sandinistas, however, thought these were counterrevolutionary stands. They didn't understand not participating in the military as a matter of conscience.

Parajón and Gilberto Aguirre from CEPAD met with René Núñez from the government's Department of Religious Affairs to hammer out an agreement. With background provided by Mennonites, Parajón suggested the models from the U.S. and Canada, where religious conscientious objectors could do alternative service for the same term as military draftees, working in hospitals, laboring on conservation projects, and staffing education programs in poor communities. In some early cases, CEPAD was able to get imprisoned young people released if they worked on farms instead of in the military.

However, the pastors in CEPAD didn't support the idea of alternative service. They noted that Catholic priests and seminarians had full exemptions with no alternative service, so why should they not be accorded the same rights? Eventually Núñez agreed to a full exemption of Protestant pastors and seminary students from the military draft. To be eligible, such persons had to have the support of both CEPAD and their denomination.

Over one thousand requests came in, creating a huge amount of paperwork. Sixto Ulloa was CEPAD's point person related to the Sandinistas. Sixto's office, including Carlos Mejía Ruiz, was tasked with handling the applications and communications. Dámaris Albuquerque and Sixto's secretary handled the heavy load of correspondence. Some of the pastors and seminarians who received exemptions were already in the Nicaraguan army, so Carlos had to drive to military bases around the country to get them demobilized and released.

In one case, Dr. Parajón asked Carlos to go to Río Blanco to find Brother Bienvenido López, who later became the superintendent of the Church of God. Carlos drove CEPAD's red Toyota Jeep that had the organization's name on the side. López thought they might need more protection as they drove through areas where both Nicaraguan soldiers and Contras were operating. So they put a Bible visibly on the dashboard, and tied a white handkerchief to their vehicle. Carlos passed safely through the conflict zone.

Sometimes pastors were even jailed on anti-government suspicions. CEPAD would advocate for those pastors. Gustavo and other CEPAD leaders repeatedly talked to government officials, eventually securing the release of those pastors.

In all, more than 1,600 pastors and seminarians received exemptions from military service through CEPAD. Not a single person was turned down. Some of them, who were against the Sandinista government, eventually fled the country. CEPAD, however, felt their role was to stand for and work out the rights of the members of the churches to follow their consciences about war.

Empowering the Poor Amid War and Disaster

PROVADENIC and CEPAD

When the Sandinistas came to power, there was a medical paradigm clash between the new government and PROVADENIC. In spite of some of their revolutionary ideology, they didn't believe in the capacity of local leaders to provide health care. For them, the primary health care providers were always to be the doctors and the nurses. Dr. Parajón had many conversations about public health paradigms with government officials, especially about local health promoters administering vaccines.

After making little progress, Dr. Parajón contacted one of his global public health colleagues, Dr. Mabelle Arole from India. She and her husband, Raj, ran a village health project in Jamkhed. The plan was to send a team from Nicaragua, including government representatives, to learn from the public health work in India that utilized local health promoters. Two representatives from the government were on the team, along with Lilliam Escobar and Dámaris Albuquerque from PROVADENIC. Though the government health officials could have seen the incredible health impact of PROVADENIC's work close at hand, seeing the impact of the health promoters in small rural communities in India opened their minds. Shortly after that trip, PROVADENIC received permission to have health promoters vaccinate people in their communities.

The trip back from India became a challenge when a connection was missed. Dámaris had never traveled internationally alone or in charge of a group before this trip. She was exhausted from the long trip and delays, but when she arrived in Miami to catch the final leg to Nicaragua, she was greeted by Dr. Parajón. Knowing the challenges they faced, he flew to Miami to ensure they were okay and give support for the rest of the way home. Such was his care for the staff that worked with him.

Meanwhile, the work in the rural clinics continued by PROVADENIC. A small clinic up in remote rugged mountain communities brought relief for the isolated people suffering from many common illnesses. People in those communities thought of Dr. Parajón as an angel of mercy. However, as the war progressed, some of the clinics had to be closed down, while some were deliberately attacked and destroyed. The war made the health challenges far more difficult to address and far more risky for the PROVADENIC staff.

Basic childhood diseases did not take a break because of the war. In 1982, Dr. Parajón supported the government's Health Ministry vaccination campaign. He approached various funders, securing a major grant from a German nongovernmental organization (NGO). With this support, PROVADENIC worked alongside the various government public health personnel to build on the earlier vaccination efforts to keep Nicaraguan children protected from childhood scourges.

CEPAD took up the work of ministering to displaced people. They provided food to some of the camps set up for people whose communities had been devastated in the war. They provided rice, corn, beans, oil, and sugar. The Mennonite Central Committee became a key partner during this time, bringing in food from agencies such as the Canadian Food Bank. CEPAD-USA was started as a loose network organized by Bob Buescher to channel funds from the U.S. for CEPAD, getting around the U.S. embargo. He helped expand the communication network so that more people and churches knew of the vital relief work being done. War is as much of a disaster as an earthquake or a hurricane for those whose homes are destroyed and lives uprooted.

Habitat for Humanity

Don Mosley of Jubilee Partners, a Christian service community in northern Georgia, was one of the original founders of Habitat for Humanity (HFH). He also became active in Witness for Peace (see later in this chapter). Millard Fuller, the executive director of Habitat, had discussions with Don about launching Habitat in other countries. Fuller was heading to Zaire (now Democratic Republic of the Congo). A key component of the work of Jubilee Partners was assisting refugees from Central America. Don thought Nicaragua would be a great place to launch a Habitat project and headed down to Nicaragua to explore the possibilities. He wrote a letter to Millard about how good it looked and suggested that they might be able to get Jimmy Carter to be part of the project. Carter showed up at the HFH work site in Americus, Georgia, and Millard showed the letter to him asking what he thought. "Go for it!" the former president replied. Carter expressed interest and said he would talk to Don as soon as he got back.

In Nicaragua in March 1984, Don explored several sites with Gustavo. Gustavo recommended a site in the impoverished village of German Pomares, the first village where PROVADENIC worked, formerly called General Somoza Colony. The houses were basically thatched shelters with occasional walls of mud or sticks. The poverty was stark.

Don went back to Georgia and met with Jimmy and Rosalynn Carter at their home. He showed photos of German Pomares and discussed the project.

At one point Rosalynn said, "The Contras—they're ours, right?" Carter quickly responded, "Not *mine*! They're Mr. Reagan's."[10] At the end of the visit, Carter asked Don, "What would you like me to do to help?"

Habitat launched the building project in Nicaragua. In February 1986, Carter was ready to go. Joan recalled, "Everyone was so gloomy about the constant war going on in the country, and Jimmy's visit cheered us up. He also encouraged Habitat for Humanity in their building projects in the countryside. He, of course, went out himself and picked up a hammer!"

Carter did pick up a hammer. He was joined in the trip to German Pomares by President Ortega and other top officials. They toured the fifty-house project, made some speeches, then got to work. Jimmy cut wood and laid bricks with Rosalynn. Carter and Ortega installed a door frame together. A ceremony was held to give the keys to two completed homes to the two families who would live in them, families that contributed their own "sweat equity" to the project according to the Habitat model.

The morning of the trip to German Pomares, Jimmy Carter joined the Parajóns at their home for breakfast. While Carter's Secret Service detail stayed outside, the three of them enjoyed a meal and conversation. Joan remembers: "I got up early and baked a sour cream coffee cake for the occasion. It was so nice for the three of us to sit, eat, and talk around the table. We were like old friends right away!" Jimmy talked with Gustavo about the reports circulating in the U.S. about alleged persecution of the religious communities.

Ever the peacemaker, during that same trip, Carter met with a Contra leader in El Salvador Arturo Cruz to explore possibilities toward a peace agreement. Cruz was open to the idea of halting U.S. aid to the Contras in response to the Sandinistas meeting certain demands. Once in Nicaragua, Carter met with President Daniel Ortega, who responded favorably to Cruz's stipulations. Later, Cruz backed away from his initial offer. Carter kept working on his diplomacy with the Contadora Group (Mexico, Panama, Venezuela, and Colombia) and the United Nations, but U.S. diplomacy undercut every mediation effort in order to keep up the war against the Sandinistas. Another 10,000 Nicaraguans would die as the war raged on.

Jimmy and Rosalynn Carter visited First Baptist Church the Sunday they were in Managua. Before the service, Jimmy met with a Witness for Peace dele-gation. Then he participated in the worship and gave a short message in Spanish, delighting everyone. Afterward, the Carters and the Parajóns had lunch together, continuing to build their friendship.

---

10 From Don Mosley's *With Our Own Eyes: The dramatic story of a Christian response to the wounds of war, racism, and oppression,* Herald Press, Scottsdale, PA, 1996.

At a press conference before flying back home, Jimmy Carter expressed his belief that dialogue was necessary to bring peace to Nicaragua. He said he opposed aid to the Contras because he wanted to see "an end to the fighting and bloodshed." He criticized the Reagan administration for not supporting the efforts of the Contadora countries: "We have to adequately explore how to solve the differences among the Nicaraguan people in a peaceful way."[11]

Over the years, Habitat for Humanity built thousands of houses across Nicaragua. CEPAD remained their in-country partner, enabling many poor families to own decent homes.

Walk in Peace

On October 20, 1986 a crowded truck was heading in pre-dawn darkness down the bumpy dirt road to Jinotega in northern Nicaragua. Fifty-one people were jammed into and on top of the truck, most headed for the market. People were holding onto the top of the cab and the frame over the bed of the truck. Children and older women were seated on bags of grain and other supplies in the truck. The Contras were operating in that area, and people knew that travel was a risk. But life has to go on, including buying food and other necessities.

Nineteen-year-old Carmen Picado was excited because she was going into town to make preparations for her upcoming wedding. She sat next to her married sister Cristina. Cristina's husband was Amancio Sánchez, 30 years old and pastor of an evangelical church in Pantasma. He was headed into Jinotega to join in planning a CEPAD prayer vigil for peace. Several of the Sánchez children were traveling with them, including the vibrant 7-year-old Elda.

Pastor Sánchez was standing on the frame over the right rear wheel with another pastor, Juan Rizo. As the light of the new day grew, that wheel hit a landmine embedded in the road. A huge explosion ripped through the truck and people, flinging twisted metal and torn bodies everywhere.

As Amancio said later, "It happened so quickly I didn't even feel pain at first. I started to fall and grabbed the side of the truck. My legs weren't working." He crawled away from the wreckage and lay on the ground. "I looked down and saw that my right leg was missing from the knee down."

Four passengers died instantly in the blast. Two more later died from their wounds. Forty-three others were seriously injured, twelve of them losing one or both legs. Carmen lost both legs. She never heard from her fiancé again. Little Elda would be in a coma for two weeks. One of her legs was blown off at the knee; the other was broken in eight places.

Don Mosley was leading a Habitat for Humanity delegation to Nicaragua that arrived the same day the mine blew up the truck and its passengers. The group

---

11 CEPAD Newsletter, March, 1986, "Jimmy Carter Visits Nicaragua," pp. 1-3.

visited Pastor Sánchez and his still-unconscious daughter, Elda. Amancio allowed them to take a photo of Elda. That photo became the centerpiece for the delegation's meetings and devotions.

The last night the group was in Nicaragua, Don felt something rouse him at 4 a.m. with a clear message: "Get up now and pray, and something wonderful will happen." Another delegation member was up as well with a similar prompting. The two men prayed in silence until the sun rose. Don's mind was flooded with exciting thoughts that Don wrote down furiously in his notebook. This was the moment of conception for Walk in Peace.

Don called Gustavo, whom he had known through the work of Witness for Peace and Habitat for Humanity. He said, brimming with excitement, "Dr. Parajón, if Elda Sánchez comes out of this coma—and I believe she will—I want to arrange for her to come to the United States, both to get a new leg and to show people there what our government is doing to the Nicaraguan people." Parajón loved the idea but pushed it further. He had just come back from visiting the wounded family members scattered in the hospitals in Jinotega and Matagalpa. He said that the whole family should go too, especially Amancio and Carmen.

Upon his return home, Mosley worked on arrangements to get the family to Georgia for their recovery and rehab. Jimmy Carter helped secure the visas. In February 1987, Mosley flew back to Nicaragua to pick up the Sánchez family. At the last moment, the doctor who had committed to help oversee the necessary surgeries and therapy backed off because it was too "controversial." However, another doctor, a member of the Fellowship of Reconciliation, stepped up to make all the medical connections. Additional surgery was needed for Carmen, and the three injured family members were fitted for new prostheses to be constructed.

Walk in Peace was launched to help amputees from the war in Nicaragua without regard for political or religious affiliation, connecting with Nicaraguan people and organizations through CEPAD. At the press conference in Georgia with his full family present, Pastor Sanchez told his story of the explosion and all that had happened. At the end he said, "As a Christian, I solely desire peace in my country so the suffering of so many families, like mine, can stop." In response, statements from the U.S. government and Contra leaders insisted that the mine could have come from the Sandinistas and that there was no conclusive evidence of human rights abuses by the Contras. The U.S. media generally favored the government and not the testimony of the Sánchez family and Walk in Peace.

Soon the day came when Amancio and Elda had their new legs. Carmen needed more surgeries, but when she finally got her two prostheses and saw herself in a mirror walking with support from the parallel beams, a smile lit up that hadn't been there since the explosion.

Eventually, the Sánchez family returned to Nicaragua. Dr. Parajón welcomed them to the annual meeting of CEPAD, where Amancio spoke to hundreds of fellow pastors. Parajón said the love that was demonstrated in helping the Sánchez family showed that not everyone in the U.S. supported President Reagan's violent policies.

Walk in Peace partnered with efforts to provide prostheses constructed in Nicaragua for those who lost arms or legs, in most cases from the war. They endowed the Nicaraguan factory so it could continue the construction of artificial limbs, including fitting and making of new prostheses for children and teens as they grew and needed a larger size. Child amputees generally need a new prosthesis every year, and adults need new ones every three years because of normal wear and tear. With such a huge population of people who lost limbs in the war, thousands of prostheses were needed each year.

Walk in Peace also worked with the Aldo Chavarría Rehabilitation Hospital to support the physical therapy extensively required by such patients. The Vélez Páiz Hospital in Nicaragua was the largest children's hospital in the country. Besides all the typical diseases that can ravage children, the burns and maiming of war filled the hospital way beyond its capacity. Not all the suffering of the children was produced directly by weapons of war, the bullets, shells, and landmines. The Contra attacks also deliberately targeted water systems, resulting in children suffering and dying from severe diarrhea. Walk in Peace leveraged assistance for some of these other vital health needs for children.

Injured civilians who needed more extensive treatment, both adults and children, were brought to Georgia for medical care and therapy. They stayed at the Jubilee Partners community in Comer. Jubilee Partners' Walk in Peace campaign got national media attention in the U.S., especially from *People* magazine, which visited the children's hospital in Nicaragua. Between his work with Witness for Peace, Habitat for Humanity and Walk in Peace, all initiatives connected to Gustavo Parajón, Don Mosley went to Nicaragua over thirty times.

In May 1995, a sad ending to part of the story occurred. Amancio Sánchez had resumed pastoring his church, though it was an extremely poor congregation. He became president of his denomination and taught at a seminary. Amancio was riding in the back of a truck just a few kilometers from where the landmine had blown up another truck almost nine years earlier, taking his leg. Suddenly, the truck hit a large hole and skidded off the road. Amancio was thrown from the back of the truck, then crushed as the truck rolled over on him. He was rushed to the hospital in Managua in critical condition. He hung on for a few days, with Dr. Parajón as part of the team attending to his care. Dr. Parajón had to tell the family and friends from Nicaragua and the U.S. that Amancio was beyond physical help.

Over a thousand people gathered at Pastor Sánchez's funeral. This humble pastor, through personal war disaster, became a pioneer for the work that would impact countless other victims of war violence. His willingness to talk about his journey, to answer questions, and to speak about the hope he had through his faith in Christ touched far more hearts than could ever have been imagined for this rural pastor from a poor Nicaraguan community. As his body was laid to rest, his family and friends were comforted by the vision of him enfolded in the love of Jesus.

Hurricane Joan

One might think a brutal war would be enough suffering for a poor nation, but Mother Nature seems indifferent to where natural disasters might strike. When Hurricane Joan crashed into the east coast of Nicaragua on October 21, 1988, it caused extensive flooding and damage. Over two hundred people died. Corn Island off the coast was severely damaged, along with Bluefields, the major town in the east.

The hurricane hit during the weekend, so Dr. Parajón told his crew at CEPAD to come in early. They organized a team to go with him, including Milton Argüello, Dino Andino, and Carlos Mejía Ruiz. Carlos went to film the damage and determine community needs. The Nicaraguan army lent them a helicopter so they could quickly access the disaster area.

The team first went to Corn Island, 70 kilometers east off the Nicaraguan east coast. All the trees and houses were flattened. Of the 100,000 trees on the island, only about a thousand were left standing, leaving a devastating landscape for the survivors. The lobster traps and boats of the fishing community were shattered. The team met with the survivors to assess the needs, committing to build four hundred new homes. They left some limited initial supplies, then flew on to Bluefields.

Again, there were no houses standing. The only upright building was a school that had a small room with a secured zinc sheet roof, but no walls. Dr. Parajón decided to make the school their operations center and the place they would sleep. They scrounged some black plastic and a few teacher's desks to use as beds. Parajón impressed his staff by insisting that they sleep on the desks while he slept on two boards on the floor. Before the team slept, the doctor gathered them together, took his small travel Bible, and read an encouraging word from the Scriptures. Then they prayed. Parajón used his bag as a pillow and had no blanket. One of the team members had a blanket he offered the doctor, but Parajón refused, sleeping only in his clothes on the floor. The younger men on the team remembered that experience as a powerful lesson in Christian leadership, caring for the needs of those with you before tending to your own needs.

When the team woke up, there was no potable water. They washed with rainwater in a bucket. Dr. Parajón walked the streets of Bluefields, surveying the damage and talking to the people who were out in the early morning. The team shared what supplies they were able to bring in the helicopter. Later, as more aid came in, the team helped with delivery of the goods. Throughout this experience, everyone was deeply moved by the president of CEPAD living with them, eating simple rice and beans. Those on the team knew Gustavo loved his chili, which wasn't available, but he ate the plain food with gusto that brought delight in simple things amid the disaster.

As the relief effort continued, one of the biggest sources of aid through CEPAD came from Jubilee Partners, Habitat for Humanity, and Koinonia Partners in Georgia. These three groups together raised some $200,000 for hurricane relief. The first DC-8 plane arrived in Managua about a week after the hurricane with a crew who donated their services. Gustavo and other CEPAD leaders unloaded the plane, inventoried the material as they loaded it onto twenty-one trucks, and sent the aid to the disaster zones. The Georgia groups later brought in four or five planeloads of medicines and other relief supplies for CEPAD to use. Gustavo said that the aid from U.S. mainline denominations and other U.S. sources was only a fraction of what came from these concerned activists in Georgia. Some denominations wanted to minimize their involvement in Nicaragua because of the political controversy it might stir. The U.S. government sent nothing. The people of Bluefields and Corn Island didn't care about the politics, but they noticed the love with which Parajón and his team brought them help in a time of great need.

The Mennonite Central Committee, who was seconded to CEPAD for their work in Nicaragua, secured a four-seater airplane with some cargo space. Because the hurricane hit just before harvest, many of the anticipated crops were lost. MCC focused on food aid. The Mennonites, with their concern for peace and political non-partisanship, noticed how Gustavo built relationships and trust with the Moravian leaders in the disaster. He had been viewed as pro-government and a Sandinista supporter, but the Moravians and the Mennonites saw that his ultimate purpose was the Kingdom of God and the meeting of human need.

After the immediate needs for food and temporary shelter were met, CEPAD began to work on the long-term needs. They helped rebuild houses, but perhaps more importantly they supported the process of organizing the communities so they could participate in their own reconstruction. Long after the news cycles had forgotten about the hurricane, CEPAD staff and volunteer teams continued to help rebuild Corn Island and the Caribbean Coast.

Attacks on PROVADENIC

One of the hideous dimensions of the Contra War was the deliberate targeting of civilians and infrastructure, including public health infrastructure. The rationale was that anything that destabilized the Sandinista government was acceptable, even if such actions were considered violations of human rights. The U.S. government denied that such activities were going on, but people on the ground in Nicaragua saw countless incidents of such violations. Two of the ugliest attacks directly impacted PROVADENIC.

Ana Julia was the first health promoter to work with PROVADENIC. She was involved in the children's vaccination program. To undercut the health work, the Contras spread rumors that the vaccines were being used to brainwash children and adults who received them. The Contras said that a Sandinista group was coming to kidnap children and make them into sausages. These vicious lies were intended to sow misinformation and fear that would disrupt the health campaigns. Ana Julia continued her work with deep commitment.

In the village of North Cubul, Contras kidnapped Ana, her sister, her brother-in-law, Marcos, and a 9-year-old girl named Magdalena. The prisoners were taken down to the Matagalpa River, where Ana and Marcos were shot. Ana's sister and Magdalena were released. Carlos Escobar, a staff person with PROVADENIC said, "Her death hurt us deeply in the soul."

Dr. Parajón wept as he announced to the church, "They have killed our health promoters." Later, he met with all the PROVADENIC staff and asked those who were traveling, "I want you to tell me if you are willing to continue traveling to the communities despite what is happening because I do not want another PROVADENIC worker killed. I'd rather close this program." They didn't close the program, but the staff courageously continued on to bring health care amid the violence of the war.

PROVADENIC had established a clinic in the village of San José de las Mulas in Matagalpa. A young man named Néstor Antonio Castilblanco began working as a health promoter in 1984. He was dedicated to his work for the health of those in his community, but he knew there was a huge risk. Contras had spread the word that they were against the public health work, saying the medications were from Cuba and from the Sandinista army. They saw those in the health committees as well as the health promoters as being fronts for the Sandinistas and thus legitimate targets.

During one attack on the village by the Contras, the clinic was intentionally burned, but all the people were able to slip away. Medical records in the clinic were taken out and burned deliberately. Supplies were shattered and scattered about.

The villagers set up the clinic again in Néstor's house. The second attack by about one hundred Contra soldiers was a focused search-and-destroy mission targeting the clinic and the health promoter. The Contras found Néstor in his home, looking for him specifically by name. Néstor was stripped and led away. His wife, Meylin, tried desperately to follow, but Néstor dissuaded her saying, "Go and care for our children." The Contras stole food, dishes, and all the medicines from the house, then they torched the Castilblanco home with the clinic.

The Contras continued their journey through San José de las Mulas, where the simple wood or even mud homes are spread out through the valley and surrounding hills. They found and seized health committee members Jesús Barrera and Daniel Castilblanco, as well as the Catholic Delegate of the Word Filemón Castilblanco, who was Néstor's brother. Jesús also served on CEPAD's local development committee. Daniel's guitar was stolen, and the homes set on fire. The Contras stole clothing and whatever valuables they could find. As they left the area around 3 a.m., they were heard singing to the accompaniment of Daniel's guitar "viva la Guardia Nacional!" ("long live the National Guard!").

In mid-morning, a search party was organized to look for the four kidnapped men. Their bodies were found about a kilometer from the last ransacked home. Their bodies showed repeated stab wounds to their necks and abdomens. One man had his testicles cut off, and another had an eye gouged out. Néstor's head had been hacked off and put on a post. Néstor was 24 years old when his life was taken from him.

The bodies were carried back to the village, where an all-night vigil was held. The next morning, they were buried behind the clinic site in coffins made from wood salvaged from the walls of the destroyed clinic. Dr. Parajón came to the village after Néstor and the others were killed. CEPAD committed to provide for the families of those killed as long as needed, including helping them resettle. Parajón realized the community was still under severe threat. He advised the rest of the family to move to a less dangerous place, which they did by emigrating to a community near Matagalpa. Most other families fled as well, leaving behind their houses, lands, and their unharvested crops, including their coffee plants.

The day after the killings, Parajón led devotions for a small group of agency representatives who worked with CEPAD. He read Psalm 73 (NIV): "But as for me, my feet had almost slipped; I had nearly lost my foothold. For I envied the arrogant when I saw the prosperity of the wicked ... Therefore pride is their necklace; they clothe themselves with violence. From their callous hearts comes iniquity; their evil imaginations have no limits." But then the psalmist goes into "the sanctuary of God." There he finds the justice of God to be revealed, finally concluding: "My flesh and my heart may fail, but God is the strength of my heart and my portion forever." Parajón then turned to Revelation 12, the allegorical story of the woman giving birth, war in heaven, the dragon being cast down from heaven and then trying to devour the woman's child. Gustavo read verse 17, "Then the dragon was enraged at the woman and went off to wage war against the rest of her offspring—those who keep God's commands and hold fast their testimony about Jesus." (NIV)

With the brutal killing of Néstor and the others in San José de las Mulas, evil had been exhibited. The ultimate evil, though, was not the soldiers who committed the horrific acts, but the "dragon" Satan behind the evil of war in all its manifestations. Parajón could see the real ugliness of evil and feel the weight of it in his soul. However, he emotionally survived and even continued strong in his work through his close walk with Jesus, who also suffered and yet was victorious in love. Parajón would later meet Contra leaders who had ordered and participated in similar atrocities and in love call them out of the ways of evil and into the ways of peace. He had no illusions about how bad things were on the ground, but he also had no doubt that Jesus' love was deeper and stronger.

After the war, in 1996, many of the surviving community members from San José de las Mulas returned and reestablished their village. A new health community was formed with the help of PROVADENIC. Oscar, a relative of Néstor's, was chosen as the health promoter. After a few years, he stepped down and Juan de Dios Blandón became the health promoter for the next fifteen years.

PROVADENIC lost other health promoters in the war, and CEPAD lost some workers. Ana Julia López was kidnapped from the PROVADENIC clinic near Rio Blanco. She was forced to treat Contra wounded, then was tortured and executed. Morgan Almanza was a Miskito agricultural promoter for CEPAD on the east coast. He was taking aid from Managua to Bilwi with two other companions. They were kidnapped by Contras from Honduras and never heard from again. Five PROVADENIC clinics were destroyed by the Contras. Dr. Parajón said, "While most of us are working hard to achieve peace, the Contras blow up a clinic which provided important services to a needy population."[12] Violence wasn't the only cause of death to CEPAD workers. Toñito Hernández was a CEPAD driver who was killed in an accident. He was bringing help to Somoto following severe floods and died as he came down the steep descent on a mountainous road.

A footnote to this story shows how the ideology that supported killing civilians involved in health care as a legitimate military mission had a religious justification in the heart of some U.S. churches. Dan Buttry, the co-author of this book, was doing peace workshops in the 1980s related to the war in Nicaragua. In one seminar, he told about the attack on the PROVADENIC clinic and murder of those working for health in their community. Buttry was vociferously challenged by a seminary classmate. This classmate was pastor of an American Baptist church, the same denomination that sent Gustavo and Joan Parajón to Nicaragua as missionaries and that provided mission support for PROVADENIC and its work.

---

12 CEPAD Newsletter, December 1987, p. 5.

That pastor said that the Contras were justified in killing these unarmed civilians associated with mission work because anything that destabilized the Sandinistas was morally and ethically justified. In his eyes, the communist Sandinistas were such a huge evil that human rights concerns didn't matter, and even denominational mission connections didn't matter. Such was the nature of the ideology that wreaked such carnage in Nicaragua. That pastor baptized the bloodbath in his own crusading ideology and ultimate demonization of the enemy. Sadly, he was not alone in his thinking.

International Partners for Witness and Resistance

Many organizations, especially in the U.S. and Europe, supported the Nicaraguan people in the face of the U.S.-funded Contra War. Some of the organizations developed to bear witness to what was really happening on the ground and counter the U.S. media that supported President Reagan's war policies in their reporting. Other organizations helped directly meet some of the needs of suffering people because of ongoing poverty and the war. Civilians were victims in far greater numbers than military personnel, both directly from the violence and indirectly from the damage done to structures that affected public health. Still, other groups in the U.S. were involved in resistance to the U.S. government support of the Contras.

With many of these groups, Gustavo Parajón became the key contact because of his leadership with CEPAD. He would often be the first to meet with groups as they arrived in Nicaragua. He would orient them with briefings that became famous for the various delegations. Groups would get to know other CEPAD folks, especially Gilberto, as they engaged in whatever activities were their particular focus. None of these amazing initiatives would have been possible without the leadership of Dr. Parajón and the committed staff of CEPAD. They brought a positive, healing, and hope-filled impact amid the war, unlike with so many of the other wars around the world.

Witness for Peace

Witness for Peace was a dynamic program that brought thousands of U.S. citizens to Nicaraguan war zones to establish a prayerful and protective presence on the ground. It started when a group from North Carolina led by Gail Phares went to Jalapa as part of a four-day trip. Jalapa is in northern Nicaragua in a tiny bit of land that juts into Honduras. That made it a prime target for attacks from the Contras in Honduras. The team learned that the fighting stopped when this visible group of Americans visited. Evidently the Contras didn't want the negative publicity about killing U.S. citizens. Phares discussed with Gustavo Parajón and Sixto Ulloa of CEPAD the idea of bringing more North Americans to vigil at the border. Gustavo and Sixto then arranged for them to meet some leaders in the government, including the Catholic priest and poet Ernesto Cardenal and Interior Minister Tomás Borge. Borge was reluctant to put U.S. citizens in a place that might give President Reagan an excuse to launch an invasion, but the idea remained on the table. The folks in that team debriefed their experiences on the way home and knew they had to take their experience further.

Phares contacted Sojourners and other peace groups about what they discovered in Nicaragua. She was invited to a gathering in Philadelphia of some of the faith-based peace and justice organizations. After hearing of the experience of the North Carolina group in Jalapa, someone suggested that if the presence of U.S. citizens could stop Contra attacks, maybe they should establish a permanent presence, some sort of "shield of love." So Witness for Peace was born to bring that prayerful and hopefully peaceful presence to the front lines in Nicaragua.

Just as important as going to Nicaragua was coming back home to the U.S. The war was being financed and driven from Washington, D.C., with the Reagan administration portraying the Contras as Nicaragua's "Freedom Fighters." To transform the situation on the ground in Nicaragua, the narrative would have to be shaped by people with first-hand experience getting into the U.S. media and to people in Congress.

People would be risking their lives to go to conflict zones. For many people from the U.S., their trip to Nicaragua was the first time they had ever entered into such a high-risk place. Witness for Peace didn't want to be another "invasion" from the North; rather they awaited an invitation. At first, Gustavo was reluctant to give that invitation because he knew it was possible someone could get killed. However, he himself was willing to take huge risks to go to dangerous places to support those who were most vulnerable. He saw, reflected in these U.S. Americans, his own faith about following Jesus for the sake of justice and peace, wherever Christ might lead. So Gustavo gave the invitation to Witness for Peace to come.

That invitation then took shape with CEPAD as the partner to handle all the logistics. CEPAD hosted Witness for Peace teams, providing on-the-ground support, transportation, translation, and housing, which often meant team members sleeping on the floors of CEPAD-member churches. Gustavo's connections enabled them to visit a wide range of people to hear different perspectives about what was happening in Nicaragua: students, pastors, health workers, government leaders like Daniel Ortega and Foreign Minister Miguel d'Escoto, people in the Catholic hierarchy who opposed the government, indigenous Miskito leaders, the editor of *La Prensa* (the opposition newspaper), and sometimes the U.S. ambassador. Gustavo was connected to people to all sides. There was also the matter of Nicaraguans putting trust in an organization of people coming from the same country that was funding the attacks against them. The relationship of WfP to

CEPAD was vital. As one organizer said, "If a partnership with CEPAD had not existed, we would not have gotten to square one."[13]

Gustavo, with his experience living and studying in the U.S., also helped the U.S. delegations frame what they would say back in the U.S. regarding the cultural and political context of the Nicaraguan reality they experienced. Many solidarity groups had come to Nicaragua in support of the ideals of the Nicaraguan Revolution, but Gustavo was adamant that Witness for Peace must be politically nonaligned. They were involved in living out gospel values of human rights and freedom. That political independence proved crucial in maintaining the credibility of the organization and its witness, both in Nicaragua and in the U.S.

There was also confusion about the name of the organization. Some in CEPAD were concerned that "Witness" would suggest Jehovah's Witnesses, so the organization became known in Spanish as Acción Permanente Cristiana por la Paz (Permanent Christian Action for Peace).

As teams gathered in the U.S., a local send-off event was organized with as much publicity as possible. Publicity was vital in order to shine a light on what the U.S. was doing in this poor Central American country. The send-off included prayer, with the poignant awareness that some on the team might not come back. Over the period of the Contra War, more than five thousand U.S. citizens went to Nicaragua. Such engagement by volunteers in another country is amazing when one considers that no U.S. soldiers were dying in Nicaragua. The church connection was the driving force of this solidarity in action for peace. Over the years, Witness for Peace expanded its model of public accompaniment to other war zones, such as Colombia, Mexico, Haiti, Guatemala, and Honduras. Similar initiatives were launched in Palestine and Iraq.

Sixto oversaw most of the logistics and became the face of CEPAD to the delegations. However, the orientation provided for every Witness for Peace delegation was usually conducted by Gustavo or Gilberto Aguirre. Gustavo sometimes accompanied teams to the high-risk areas, sharing the experiences with them and helping make the connections between what they were experiencing and the larger political context. Micah 6:8 was one of the pivotal texts for Gustavo: "What does the Lord require of you but to do justice, love mercy, and walk humbly with your God." The team members saw that verse lived out in the actions and demeanor of Dr. Parajón. They spoke later of the humility he showed, along with the incredible strength to walk into difficult situations. He modeled equal respect for everyone while raising a prophetic voice for people who were most marginalized. The WfP teams tried to act and reflect what they saw in him.

---

13 From *Witness for Peace* by Ed Griffin-Nolan, Westminster/John Knox Press, Louisville, Kentucky, pp. 123.

In his orientation, Gustavo sometimes made a very earthy connection to the team members' experiences and the Scriptures. He said, "Some of you are suffering from diarrhea. In the next few days, many of you will become ill. You will drink the water in our countryside, and unfamiliar organisms will wreak havoc on your intestines. You will suffer, you will be uncomfortable. If you are not careful, you will get dehydrated. But you will recover. In a day, three days, a week or two at most, it will be something you remember and never wish to repeat. You will recover because you come from a first world country with advanced medical care, and, thank God, you have access to that medical care."

Then Gustavo would bring his message home to Nicaragua: "Remember when you are feeling those pains that here in my country diarrhea has been the number one cause of death for infants." He talked about all the poverty-related problems that lead to those infant deaths. But health care for the poor changed with the revolution. He said to the WfP teams, "This is how more than half of our babies used to die. This revolution is bringing health care to rural areas. It is bringing clean water, health education, and medicine to those families who were forgotten before, and to those babies who used to die with no name. Now babies will no longer die in infancy, but will live out their normal life span."[14] Then Gustavo took the group to the powerful passage in Isaiah 65 that talks about a time when children and old people will live out full lives. This was the hope they were trying to build upon that was under a direct assault by the Contras.

The goal of Witness for Peace was to confront the Contras at the war zone, usually near the border with Honduras. This was intentionally done in a very public way. Teams would take a bus from Managua to a community such as Jalapa. As they approached the war zone, sometimes mortar rounds would go over the bus, including the very first time. Sometimes team members were in tears, shaken by their initial, sobering experiences. They stayed the course, buoyed by the strength of the people they had come to stand alongside.

The first team felt that strength from the sustenance in the breakfast served at Ocotal before they traveled to Jalapa. They slept on the floor of a CEPAD-related church in Ocotal, sharing the floor with many women and children who had been displaced. Through the night they could hear gunfire that triggered the children's crying. The team held a vigil in the church and prayed with those staying there. Before dawn, the displaced women got up, fired the adobe ovens, and made tortillas and coffee. Those who had nothing and didn't know what the next day or week might hold shared their tortillas and coffee with strangers who had come for the sake of peace.

---

14 From *Witness for Peace* by Ed Griffin-Nolan, Westminster/John Knox Press, Louisville, Kentucky, pp. 30-31.

The first Witness for Peace team went to the ill-defined border, to a woody area just outside Jalapa. Contras were watching from the tree line. The team planted a cross in the field in front of the soldiers. They then conducted a Eucharistic service. The Nicaraguans with the group were wary of being marked by the Contras, so Jim Wallis led in the celebration of the Eucharist. No violence took place during the time that the WfP delegation was in Jalapa.

However, the continuing violence of the war marked the teams even if there was quiet while they were in a vulnerable community. On Pentecost Sunday in Cleveland at the Episcopal cathedral church, a new team was commissioned as a returning team was welcomed home. As the teams were meeting, they received a call from Sojourners. The Contras had executed a number of civilians in front of Maryknoll Sisters in Ocotal, from which the team had just returned. The team asked for the names of those who had been slain, and they wept as they heard names of their friends from their recent trip. The toll of the violence in the war became very personal for the team members, as they had spent two weeks with the people of that community. The commissioning service was then expanded into a press conference to tell about their experiences and about the murder of civilians in Ocotal by the Contras. The next morning the front page of the *Cleveland Plain Dealer* proclaimed "American Mercenaries Kill Civilians."

Such public outcry about Contra activities was key to changing the narrative about Nicaragua in the U.S., a narrative that had been controlled primarily by the Reagan administration. Witness for Peace and participating churches were exposing a different narrative to the American public. They became a major source of information to U.S. media about what was happening on the ground in Nicaragua. They showed how the Contras were engaged in terror against civilians, deliberately targeting noncombatants in an attempt to destabilize the Sandinista government. Human rights activists, including Witness for Peace, documented the kidnapping of pregnant Nicaraguan women by the Contras. The Contras would cut a child out of the mother's womb, then kill both mother and child. Often, Contras would behead prisoners and deposit the bodies on people's doorsteps. The Contras, many of them former National Guardsmen from the Somoza era, were paid and armed by the U.S., sometimes legally, sometimes through backdoor channels. When Congress finally halted funding for the Contras, the U.S. State Department blamed the churches for the pressure that put a stop to that support.

Some members of Witness for Peace ended up in the thick of combat. Some were taken prisoner by the Contras, often in the company of Nicaraguan civilians. Richard Boren was with a Witness for Peace group in northern Jinotega when the community he was in was attacked at night. He was staying in a home with a 13-year-old girl named Reina, who was shot as Contra bullets raked her house. Boren tried to put a tourniquet on the girl to stop her bleeding. Suddenly, some

Contra soldiers burst through the door, seized Boren, and dragged him out. Boren yelled, "There's a little girl in there bleeding," but the Contras wouldn't listen. Boren was taken to the Contra camp, where he was held captive for two to three weeks. Thankfully, Reina survived.

Boren was held along with a Nicaraguan captive, Víctor Rodríguez. They hiked with the Contras over rugged terrain, sleeping out in the open or in huts. In the U.S., a huge movement demanding Boren's release was putting pressure on Washington. In the jungle of the Nicaraguan/Honduran border, Boren was more concerned about Rodríguez. The Contra commander was threatening to kill Rodríguez for collaborating with the Sandinistas, but Boren said he would refuse to be released without taking Rodríguez with him. When the negotiations for Boren's release led to a meeting with a team from Witness for Peace, Boren still had to refuse to leave until the Contra commander finally relented and freed Rodríguez as well. When he heard Reina survived, Boren broke down in tears.

In 1985, the Contras tried to open a second front in the war, establishing bases in Costa Rica just across the San Juan River. The Nicaraguan government was concerned about having to fight a two-front war, so they appealed to the Contadora countries (Colombia, Mexico, Panama, and Venezuela) to provide a peacekeeping force at the border. They refused. So Ed Griffin-Nolan, one of the in-country coordinators for Witness for Peace, suggested to Foreign Minister Miguel d'Escoto that Witness for Peace patrol the border. The foreign minister agreed, somewhat skeptically.

Witness for Peace hired a boat to patrol the San Juan River, but before they left, their trip became a media event. With part of their *modus operandi* being to bring public attention to what was going on, WfP announced the trip and the Nicaraguan concern about the second front. Edén Pastora, head of the Southern Contras, threatened to kill them if they tried to patrol the border. Griffin-Nolan said WfP was going through with the project. The media picked up on the potential clash, with many organizations sending journalists, including NBC. Later, WfP discovered that the CIA had also sent an agent disguised as a journalist.

As the boat came near to a Contra camp right on the river, gunfire erupted. The Contras seized the boat and everyone on it. For a day and a half, they were held at a camp a bit back into the forest. Ed talked to the officer watching over them. The Contra officer said he was just following his orders. Ed asked what if he was ordered to kill them. "Then I'll kill you," was the simple reply. Extensive lobbying by WfP members across the U.S. brought about the pressure on the U.S. government to have the Contras release the prisoners unharmed.

However, the Contras had other ideas about the Nicaraguan crew of the boat hired by the WfP party. The soldiers tried to separate the Nicaraguan civilians, perhaps to turn them into Contras or to kill them. Without a word, the U.S.

members of the WfP team quickly surrounded the Nicaraguans in a nonviolent protective shield. In that tight formation, they made their way to the river to safely depart on the boat.

Jim Wallis of Sojourners often went to Nicaragua to facilitate Witness for Peace work and report back through *Sojourners* magazine. He would usually spend time with Gustavo, often eating dinner with the Parajóns. Gustavo helped Witness for Peace navigate arrangements with the authorities, such as getting authorization for teams to enter war zones. Wallis and Parajón once met with Nicaraguan President Daniel Ortega and Foreign Minister Miguel d'Escoto. Even in such settings, Gustavo humbly carried authority in his own personhood.

Jim and Gustavo went on a trip to the Caribbean Coast, where there was resistance from the indigenous communities. That resistance wasn't directly connected to the larger Contra movement. They met with the Moravian Miskito leaders. The Miskitos generally didn't trust either Somocistas (as they called the Contras) or the Sandinistas. The Miskitos asked if they could meet with Jim Wallis alone, specifically they asked "Spaniards" to leave, referring to the Spanish-speaking Nicaraguans. Gustavo quickly agreed; he understood what was happening and treated the indigenous people with respect. His willingness to give the Miskitos space was one of the small things that built the trust that Gustavo earned from the Moravian Miskito leaders. That trust would later prove invaluable as they became partners in peace efforts.

As Jim Wallis later said about Gustavo Parajón from his work with Witness for Peace: "He didn't have the best infrastructure; he had the best theology, helping people understand that charity is not enough, that justice had to be done. He was even-handed; the Sandinistas sought his counsel, but he could be critical of them, too."[15] Meanwhile, when ordinary Nicaraguans were asked how they felt about Witness for Peace, they said, "It made us feel like we weren't alone."[16] Gilberto Aguirre said succinctly that the work of Witness for Peace on the ground in Nicaragua and through their pressure on the U.S. government "saved lives."

Pastoral Letters

As the Baptist churches in Nicaragua struggled with the suffering going on in their country and their uncertainty about the future, Dr. Parajón was one of the guiding voices and motivators, with his deep biblical rootedness and the testimony of service he had established over the years. Parajón served on the board of directors of the Baptist Convention of Nicaragua. As someone keenly aware of the connection of churches in the U.S. to churches in Nicaragua, he inspired the Baptists as a body to write a series of pastoral letters to the churches in the U.S.

15 Church Times, "Obituary: Dr. Gustavo Parajón," 30 March 2011.
16 From *Witness for Peace* by Ed Griffin-Nolan, Westminster/John Knox Press, Louisville, Kentucky, p. 83.

Those letters were signed by the board of directors, including the president of the convention, the executive secretary, and the recording secretary.

A series of ten letters was sent. The first one in January 1983 focused on the atrocities committed by the Contras. The text urged churches to "denounce the atrocities committed by the counterrevolutionaries attacking our country, of which our brethren are victims. These groups are clearly trained and financed by the government of the U.S., and as they invade our country they are planting death, panic and desperation among our people."

The response of the churches in the United States and Europe in general was positive. Denominational bodies, pastors, priests, and general church members responded by sending letters to Congress to call for an end to the financial and military support given to the Contras. Some Nicaraguan Baptists believe that these letters and the resulting response in U.S. churches helped prevent a military invasion from being launched against Nicaragua, as happened in Panama and Grenada during those years of the 1980s.

Following a speech by Ronald Reagan requesting funds to support the Contras, the Baptist Convention of Nicaragua issued a letter on May 5, 1983, to the American Baptist Churches (ABC). In the letter they spoke about the suffering experienced by those who had been attacked by the U.S.-backed Contra forces. The letter condemned the U.S. embargo of Nicaragua as "anti-Christian, anti-biblical, inhumane, unjust, illegal, and arbitrary." It went on to directly challenge the U.S. president: "We cannot conceive how the same president who was sworn in with his hand on the Bible can issue a decree that goes totally against the Bible and is aimed at annihilating an entire people." Then Nicaraguan Baptists asked the ABC to "have the U.S. government stop backing and promoting the groups that are trying to overthrow our government."

The General Assembly of CEPAD also sent an open pastoral letter in May 1983. As president of CEPAD, Dr. Parajón's signature was the first on the letter. It was addressed to "Fellow Christians throughout the whole world." The letter begins with a quote from 1 Corinthians 12: "If one member of the body suffers, all the rest suffer also." The letter declared, "As Christians committed to justice and to love, we can do no less than denounce before all of you and before the world, the atrocities committed by counterrevolutionaries attacking our country, of which our brethren are victims." The letter identified the government of the United States as the source for training and financing those attacks, then made a direct plea to the churches in the U.S. "to intercede before your government on our behalf, that it might halt the undeclared war it is making against the Nicaraguan people." They appealed for dialogue, peace, and assistance with relief supplies to those who are suffering.

Other letters were sent by the Baptist Convention of Nicaragua over the next few years, sometimes inspired by specific actions, such as the killing of health workers and destruction of clinics. A letter in March 1984 sent to Baptists in the U.S. poignantly spoke of "the tears of mothers who cry for their children, the tears of desperation and impotence before the powerful who impose themselves on the weak, the tears of wishing for peace while war is being imposed, the tears of wanting to build while our work is being destroyed, the tears of scarcity, poverty, and misery as the price for the dignity God gave us as a right." That letter spoke about peacemaking efforts being rebuffed while catastrophic violence was pursued. They urged their Christian kin in the U.S. to urge their government toward peace, saying in capital letters, "WE NEED YOU TO HELP US BUILD PEACE, as is the will of our God."

In 1985, an appeal was sent to Baptists in the U.S.: "It is urgent that we make an all-out effort, now while there is still time, to stop the plans for war and destruction designed against us. We need your help to achieve peace." In a letter sent July 4, 1986, the convention asked, "What right does the most powerful and rich nation of the world have to impose misery, pain, and death on a poor and weak people like Nicaragua? What right does the Reagan administration have to decide the destiny of Nicaragua?" They urged North American Christians to "act so that the United States government will leave us in peace." In another letter, the Nicaraguan Baptists wrote in support of The Hague International Court of Justice decision that condemned the U.S. government's policies as violating international law and rights and calling for reparations of $12 billion (the U.S. withdrew from the court, saying they had no authority in the relations of sovereign states). The Nicaraguan Baptists later wrote in support of the 1987 Esquipulas II peace accords signed by the Central American presidents, including Daniel Ortega.

One American Baptist church in Boston had a peace group involved in the protests against U.S. policies in Nicaragua and El Salvador. When the pastoral letter was issued by the Baptist Convention of Nicaragua in March 1984, the church received a copy through denominational sources. They took one of the quotes from the letter and painted it in big black letters on a bedsheet: "The government of the richest, most powerful nation in the world is blocking, attacking and destroying the life aspirations of our people—Nicaraguan Baptist Convention." The members of that church felt they were a megaphone to expand the voice of their Baptist brothers and sisters in Nicaragua. During one demonstration, as the bedsheet was held up by two church members, it was photographed by someone from the Evangelistic Association of New England. EANE had a weekly newsletter that was sent to every church in all the New England states. The message from the Nicaraguan Baptists on that bedsheet appeared on the front page, getting the word out to every church of any denomination in the region.

Pledge of Resistance

In the 1980s, religious peace groups in the U.S. met annually for a retreat at the Kirkridge Retreat and Study Center in Bangor, Pennsylvania set in the beautiful Pocono Mountains in the eastern part of the state. Their 1984 retreat was historic, sparked by a phone call from Gustavo Parajón.

Gustavo initially called while the group was in session, so he left his number for Jim Wallis. At the break, Wallis called back. Gustavo began, "We have intelligence that the U.S. is planning to invade Nicaragua." A bit earlier in October 1983, the U.S. had invaded Grenada, so this was no idle fantasy. Gustavo said he had access to concrete data. He and Nicaraguan friends were praying about what to do. He told Jim, "God told us what to do." Jim responded with anticipation, "What?" Gustavo replied, "To call you and ask you to stop the invasion." Jim asked, "How can I do that?" Gustavo simply said, "God didn't tell us that." Then he pleaded, "For God's sake, please try to help us!" Jim didn't know what to say.

So Jim returned to the group and relayed his conversation with Gustavo. For a while, the group talked about typical actions peace groups had taken: going to congressional offices, demanding the invasion be called off, risking arrest. Then Jim Rice, director of Peace Ministry for Sojourners suggested that they could get people to sign up for a massive national phone tree. Sojourners had a huge mailing list across the U.S. They could invite people to sign a "Pledge of Resistance" to commit acts of civil disobedience if the U.S. invaded Nicaragua. The phone tree could mobilize the signers of the pledge to rapid action. In the next few weeks, over 80,000 people across the U.S. signed the pledge.

Wallis then met with the U.S. Assistant Secretary of State for Latin America. He promised the official that if the U.S. invaded Nicaragua, he would have to arrest 80,000 U.S. citizens, including clergy in their ministerial collars and Catholic nuns in sisterly garb. The official seemed sobered by this promise, according to Wallis.

The invasion didn't take place. According to Wallis, one person who was in the room when the invasion was debated said the Pledge of Resistance was one of the biggest reasons they decided not to do it. A general said they could have invaded Nicaragua "... if we could have gotten the damn Christians out of the way." The mobilization of all "the damn Christians" was triggered by that call from Gustavo Parajón.

However, the Reagan administration continued to pursue action to undermine the Sandinista government in Nicaragua. Rather than launching an invasion, they turned toward what was called "low intensity conflict." This conflict was low intensity as far as U.S. forces were concerned, but involved highly intense brutality in the hills and communities of Nicaragua. Funds would be channeled to the Contras, pulled together from the remnant of Somoza's National Guard and anybody else who could be lured into the fight either from disaffection with the Sandinistas or the money provided by the U.S.

The battleground shifted for the Pledge of Resistance from a U.S. invasion that had been stopped, to congressional funding, a very live issue. When Congress passed a bill to fund military aid to the Contras, the phone tree was triggered calling for action by the signers of the Pledge of Resistance. Tens of thousands of people across the U.S. took action. Boston and San Francisco had two of the largest Pledge networks. A total of 586 people were arrested in Boston as they nonviolently occupied the Federal building downtown, while thousands outside demonstrated in support of those inside. In San Francisco, 443 people were arrested. Similar actions were held in almost every major city.

In the weeks and months that followed, further actions took place, depending on the latest twists and turns of U.S. policies. To avoid the news exposure of the massive arrests, in many cities police stopped making arrests and used more physical force against protesters. Most of these protesters came from religious groups, woven into the protest movement through Sojourners, the Fellowship of Reconciliation, and denominational peace fellowships. These groups had launched this massive movement at that Kirkridge retreat, in response to a call from Gustavo Parajón.

In March 1986, a vote came before Congress to provide $100 million in military assistance to the Contras. Demonstrations sprang up across the country using many crosses with the names of Nicaraguan civilians killed in the war as their visual message. The demonstrators in Washington were joined by Gilberto Aguirre from CEPAD and Pastor Norman Bent of the Moravian Church. Despite massive protests, extensive lobbying, and the disapproval of the majority of the U.S. public, Congress passed the military aid package. After the vote, Gustavo asked U.S. Americans in Nicaragua, "What have you learned about your democracy?"[17]

Music

Joan and Gustavo were very musical people, Joan in a far more professional sense. Gustavo loved to sing and had a good tenor voice. Joan directed the choir at First Baptist, Managua. Together, with Witness for Peace and working with the poor, they had an impact on many musicians.

Ken Medema is a singer/songwriter/pianist who writes and plays Christian songs with a strong social consciousness. In the early 1980s, he was invited by the Baptist Convention of Nicaragua to perform a series of concerts around the country. They hoped, through Ken, to show that there were Baptists in the U.S. who didn't agree with Ronald Reagan's Contra War. A delegation from Ken's church, Dolores Street Baptist Church in San Francisco, went to Nicaragua for a month.

17 From *Witness for Peace* by Ed Griffin-Nolan, Westminster/John Knox Press, Louisville, Kentucky, p. 181.

They met Gustavo and Joan on a Sunday at FBC Managua. Ken learned from Joan that the choir had sung his Moses song in Spanish. Ken said, "It blew my world!" Then he heard Gustavo preach, and Ken felt so at home. He relished the truth being told with love that had firmness and directness, a rare combination.

Ken spent the afternoon with Gustavo and Joan. He wanted to learn about Gustavo; but Gustavo wanted to learn about Ken, especially about the Dolores Street Church and their ministries to the homeless. Ken noticed that for the Parajóns what mattered most were their guests, being hospitable, and supporting the work of the guests. He was deeply moved by the guest-centered hospitality he received from them.

Medema then traveled around Nicaragua, performing concerts in many different towns. In Ocotal, a town near the Honduran border, Ken played in a theater that had been bombed out by the Contras the week before. They still held the concert there, amid the damage. Ken brought greetings to the crowd from Gustavo and Joan. In response the crowd stood and applauded. On his tour, Ken discovered that Gustavo was deeply beloved, not just by Baptists, but by everybody.

Another musician who connected with Gustavo was Bono from the Irish rock band U2. Bono and his wife, Ali, went to Nicaragua with David Batstone of Central American Mission Partners. They met with Gustavo for an afternoon, impressing Bono enough that he would intentionally see him later in the U.K. Bono was deeply moved to see Christian leaders like Gustavo with a strong faith who were directly engaged in the struggles for justice and meeting the needs of a hurting world.

Bono and Ali visited El Salvador as well as Nicaragua. Seeing firsthand the impact of U.S. military support and weaponry in the conflicts shaped much of the music in U2's *Joshua Tree* album. In El Salvador, Bono and Ali witnessed an air attack in the next valley. He said of that experience, "I remember the ground shaking, and I remember the smell, I suppose, of being near a war zone. I don't think we were in danger, but I knew there were lives in danger or being lost close to us, and I felt for them. It upset me as a person who read the Scriptures, to think that Christians in America were supporting this kind of thing, this kind of proxy war because of these communists."

Some say Bono's song "Where the Streets Have No Name" comes from Managua's unnamed streets that can leave a person feeling like they are in a rabbit warren. Maybe so, but Bono was also lifting up a vision counter to his experience in Ireland of someone knowing your religion because of the name of the street where you lived. Bono's visions for peace were certainly deeply stirred by his experiences in Central America and later in the refugee camps of Ethiopia.

Bruce Cockburn went to Nicaragua having heard already about CEPAD. He was intrigued that evangelical Christians could be on friendly terms with the Sandinistas. As a progressive-thinking Canadian folk-rock musician with an engaged faith, he was interested in seeing how Christians interacted with the leftist revolution. He first went to Nicaragua in 1983 but didn't meet Gustavo, though he heard a lot about him.

Two years later, he made a point of meeting Dr. Parajón. Gustavo and Joan invited him for dinner. He had brought his guitar, and Gustavo asked Bruce to play a couple songs. The singing went on much longer than that! Bruce Cockburn's song "Nicaragua" captures vividly what he experienced and felt while in that country.

Kris Kristofferson was deeply affected by his visits to Nicaragua, expressed in his song "Sandinista," which he often sang in concerts with an opening commentary. He spent a few hours in deep conversation with Gustavo during one of his visits. Some of the musicians, such as Kristofferson and Jackson Browne, spent time with Nicaraguan musicians and wove their concerns into their music and their political critique of the U.S. government.

Garth Hewitt, the Anglican priest and singer/songwriter from the U.K., was very involved in Nicaragua and with the Parajóns, along with his wife, Gill. (See more in Chapter 10.) His song "O, Nicaragua" had a line in one of the verses inspired by Gustavo and the work of PROVADENIC. Each set of lines in the verses celebrated some of Nicaragua's geographic, social, or political experiences, sometimes with joy, sometimes despair. He sang in celebration, "You're a health clinic up some mountainous road, working for the future and lifting the load." He recorded a video of that song inside the CEPAD compound.

Garth and Gill toured Nicaragua with Sue and Simon Plater in 1993 specifically to select a CEPAD project for Garth's foundation, Amos Trust, to support. They traveled with Gustavo and Gilbert Andino, not just seeing CEPAD projects, but experiencing Nicaraguan culture. Garth produced an album out of his experiences on this trip, "Stronger than the Storm." When in Managua, they all stayed at the Parajón home, deepening the family ties. Over the years, the Hewitts and Platers visited Nicaragua many times, and Amos Trust became a major partner with Gustavo's ministries.

Scottish Christians for Nicaragua

Solidarity groups from the U.S. weren't the only folks interested in what was happening in Nicaragua. In other countries, small groups, especially of Christians, were interested in how they could support Christians under assault from the military and economic might of the U.S. A small number of Scottish Christians who had become interested in liberation theology were energized by the Nicaraguan Revolution. They saw a revolutionary movement that wasn't purely Marxist-Leninist, rather one where care for the needs of the poor was also shaped by Christian thinking, including radical priests in their leadership, such as Ernesto and Fernando Cardenal and Miguel d'Escoto.

They initially helped raise funds for medical assistance through the organization Scottish Medical Aid for Nicaragua, attending the monthly meetings of that network. They leafleted cinemas showing the powerful movie "Under Fire" about a Scottish bus driver and a Nicaraguan woman who had fled the violence. Their efforts helped fund a medical clinic in Belén. However, they felt a particularly Christian perspective was important in the effort, so they formed Scottish Christians for Nicaragua (SCN).

The group continued raising money for the medical work. One of their favorite activities was "busking," forming a small band to play on the streets and get passers-by to donate. On a good afternoon they could raise £1,000 to £2,000 for medical relief. They spoke in churches about the Christians working alongside the revolution. They led in worship services, singing Nicaraguan Christian songs such as "You Are the God of the Poor." SCN sold books, including *The Gospel of Solentiname* by Ernesto Cardenal. They wrote many letters to urge political and financial support for the people of Nicaragua. They had picked up a quote from Gustavo Parajón, likely from a *Sojourners* magazine: "The threat of Nicaragua was that of a good example to the United States." Thus the U.S.-funded war to strangle the hope rising in Nicaragua before it spread too far.

But one question prompted David McLachlan and a few others to go: How could they give a credible witness unless some of them had gone to Nicaragua and seen the situation for themselves? So, the small team went in August and September 1985 to see what they could, including the clinic in Belén.

They arrived unannounced at the CEPAD offices just as Gustavo was giving an orientation to a large group of young church folks from the U.S., very similar to the Scots. Gustavo talked about the war, the impact of the U.S. intervention on the people, especially upon public health. For example, dengue fever was on the rise. Children were also being maimed by explosives in children's toys. The economy was in tatters. "This is what American intervention means for us," Parajón said. One of the young Americans asked, "Well, what kind of intervention do you want?" Gustavo responded "We don't want any kind of intervention. We'd like you to leave us alone!" The Scots were struck by how the visiting Americans assumed that everything the U.S. did was for good even if mistakes were made along the way.

The Scots joined a Witness for Peace group going up to Esteli. They met with Julie Beutel, a Witness for Peace participant who had been captured by the Contras and later released. David and his wife went up to a nearby village up in the mountains to bring a thousand pencils to the school. They could hear weapons firing in the distance, leading to difficulty getting a taxi to evacuate them. Eventually they got out and back to Managua. The Scots joined in a protest picket line in front of the U.S. Embassy. They had dinner with Gustavo and Joan at their home. Once they returned to Glasgow, their credibility went up as they spoke about what they experienced.

After the SCN trip to Nicaragua, Gustavo Parajón was invited to Glasgow. He stayed in the homes of members of SCN, spoke in their churches, and touched their hearts. He spoke about the reforms in medicine and education achieved by the revolution, positive achievements under threat in the war. When asked how long he would support the Sandinistas, he responded, "We will support them as long as the people are with them." David McLachlan took him to the headquarters of the Church of Scotland (a Presbyterian denomination) to meet with leaders there. While in Glasgow, Gustavo stayed with the Smillie family, who had small children. He taught the kids "Dios es Amor."

Later, when Gustavo participated in the Greenbelt Festival (see Chapter 9), Scottish Christians for Nicaragua held an event called Cabaret Nicaragua in the biggest tent in the festival. Gustavo was the main speaker, with musicians such as Bruce Cockburn playing along with their own busker band. A "Cabaret Nicaragua" album was produced with songs by Cockburn and others as well as clips from Gustavo's talks. One word of Gustavo's that struck deep for the Scots was, "It appears to be bleak, but we are people of hope."[18]

Criticism and Prophetic Witness

As part of the information and psychological war waged by the U.S., many false accusations were made about Gustavo Parajón and CEPAD. The fact that they had a working relationship with what some conservative churches in the U.S. viewed as a communist government was enough to show that Parajón and CEPAD must be evil. Falsehoods were circulating in abundance. One such propaganda lie was that CEPAD gave fourteen Jeeps to the national police. CEPAD never had that many vehicles and never gave any to the government, but the lie circulated widely. At an open-air preaching meeting in Diriamba in October 1985, local police came to ask that the sound be turned down. The story was told that the police shut down the event, one supposed example of the persecution of churches. However, the church organizers said that wasn't true. They simply turned the sound down and continued without a problem. Yet the story circulated to show how the Sandinistas were persecuting Christians. Truth didn't matter for many involved in these campaigns of criticism, and Parajón and CEPAD were their favorite targets.

"The Other Invasion" was the propaganda war both inside and outside the country. The U.S. Embassy funneled money to conservative churches, seeking to stir up trouble even within CEPAD churches. There were monthly meetings with CEPAD and various Sandinista government officials to coordinate health care,

---

18 Church times, "Obituary: Dr. Gustavo Parajón," 30 March 2011.

development projects, and some of the logistics regarding all the international teams coming to Nicaragua. These ties gave fuel to the accusers.

There was a group of about fifteen pastors and older leaders among the Nicaraguan Baptists called the Dialogue Group. They thought the Baptist Convention in general, and Dr. Parajón in particular, should stay out of political matters and focus on saving souls. After many meetings with the Dialogue Group, the matter was brought before the General Assembly of the Baptists. By a majority vote, that body of all the Baptist Churches asked the Dialogue Group to desist from their actions and not to obstruct the peace and reconciliation work of Dr. Parajón and the board of directors.

A representative from Trans World Mission accused CEPAD, saying, "The Communist Sandinista Government of Nicaragua has ordered 1,300 pastors to sign up with CEPAD, join the army or go to jail. If they join the army, they will be killed by their own troops who will then report that they were killed by the Contras." When asked about this Gustavo replied, "Well, it's a hilarious comment, and I wish it were hilarious only, but it is also tragic because it is not true." The real picture was very different. Evangelical churches were growing, making up to 15% of the population in Nicaragua. CEPAD at that time had put together a list of nine hundred young people of draftable age who were pastors or seminarians. CEPAD was able to secure draft exemptions for all of them, a number that eventually grew to over 1,600. Another fallacy promoted by Trans World Mission was that in order to preach legally in Nicaragua, a pastor must have a card signed by CEPAD. In order to get this card, the pastor must sign a document stating that he will preach Marxism-Leninism and the revolution half the time and the Bible the rest of the time. No such requirement ever existed. Instead, Gustavo talked about churches having the freedom to share the Gospel and bring people to Christ. Churches were packed. It was sad to see Christian bodies spreading disinformation that was damaging to other Christians as part of the ideological war against the Sandinistas.[19]

The spreading of falsehoods was even more painful to Gustavo when it was done by people he knew. One pastor accused him of turning the names of non-sympathetic pastors over to the Sandinista Secret Service so they could be persecuted, tortured, and even killed. Gustavo agonized in prayer, "How could a colleague, a pastor, lie and slander others?" At the same time, it was the supposed "enemy" who was encouraging him in how he followed Christ. The Sandinistas saw how he served the poor and appreciated him for that with no religious restrictions.

The main driver of the accusations in the U.S. against CEPAD as an organization and against Gustavo Parajón personally was the Institute for Religion and Democracy (IRD). For quite a few years, Dr. Parajón was in the crosshairs of IRD's slander. The IRD called CEPAD "a government commission" and Parajón "a loyal

---

19 May 9, 1987 interview with Ronald G. Taylor, International Ministries.

Sandinista." They said Parajón recorded CEPAD meetings and passed the information on to government security offices. They said funds raised in the U.S. were channeled into government-approved projects. The Reagan administration took the IRD accusations verbatim to include them in press briefings about Nicaragua.

IRD's main goal was to cut U.S. church funding to CEPAD. IRD's September 1984 newsletter, said "... hundreds of thousands of our church dollars are going to organizations that support those who are persecuting Christianity in Nicaragua." CEPAD was at the top of IRD's list of such groups. IRD called for all funds from U.S. churches and denominations to be suspended for "church and educational organizations which support that [Nicaraguan] government," particularly CEPAD. IRD showed no concern for the poor in need of education, health care, housing, and public health. Rather, for the IRD and the Reagan administration, the Sandinista government was so evil that anything was justified that would destabilize the country, including damaging church-based programs for suffering people.

It is true that CEPAD coordinated a lot of their work with the Sandinista government. It is true that Gustavo Parajón viewed the Sandinista revolution as a vast improvement over the Somoza regime because of dramatic increases in programs to lift up the poor. However, Parajón and CEPAD would also raise prophetic voices against Sandinista policies and actions that damaged people, especially with regard to the indigenous people on Nicaragua's east coast. Parajón and CEPAD stood against the Sandinista repressions in the early years of the revolution and succeeding war. They became the main advocates outside the indigenous community about the Miskito concerns, calling for justice and reconciliation. In a CEPAD newsletter, they referred to the "brutal errors of the new government."[20] Through CEPAD's work, government insensitivity toward indigenous people was reversed for the most part, and the path was paved for reconciliation.

CEPAD became the key mediator between the government and conservative churches and even groups like the Jehovah's Witnesses, who were either unengaged with government concerns or even opposed to the government. They worked out the exemption from the military draft for evangelical pastors and seminarians.

A *Sojourners* magazine editorial by Jim Wallis put the questions of truth, integrity, and government complicity with pointed accuracy: "What emerges from this campaign of falsehood and innuendo is not the subservience of CEPAD to its government, but rather the subservience of the IRD to its government. Indeed, CEPAD has demonstrated a more independent and critical posture in relation to the government of Nicaragua than the IRD has shown toward the government of the United States. The IRD has virtually become the official seminary of the Reagan administration. With ready access to the government, lots of conservative

20 CEPAD Newsletter, March, 1986.

money, and highly placed media connections, the IRD has become in the United States what it falsely accuses CEPAD of becoming in Nicaragua."[21]

To try to bring an ethical solution to the conflict around these accusations, Vernon Grounds, president of the Evangelicals for Social Action (ESA), invited the IRD to go on a joint fact-finding trip to Nicaragua with ESA. Each organization would put forward people to interview and listen together to what was said. The IRD initially agreed to the proposal, but then they backed out. In the end, the IRD showed no interest in pursuing a path of integrity and seeking the truth with any Christian organization, preferring to continue their slanderous campaign for the sake of the ideology that was attacking a leftist government. Not once did the IRD raise a voice of criticism about the Contras killing civilians, health workers, or even clergy. Wallis used a quote of IRD board member Michael Novak: "The first step in combatting terrorism is to condemn it, no matter who commits it, or whatever party or ideology. Terror is the murder, maiming, or menacing of innocent civilians, and must always be forthrightly condemned, universally, across the board." The Contras were clearly engaged in such terror as a persistent strategy, something documented over and over again. The IRD instead chose to continue its attacks against Christians inside Nicaragua working to help the poor, to stand with the victims of the war, and to raise a prophetic voice against the politics that continued to support and fund that terror.

Three years after Wallis' editorial, the IRD was still going strong, making false accusations in order to undermine Christian work in Nicaragua that made things better for the poor and marginalized. An IRD newsletter quoted the National Council of Evangelical Pastors (CNPEN) about CEPAD diverting funds from U.S. churches to the work of the Sandinista regime. In response, CNPEN wrote a letter rejecting what IRD claimed about them, but the IRD refused to publish CNPEN's statements. CNPEN said they had no ties with IRD and some CNPEN pastors felt they had been used by that organization.

Parajón's own peacemaking centered on the call of Jesus to simply go and talk to the other person or party, whoever could be considered to be at fault (Matthew 5:24 and 18:15). On March 13, 1986, Parajón was in Washington, D.C. speaking at an ESA breakfast. He raised the issue of the false accusations coming from IRD and asked to be able to reply in an IRD publication to the charges made against him. So, later that day ESA Executive Director Bill Kallio took Gustavo to meet with IRD board members and staff. IRD leaders agreed to publish an interview with Parajón, but after a year, no action was taken. Kallio checked up on IRD and asked when the interview would take place, but IRD rescinded the offer of an interview. Then, about a year and a half after that first meeting, Parajón had an unplanned encounter with one of the IRD leaders. He asked her why nothing had

---

21 *Sojourners*, November, 1984, "In Defense of CEPAD" editorial by Jim Wallis.

been done to address his grievances about the falsehoods. She replied, "Oh, but we haven't written anything negative about you for months." Joyce Hollyday of Sojourners followed up and was given repeated equivocal responses. Staff said they couldn't remember meetings or that they weren't "sure Dr. Parajón really wanted to do anything." The IRD refused to retract anything they said or to make a public apology. One person said about what IRD published regarding Parajón, "I don't know if it's true, and I don't know how to find out." IRD repeatedly showed a lack of journalistic integrity or concern for Christian ethical behavior. They slandered a major Christian leader and refused to be held accountable for their repeatedly stated falsehoods that were weaponized by the Reagan administration as part of its propaganda war. IRD's ongoing behavior gave no counterevidence to Jim Wallis' assertion that "... the IRD has become in the United States what it falsely accuses CEPAD of becoming in Nicaragua."

Hollyday later wrote about the reason IRD and the U.S. government continued to attack Parajón: "A man like Gustavo Parajón, who has shown a steady stream of U.S. visitors a picture of Nicaragua entirely unlike the propaganda emanating from the Reagan administration and its friends, is a threat to the policy of falsehood. Because he is so well respected, Gustavo Parajón is more dangerous to the IRD and the White House than anyone who might actually fit their accusations. For the lies to stand up, people like Gustavo Parajón must be discredited. Gustavo Parajón's rejoinder to the IRD's defense is to the point: 'Such actions serve neither religion nor democracy.'"[22]

So how did Gustavo Parajón operate in the face of the nastiness and distortions of IRD and other critics? Those close to him were amazed at his demeanor. He would always try to make a connection, calling critics "brother" or "sister." Some friends felt he was too soft on his critics, but Gustavo would respond, "Did you read the Bible?" Stories of reconciliation in the Bible between Jacob and Esau and between Joseph and his brothers shaped his approach more than the ideological struggles. As his International Ministries area director José Norat-Rodríguez said of him, "He lived what he believed. There was a coherent element between theory and practice."[23]

Some people vilified Parajón as a conservative for his use of the Bible and Baptist doctrines. Others called him a "liberal softie" because he would meet with "sinners." (A criticism made of Jesus as well!) He was called a "communist Sandinista" for partnering with the government on various projects and for supporting the revolution as a dramatic improvement over Somoza. He was called a "counterrevolutionary" because he worked for peace and would meet with insurgents.

---

22 Joyce Hollyday, *Sojourners*, March, 1987 "Usual Operating Procedures."
23 Interview of José Norat-Rodríguez by Daniel Buttry.

Gilbert Andino was a young person shaped by Dr. Parajón who went on to work for both PROVADENIC and CEPAD. He noticed how Parajón never declared himself on the side of any party. The doctor was offered positions in various governments and simply said, "No thank you." Andino recalls him saying, "I do not feel that the Lord has called me to that." As Andino saw up close, Parajón "did not allow himself to be entangled with flattery, nor with power." In all the years Andino knew Dr. Parajón, he never heard him speak ill of anyone or judge them, not even his detractors. If he heard someone else being critical of another person, Parajón would gently correct and try to emphasize the positive.

In his close time with Gustavo, Jim Wallis saw him as independent of Sandinistas.

He never capitulated to political power. Rather, he was an independent, Christ-centered pastor and doctor who simply wanted to take care of people. Yes, Parajón was in favor of building the new government that was such a vast improvement over the previous one. However, he would also keep doing what he thought was right, whatever that might mean for the politics.[24]

Despite all the ugly and baseless criticism, Parajón continued his service to those who were needy and to bring peace to Nicaragua. Soon, his passion for peace would open up opportunities to end the war and help heal the shattered land. He eagerly and courageously moved in that direction.

---

24 Other sources in this section are interviews by Daniel Buttry with Jim Wallis and Joyce Hollyday in Jim Wallis' "Letters on Nicaragua," *Sojourners*, December 1987.

Gustavo with peace commissioners in Bilwi listening to concerns.

Dr. Parajón, President Ortega, and Cardinal Obando y Bravo discuss the peace process.

Discussion of peace concerns with Gustavo Parajón at one end of table and Daniel Ortega at the other.

Peace talks with Contras in mountains of Nueva Guinea.

6

Peace Process and Reconciliation

Before anything serious had been done for peace on the level of national leaders or diplomats, Gustavo Parajón had been at work building peace in the harsh environment of war zones. Driven by his commitment to Christ, the Prince of Peace, Parajón acted on a dream at a time when few others could even imagine it.

CEPAD's Local Peace Commissions

In 1984, CEPAD began to develop local peace commissions based on some of the local development and public health committees from their grassroots empowerment of community leaders. With CEPAD's extensive connections around the country and strong relationships with local community leaders, they were close to the suffering of people during the war. They talked with people who had been jailed by the government. They listened to people who had been kidnapped by the Contras. Contra terror tactics, land mines, and disruption of the economy created much hardship. CEPAD also knew of the discontent over government surveillance, the centralized economy, and censorship. CEPAD worked to build up the local capacity to address some of the particular concerns that affected the lives of people in the communities.

Hundreds of ordinary citizens became involved in these local peace commissions. Often, a local Catholic priest or lay pastor (known as a Delegate of the Word) would head a commission. Evangelical pastors, with their connections to CEPAD, were usually involved. Farmers and businesspeople participated. CEPAD staffers and representatives of the International Red Cross served. They sought to be politically neutral, though sometimes people from opposition parties and even former Contras joined the commissions. Though members often held different visions for their work, the commissions sought to find the middle ground where dialogue could be established and where work could be done in addressing community concerns with both the government and the Contras.

In this context, Milton Argüello, one of the younger people working for CEPAD at the time, was fascinated by Dr. Parajón's capacity to listen. He saw Parajón actively working to get people to talk to each other. How could this be done in the middle of a war? Fear was so strong. Talking to someone from the other side was literally dangerous, and attacks could be launched without warning. Parajón and other CEPAD staff could take on this delicate work because with steadfastness they had invested themselves in the communities and community leadership. Through the work for health care and development, local evangelical leaders also had credibility from their work with CEPAD and PROVADENIC. Trust had been built, and the fruit of the trust built over those years was harvested in the reconciliation efforts.

One example of Dr. Parajón de-escalating a specific situation was related to Nicanor Mairena, a Nazarene pastor in the Solentiname archipelago in Lake Nicaragua. Pastor Mairena was accused by the Sandinistas of anti-government activity. Gustavo, Gilberto, and Milton went to the islands and interviewed many folks, digging into the assertions and finding out what really happened. They presented what they found to government officials, and the action planned against Pastor Mairena was halted. These are the kinds of actions that were ignored by Parajón's U.S. critics but made a huge impact in conflicted communities.

Some of the villages up in the hills were accessible only by paths, rather than roads. Gustavo would walk with others in his team. Because of his childhood polio, he had a limp, but he would press on through many kilometers of difficult terrain. Often, he took a pillow with him, and once Milton asked him why. Gustavo replied, "Now that I am old, I know that the pillow is essential for a good sleep." Sometimes one donkey was available to ride on, but Gustavo would refuse to use it unless there were more donkeys available for other members of the team. Such selfless leadership endeared him both to those on his team and to the local leaders who saw his humility in action.

Carlos Mejía Ruiz was a young worker in CEPAD who left with revolutionary zeal to do two years of military service with the Nicaraguan army. Dr. Parajón had tried to persuade him not to go, but to continue to work with CEPAD. Carlos went off anyway and experienced the horrors of war: watching friends bleed to death, seeing limbs blown off and stomachs pierced, with their viscera oozing outside the bodies. He saw headless boys and girls. When he had served his time in the army, he rejoined CEPAD, but now with a deep empathy for Dr. Parajón's love for peace and reconciliation. He was inspired when Parajón said, "It is not with a sword or with armies but with God's Holy Spirit that we are going to free ourselves from this war."

One time, the peace commission in Nueva Guinea wanted to meet with Dr. Parajón. He and his team, including Carlos Mejía and Milton Argüello, drove to the town of Santo Tomás, arriving in the late afternoon. The way ahead was merely a trail. So, while they were stopped, the team members found accommodations for dinner and the night from the pastor of a local CEPAD-related church. When they went back with their joyous news about dinner and a place to sleep, Parajón got angry, something seldom seen. He said that if they stopped just because it was evening, the peace commissioners would have gathered for nothing. "We have to go, whatever it takes," he insisted.

The team wasn't the only problem. Forty kilometers later in La Gateada, the military chief of that area told him, "Doctor, you cannot pass with your people because you do not know if there is an ambush or if there are mines. This is dangerous. You cannot continue." Parajón asked those in the truck, "Is there anyone who is afraid?" Milton confessed years later, "We were obviously fearful, but no one said anything." Hearing nothing, Parajón said, "Let's continue. Our commitment is to be there early tomorrow for the meeting with the peace commissions." The officer still refused to let them go. Then Parajón asked firmly, "Who do I have to talk to?" They contacted the minister of defense, General Humberto Ortega. Parajón found a typewriter and quickly wrote a letter that the group was responsible for their own safety and would be meeting with the peace commission in Nueva Guinea. Finally, they were cleared through the checkpoint.

The team left La Gateada as the sun went down for the last leg of the journey. They had a small convoy of vehicles, leaving their lights on as a sign of their peaceful intentions. Before they left, Parajón brought them all together for a brief talk: "We are going to travel. We are all scared. If God is with us, who is against us? We are going to travel because we cannot leave the peace commissions waiting. Today we have to be there. And what's more, I'm going ahead. Who wants to go with me?" The entire team agreed to go with him, whatever the risks. Then they prayed and headed out into the war zone. They arrived around midnight after hard driving on the rough road, even fording a river swollen from the recent rains.

A crowd of four hundred people was eagerly waiting for them. They began their discussions with the local peace commissioners and others in the community. Then they went to bed, rising to the new day with more telling of stories, raising concerns, and singing songs of peace and hope. Dr. Parajón reminded all who gathered of their hope through a song he led: "It is not with a sword, nor with an army, but with His Holy Spirit." This was the song they always sang at their meetings, and it became a favorite for the team.

Another time, Parajón and his team traveled to Nueva Guinea to press on further to the remote community of La Fonseca to meet some of the leaders of the Contras' Southern Front. Their guide was Pastor José Ángel Jirón, lovingly nicknamed "Changuito." When the road became too difficult for vehicles to pass, everyone got out. There was only one mule. Pastor José tried to get Gustavo to ride the mule so he wouldn't get tired, but the doctor refused. Instead, they loaded the cameras and other equipment on the mule. For an hour, Parajón walked with his team through the mud, the puddles, and the vicious clouds of mosquitoes. At last, they came into a valley, where they were suddenly surrounded by hundreds of armed men under Commandante Gallo from León. Soon, their meeting was underway. Parajón began the discussions by reading from the Bible and leading a devotional. As Parajón talked, many were in tears. Afterward, there were hugs all around. Carlos Mejía remembers hugging an armed boy about 17 years old, who said, "Find out how to do something for peace. We can't bear to be here anymore. This is hard." Carlos knew how hard it was, though he had served on the other side in combat. Now he was helping Dr. Parajón as an ambassador for peace, seeing the face of one who was once his enemy.[25]

As the team encountered Contras, they noticed that many of the soldiers were teenagers and even children. Most were dirty and hungry. The team would bring cheese and tortillas to feed them and watched the children devour the food with desperation. That special care for the physical needs of the soldiers eased tensions and opened the doors to trust.

In 1986, a Campaign of Prayer for Peace was launched by CEPAD. At the launch of the campaign on July 25, a vigil was held throughout the night, with passionate prayers lifted up by several hundred people. On July 20, prisoners at the maximum-security penitentiary in Tipitapa prayed for peace and celebrated the baptism of 104 prisoners. The prisoners were allowed to go out to a nearby park for an ecumenical service with eighteen pastors. They spoke of their commitment to the God who wants peace and justice for Nicaragua. The campaign continued from August through October, with special ecumenical services held in various communities. Days of fasting for peace were observed, and a national retreat for pastors was held to lift up their prayers for peace. (Pastor Amancio Sánchez and his family were severely injured by a landmine when he was traveling to Jinotega to plan one of these events—see Chapter 5.) The campaign concluded on October 31 with a massive ecumenical worship service in Managua's Plaza Ana María.

Over the years of the war, Dr. Parajón and CEPAD worked alongside grass-roots peace commissioners. They provided training for the commissioners. They

---

25 Stories from interviews of Carlos Mejía and Milton Argüello by Dámaris Albuquerque.

visited to bring encouragement. Sometimes they entered into direct talks with Contras and Nicaraguan army leaders and worked on some specific local issues. Eventually, there were over 200 local peace commissions set up, often in communities where there were no government structures in place. The CEPAD teams went where nobody else would go, and they found people who ached for peace to come. They brought hope to communities and people that had been shredded by the war.

National Reconciliation Commission

After the failure of the Contadora countries (Mexico, Venezuela, Colombia, and Panama) to come up with a peace agreement for the war in Nicaragua, a new person on the scene made an immediate impact. In 1986, Óscar Arias Sánchez was elected president of Costa Rica, the only country in Central America without a standing army. Arias took a totally different approach for the peacemaking efforts. First, he focused on a process with all five of the countries involved in some way in the wars in Central America: Nicaragua, El Salvador, Guatemala, Honduras, and Costa Rica. Second, he worked on conditions for peace that would be applied to all five countries, something comprehensive that would address not only the places where fighting was hot, but also in places where rebel groups found sanctuary.

On August 7, 1987, the presidents of the five Central American countries signed the Esquipulas II Peace Accord. The agreement called for a simultaneous ceasefire, amnesty for all rebels, and restoration for full press and political freedoms. This all sounded good, but the weakness of the accord was that there were no significant sanctions to back up the agreements. Arias had to expend his own effort, cajoling the other presidents to keep their commitments to the accord.

Furthermore, the United States was left out of the process and felt that too much had been given away by Arias, specifically recognizing the Sandinistas. President Reagan continued to pump millions of dollars into the Contras, destabilizing everything the peace accord was trying to achieve. Arias pointed out that the U.S. and Costa Rica don't think the same way. Arias said, "We both believe that a durable peace in Central America is possible only if there is democracy. But how to achieve that democracy is where we part company." Arias forged the agreement against U.S. diplomatic pressure, then he continued to push ahead in trying to get everyone to implement it. In appreciation for his efforts, Óscar Arias was awarded the Nobel Peace Prize in 1987, though some thought all five of the presidents involved should have received the honor.

Each country covered by Esquipulas II had its own journey related to working out the peace accord. In Nicaragua, the process worked far quicker than it did in Guatemala, for example. The Sapoá ceasefire was agreed to between the Sandinistas and the Contras on March 23, 1988, whereas in Guatemala the conflict dragged on until 1994. Sapoá was a tiny border post, where for fourteen days

representatives from the Nicaraguan government and the Contras held negotiations, resulting in a sixty-day ceasefire. The ceasefire was the relatively easy part,
difficult as that was to achieve and maintain. Building a working peace throughout
the country was far more complex. Violence would break out occasionally, usually
from the Contra side because the U.S. was still pouring millions into aid for the
Contras. However, the tide had turned, focusing instead upon an election in early
1990.

The Esquipulas II Peace Accord stipulated that each country would form a
National Reconciliation Commission. The commission would be chaired by a
representative from the Catholic Church and would include one person from
the government, one representing those in opposition, and one citizen-at-large.
In Nicaragua, Cardinal Miguel Obando y Bravo, representing the Bishops'
Conference, was chair. The other members were Vice President Sergio Ramírez;
General Secretary of the Popular Social Christian Party Mauricio Díaz; and
Dr. Gustavo Parajón as the citizen-at-large. The commission was launched on
September 1, the first of the Central American commissions to begin following
the Esquipulas II agreement.

The National Reconciliation Commission had plenty of internal challenges.
Cardinal Obando y Bravo did not think much of Dr. Parajón and would hardly
give him any attention. As Parajón and Díaz watched the frequent sparring
between the cardinal and Vice President Ramírez, Gustavo described it as "a university," perhaps referring to the intellectual sparring that seldom produces much
substantive fruit. Parajón didn't consider the national commission his best peace
work, but rather going out across the country to work beside local people, evangelical and Catholic, who were trying to forge peace on the ground.

The local peace commissions established by CEPAD provided a great network
for doing the grassroots tasks for peace and reconciliation. The Delegates of the
Word for the Catholic Church also provided a grassroots network to be woven
into the peace building. It turned out that the other Nicaraguan commissioners
mostly stayed in Managua, but Gustavo Parajón was the one who continued to
risk his life for peace by going to meet people face-to-face in the conflict zones.
Once Dr. Parajón was asked if he and the other commissioners with him were
afraid. He answered, "They were afraid to be captured by some of the conflicting
parties." The questioner followed up, "And you?" "I was afraid of not doing what
God asked of me."

In those high-risk areas, Parajón was always calm. He led by sharing from the
Scripture, praying, and listening. When he spoke, he had to be very careful, something he was a master at doing. He never tried to force people into a commitment,
but rather used the power of persuasion. He would lift up the vision of a better way
forward that drew people toward constructive action. More than any other person

in Nicaragua, it was Dr. Parajón who did the hard work on the ground to make the peace envisioned in Esquipulas II a reality.

Caribbean Coast Mediation Initiative

The eastern Caribbean Coast of Nicaragua is a very multicultural, multilingual region. The area had been colonized by the British, so English became the dominant language in some areas. A key ethnic group are the Creoles of African and English descent, sometimes mixed with indigenous descent. In the late 1800s, the region was traded back and forth between the U.K., Honduras, and Nicaragua, finally losing its autonomous status with a complete takeover by the Nicaraguan government in 1894. The "Spaniards" from the rest of the country were viewed as conquering enemies along the Caribbean Coast, and the news of what was happening elsewhere seemed distant to them.

Besides the linguistic and ethnic difference, there was a significant religious difference between the people living in the east and the rest of Nicaragua. Moravians from the Caribbean Islands came and evangelized the Miskito Indians in the 1840s. By 1894, most of the Miskitos had become Christian, mainly Moravians. Moravian faith was woven into their lives and culture as Catholicism was in the rest of the country.

As the Contra War began to develop, the suspicious Sandinista government took some actions that dramatically heightened the distrust of them along the Caribbean Coast. The leader of the Moravian Church was invited for a meeting in Managua, but when he landed at the airport, instead of being taken to the meeting, he was taken to prison. Other pastors were arrested and some were tortured. Andy Shogreen was the pastor of the Moravian church in Managua, and in 1983 he was elected by the Moravian synod to replace the imprisoned pastor. In the years ahead, the Rev. Shogreen would play a vital role bringing peace to the Caribbean Coast.

More grievous to the indigenous people was action taken by the Nicaraguan army in a Miskito village 64 kilometers south of Puerto Cabezas. Sixty people, all civilians, were killed as the army swept through. The bodies of those slain were left unburied. International human rights organizations visited the site and saw the bones of those killed. These groups were from the United Nations and the Organization of American States, so it was not possible for the government to stop their investigations, even though they tried to keep them from getting to the village.

Some villages were cleared out and relocated to areas that the Nicaraguan army could control more easily. In response to the government actions, a number of insurgent groups began to form along the Caribbean Coast and fight against the Sandinista army. The Caribbean armed groups were mostly made up of indigenous people—Miskitos, Sumos, and Ramas—who spoke their own indigenous languages, not Spanish. They had a separate organization, YATAMA (**Ya**pti **Ta**sba **Ma**sraka Nanih Aslatakanka, translated as "Sons of Mother Earth"), a consortium of the seven commanders of the earlier insurgent groups in the Caribbean Coast. These indigenous groups in the east had different grievances and different political aims from the better-known Contras, who had their roots in Somoza's National Guard. They sought respect for religious and indigenous rights, whereas the Contras sought regime change. The African-Caribbean Creoles centered in the south around Bluefields were less involved in the conflict.

As the war dragged on, the Moravian leaders had been involved in their own efforts for reconciliation. A commission of pastors had approached an armed indigenous group, as well as the government, about not fighting each other in villages to avoid civilian casualties. In their denominational synod in 1986, the Moravian Church passed a resolution that shared their anguish and hope: "We have heard the desperate cries of our people. The workers, the professionals, the youth, the children, and those pitched in violent conflict, all declare together that we are tired of the war, and we want peace." They went on to invite the government and armed opposition to "search for a dialogue which is fraternal, responsible, and sincere, in order that an honorable reconciliation, social justice, and a lasting peace may be attained." For these Moravian leaders, peace was a central element of the Gospel of Jesus Christ.

Meanwhile, the Mennonite Conciliation Service wanted to explore an effort to support partners of the Mennonite Central Committee in Latin America, where civil wars were going on. MCC was focused on relief related to problems caused by war, but how could they help halt the wars creating such terrible conditions? John Paul Lederach took the assignment and relocated to Costa Rica with his wife, a good central location from which to operate.

MCC already had many connections with the Moravian Church in Nicaragua from their relief and development work. Andy Shogreen was the Moravian leader, and he and other pastors had been arrested by the Sandinistas at various times. Gustavo Parajón often interceded for these pastors and for people who had been forcibly displaced by the Sandinistas. Since the 1970s, Parajón had worked in the Caribbean Coastal areas with CEPAD, developing relationships and mutual respect. CEPAD had a regional office in Puerto Cabezas directed by Anita Taylor. This work in agricultural development, leadership development, and theological training built a base for Gustavo's advocacy for justice. Then, Parajón was named to the National Reconciliation Commission, which gave him great access to the government.

Brooklyn Rivera, one of the YATAMA leaders, had met Daniel Ortega in New York City in October 1984, where they discussed the possibility of negotiations. The YATAMA leaders felt like they needed mediation help for the talks to be productive. They asked the Moravian leaders and CEPAD to open up a conduit to the Sandinista government and assist in the process. The Moravians and Gustavo then turned to the Mennonites and asked John Paul Lederach to join them as an advisor, since they had no particular skills or background in conciliation. The more they worked together as a team, the more fully Lederach became embedded in the group. The other team members, besides Andy Shogreen and Gustavo Parajón, were Moravian Bishop Headly Wilson, Miskito Pastor Silvio Díaz, the Rev. Ofreciano Julias and the Rev. Faran Dometz.

The web of relationships was key in preparing the way for negotiations. Gustavo knew the top leaders in the Sandinista government. Andy Shogreen was a personal friend of Brooklyn Rivera, one of the YATAMA leaders. Rivera had actually lived with the Shogreens when Rivera was studying at seminary in Managua. He also had been a leader among the youth at the First Baptist Church of Managua, where he got to know Gustavo Parajón. The relationships within the team helped link the warring parties together.

As the team began their work, they discovered many of YATAMA's contacts were in Costa Rica. With his home in Costa Rica, Lederach was ideally placed to convey messages back and forth. Gustavo could freely travel throughout Nicaragua, but sometimes Costa Rica limited travel for Nicaraguans due to the war. Everyone recognized that Gustavo played a key conciliation role as the informal communication worked back and forth.

In 1988, the peace mission in the east was launched. In the formal meetings with the two sides, Gustavo and Andy would take turns opening with a short reading from Scripture and a prayer. Psalm 85:10 was the favorite passage to be used. The text is much more direct in Spanish than in English: "Truth and Mercy will embrace; Justice and Peace will kiss." As the talks progressed, John Paul (known as Juan Pablo to his Nicaraguan friends) could hear each of these qualities needed for reconciliation take voice in the various speakers. One person emphasized the importance of truth, another of mercy. One person would speak on the values of justice and another would call for peace. How could all these voices be woven together to make a tapestry of reconciliation? That was their challenge.

In the first meetings, modest progress was made. Everyone made a basic commitment to continue. They then began to construct a more substantive agenda. The government and YATAMA formally recognized the Conciliation Commission. A cease-fire was not achieved, but both sides agreed to suspend offensive military operations. So far, so good.

Then Brooklyn Rivera asked that the heads of YATAMA be allowed to travel safely into their home territories to talk with people and consult about the process. Interior Minister Tomás Borge was present, and Lederach was sure he would reject the proposal. Instead, Borge surprised everyone by agreeing to Rivera's request, with one condition: That government representatives would go as well, and that the Conciliation Commission would go and prepare all the meetings. Everyone agreed to take on this initiative for a series of meetings throughout the Caribbean Coast region, with leaders from both sides together and the Conciliation team facilitating. Again, so far, so good.

The trip began well enough. The group contained the top representatives of YATAMA, Borge's right-hand people, including a controversial high-level commander from the Caribbean Coast, the Moravian pastors, Parajón, and Lederach, and a support team from CEPAD. As they arrived in a community, church bells would be rung, sometimes from Moravian churches that were roofless from bombings. They began in Bluefields, the largest town in the region. Then they traveled into some of the remote communities inaccessible by road, such as Sandy Bay. The group traveled up rivers or north up the coast in pangas, long thin rowboats with an outboard engine on the back, fitting four or five people per panga.

When a public meeting was held, Andy Shogreen would usually begin with Scripture readings. Again, Psalm 85 was often read, a psalm that speaks of an estranged people coming back together to reconciliation. Gustavo Parajón would pray. In his prayers, he would often bring up specific people from the community and pray for their families. Then there would be a time for people to speak. Some civilians spoke out against the local Sandinista officials. Everyone tried to listen to what was being said from whatever side.

Gustavo sent a CEPAD advance team of Milton Argüello, Dino Andino, and Carlos Mejía Ruiz to go up and down the Coco River and meet them at Puerto Cabezas, the largest town on the North Caribbean Coast. They traveled with YATAMA leaders Brooklyn Rivera and Steadman Fagoth. They were to tell people in the communities about the conciliation efforts by the Moravian Church and CEPAD. Milton was making notes for Dr. Parajón, Dino was interviewing chiefs, and Carlos was filming what was going on. The people in the communities welcomed them. Most spoke Miskito, so someone had to translate into Spanish. The team also met with the indigenous armed groups, as well as the Spanish-speaking Contras, known as the FDN (Nicaraguan Democratic Forces).

In one community, Carlos was approached by an FDN officer, tall, bearded, sunburnt, strong and stocky. The Contra officer told him, "Find out how to do something for peace because there have been many deaths, both the Piricuacos (the Sandinista military) and the Contras." Almost everywhere they went, people asked for peace. People were weary of the war. Far too many had died, mostly young people and children. Carlos filmed all their messages while Milton wrote them down.

But meanwhile, trouble was brewing. The next stop was Puerto Cabezas, further up the coast. The CEPAD team met up with Dr. Parajón and the rest of the

Conciliation Commission. There was a lot of tension, as this town was a stronghold for Brooklyn Rivera's group, but there also were a lot of Sandinistas present. Reports came in that things could get nasty, and some wanted Gustavo and Andy to call off the event. Brooklyn Rivera felt there was potential for violence from the other side, but also that this was his biggest platform for the entire trip.

The next morning, the local baseball stadium was almost completely full of people from the various ethnic groups in the region, many of them supporters of Brooklyn Rivera. However, surrounding the stadium was a crowd of Sandinista sympathizers armed with chains and wooden bats. The Conciliation Commission pushed through with the event because they had made a commitment to allow YATAMA leaders to speak. Andy and Gustavo escorted the YATAMA and Sandinista government speakers into the stadium, while Carlos Mejía Ruiz drove a CEPAD truck in with the sound equipment that was to serve as a platform for the speakers. The truck was parked at the pitcher's mound. The event began, and both Rivera and a Sandinista representative spoke to the crowd.

Suddenly heavy gunfire erupted outside the stadium, and the Commission realized they had to evacuate everyone. The Moravian pastors and Gustavo made a protective circle around the speakers and escorted them out. The core Commission members and leaders from both sides were not harmed.

Inside the stadium, however, the situation had quickly deteriorated. Carlos was both driving the truck and filming the event. John Paul Lederach got into the truck with him, and they tried to leave. The crowd from outside burst into the stadium and started throwing rocks. The windows of the truck were smashed. Carlos hid his camcorder under the driver's seat because he was sure the mob wanted to seize it. Then he was struck on the back of his head with a big rock, or brick. Carlos remained conscious and continued to drive through the crowd, with blood streaming from his wound. John Paul was the only non-Nicaraguan present, and he heard someone yell, "There's the gringo! Let's get him!" Lederach believes he and Carlos would have been killed if it wasn't for the courage and tenacity of Carlos. Carlos kept driving, crashing through the half-opened gate to get out of the stadium. Carlos and John Paul had to abandon the truck when it got stuck, but they were rescued by Miskito women and young people who popped open umbrellas to shield the two men from the barrage of stones. They shielded Carlos while he got the truck going again so they could get completely clear of the mob.

They went to get medical help at a temporary hospital that was staffed by Cuban doctors. It took twenty-seven stitches to close up Carlos' head wound. His arms and shoulders were covered with livid bruises from the stones and chains. That evening, Myrna Cunningham, a Sandinista representative in the peace process, came by. Dr. Parajón confronted her about Carlos, "He is an official of ours, and they almost killed him, and also this brother (Lederach) who comes to seek peace." Cunningham apologized for what happened. Later, when Gustavo got back to Managua, he made a report to the government, particularly noting the violent provocations from the Sandinista side and demanding an end to such disruptive violence.

Dr. Parajón and the Conciliation Commission members were not deterred from their mission by the violence at Puerto Cabezas. Instead, as Carlos remembers, "Rather he felt stronger and more committed to peace, with more love." Gustavo, Andy Shogreen, and John Paul Lederach all received written assassination threats along the way. John Paul's daughter was threatened with kidnapping. Lederach was accused by the Sandinistas of being connected to the CIA, while the Contras said he was selling out to the Sandinistas. Being the peacemaker in the middle can make one a target from both sides. Yet through it all, they pushed on.

John Paul was particularly taken by Gustavo's character and his way of engaging people in the process. He saw Gustavo working as both a pastor and a doctor in how he related to people in the peace work. The combination of his deep faith and medical training made him a special conciliator. Gustavo would meet with almost anybody, even those critical of him. He would usually know who people were before meeting them. If he didn't know a person, he would ask their name and use their first name, even inquiring after their family. Others spoke about how he always listened carefully and spoke to people with respect. Gustavo could speak truth into a situation in a way that nobody could write off. People recognized the way he put together truth and respecting people's humanity.

Gustavo's character was particularly revealed in two potentially explosive incidents during the preparations to bring Jimmy Carter to visit with YATAMA leaders in Puerto Cabezas. Gustavo and El Profe, along with Ana (more commonly called Anita) Taylor, CEPAD's regional director, were gathered at the Moravian church office building to go over the details of Carter's visit. Suddenly, about a dozen YATAMA soldiers burst in with automatic weapons, yelling and demanding immediate attention and food. They threatened to kill everyone there. Gustavo was calm and tranquil. He took his Bible and began, "The Word of God is telling us ..." The soldiers continued to yell, but Gustavo repeated that the Bible had something to say. As they were all crammed in the office, the soldiers soon followed Gustavo's calm tone and quieted down. Gustavo gently stood up, taking control of the emotions in the room and began preaching about peace in the Bible. Two of the soldiers asked for Bibles! Then Gustavo said, "Anita, please explain how the program runs here and how food relief is delivered to people in need. We can't give them that food." The soldiers peacefully left, carrying their Bibles, but none of the food from the relief program.

Shortly after that incident, CEPAD organized a meeting with 100 community leaders from the indigenous communities in preparation for Jimmy Carter's visit. The men, and a few women, gathered to hear about efforts to bring displaced people back from exile to Puerto Cabezas. As the meeting was about to begin, some of the insurgent leaders began to agitate, even stirring up some of the pastors. They said when the Sandinista Tomás Borge stands to speak, everyone applauds, but when a Miskito leader speaks, people just sit. The atmosphere began to get charged with hostility. Leaders said they didn't want the Commission, and some even threatened them. With Gustavo, Gilberto, and Anita sitting there, they asked "Why do Spaniards have to come to solve our situation?" Anita looked at the window of the second story room they were in and wondered if they would have to jump out to save themselves.

Gustavo picked up the microphone and his Bible. "The Word of God is telling us," he said. People were yelling, but he continued in a low, sweet voice, reading from the Bible. Eventually, everyone sat down and paid attention. Gustavo read the story of Jacob meeting Esau. He spoke about the importance of sitting together and how so many families were divided by the conflict. He encouraged them to come together as Jacob and Esau did. He especially lifted up what Jacob said about Esau, who he had feared would kill him, "For to see your face is like seeing the face of God." (Gen. 33:10 NIV) The meeting moved on to the business at hand.[26]

Two days later, Jimmy Carter and Tomás Borge arrived. They announced that an agreement had been reached for the people to come back from the other side of the Honduran border to participate in the election. Meanwhile, Gustavo enjoyed fried tortillas for dinner at Anita's mother's home.

The Conciliation Commission held two more rounds of formal negotiations with YATAMA and the Sandinista government. The government agreed to withdraw military forces from certain villages and regions, providing greater freedom of movement and capacity to farm by the civilians in those areas. The army had also mined roads around some villages, and the government agreed to demine, so the roads would be safe. These tangible steps helped build a momentum of trust. Agreements were hammered out for a cease-fire on the Caribbean Coast and parameters for the return to Nicaragua of people who had been displaced by the fighting. A measure of autonomy for the Caribbean Coast was agreed to. Meanwhile, there were major developments in the rest of the country.

Disarming and Grassroots Reconciliation

On February 25, 1990, a national presidential election was held in Nicaragua. In a surprise for many people, Violeta Chamorro of the National Opposition Union won over President Daniel Ortega of the Sandinistas. Many observers felt the election was less about which candidate was preferred and more about how to stop the U.S. support for the war that had left the country with a depressing

---

26 From interview of Anita Taylor by Daniel Buttry.

weariness. Sure enough, with Chamorro's victory, the U.S. stopped funding the Contras and lifted the embargo. However, the U.S. also did nothing to help repair the damage done to people's lives and the economy from almost a decade of violent conflict.

With the Esquipulas II Peace Accord and a new government, the war was officially over, but how could the insurgents be disarmed, and how could communities experience reconciliation as fighters from both sides returned home? The process of working on these two matters would take as long as the war itself.

Many Contras were ready to turn in their weapons, but they still viewed the Sandinistas as their enemies. Most Sandinista army officers remained in their positions, including the commanding general of the army. Part of the transition to a new government was the assurance that the police and army would be under the civilian control of the new president. However, for those living in the remote areas where people had a decade of grudges built up from the war, turning one's guns over to the people on the other side was too much to ask for. So the Contras in Nueva Guinea asked for Dr. Parajón, CEPAD, and local peace commissions to receive their weapons. They were the ones trusted by these weary fighters.

CEPAD had organized the local peace commissions, who continued to play a key role in the post-war demobilization and reconciliation phase. The local commissions had pastors and Catholic leaders working side by side to receive and destroy the weapons as they were turned in. Besides receiving arms, CEPAD sought to deliver aid where they could. The Contras were in desperate need of food and material assistance to start their new lives. Various governments had promised aid after the war, but little was actually forthcoming once Nicaragua was no longer front-page news. Once again, CEPAD stepped into the gap.

Nueva Guinea had been one of the hot spots in the war in the south. In the early 1990s, Gustavo went with his son David in response to a call from a group of Contras in Nueva Guinea. Three thousand ex-soldiers came to turn in their weapons. But they had received none of the promised food, land, and health care in return. The Contras had everything when they were fighting, but now that the war was over, they had nothing. Many felt they had been used and were now abandoned. They spoke about their needs and their disappointments to Dr. Parajón, who then carried their messages to the government. It wasn't just the soldiers who complained. The peace commissioners also raised their voices about poverty, hunger, bad roads, and other desperate needs for their communities. They felt they had been well-trained and supported in their peace work by CEPAD, but the world turned away from them once the shooting was over.

British Anglican priest and musician Garth Hewitt and his wife, Gill, went with Gustavo, and Sue and Simon Plater on a trip to Nueva Guinea in 1997. They visited areas where reconciliation work had been going on with CEPAD. As they talked with the local reconciliation commission, they heard stories shared by people from both the Sandinista and the Contra sides. Everyone, no matter their politics, appreciated how Gustavo and other CEPAD folks listened to them. Such listening and the respect it garnered laid the foundation for the hard work of reconciliation. Later, Garth performed a concert in which he sang a song in Spanish. After the concert Gustavo laughingly told him people were discussing what language he had sung in!

Some Contra groups remained at-large for years, and they even continued to sporadically fight even though the Sandinistas were no longer in power. Juan Carlos Palma was a peace commissioner in Jinotega as well as a member of CEPAD's staff. He was Catholic, so he was not initially familiar with Dr. Parajón. He thought Parajón would be difficult to approach because he was "at the very top of the ladder." He later said, "I was so wrong. He always asked me how I felt, how my family was, how the work was coming along."

Palma and Parajón faced a crisis in the community of Santa Cruz. Palma and others from the commission were trying to meet with an armed group led by Commandante Lobo (Wolf). However, Lobo had tried to ambush President Arnoldo Alemán (who was elected president after Violeta Chamorro in 1997). The ambush failed, but President Alemán gave the order to eliminate the comandante. Palma called Dr. Parajón for help at midnight. Parajón immediately called the army chief, and the operation to find and eliminate Lobo was aborted.

Moving forward, Palma and his peace commission were then able to successfully negotiate the demobilization of Lobo and his group, one of the last Contra groups to disarm. They called Gustavo and Gilberto to attend the ceremony to receive the weapons from Comandante Lobo's troops and welcome this rogue group into amnesty and peace. Lobo and his tattered band of seventeen men, many of them mere boys as young as 10 years old, came out of the forest to meet with the officials from the Ministry of Defense. Local peace commissioner Johnny Hernández received the weapons from Commandante Lobo that he then passed to the government officials. The government representatives, in turn, gave each ex-soldier a certificate to prove he had disarmed. Lobo, who was a campesino himself, spoke eloquently about the peace commissioners' role in the process. The Disarmament Brigade then destroyed the weapons.

Following the disarmament events, Gustavo, CEPAD, and the local peace commissioners participated in creating peace parks in many communities. The broken weapons that had been turned in were often buried and memorials erected. The hard work of demobilization and reconciliation would be remembered by generations to come.

As part of the peace accord, those who were displaced were invited to return home. Nancy Wheaton, a family friend from First Baptist Church in Cleveland, traveled with Gustavo to the Honduran border to receive refugees. When the bus stopped at the border to unload the refugees, Gustavo shook the hands of everyone who crossed back into Nicaragua. He was the warm face of welcome to those who had fled their homes. Whether ex-soldiers or returning refugees, Gustavo would ask people their names and then address them by their names to welcome them home.

For the Caribbean Coast groups, President Charmorro invited Brooklyn Rivera into her cabinet to facilitate the return of refugees. As the process turned to disarmament and return, the deeper issues of autonomy and indigenous rights were usually pushed aside. Under later governments, Rivera became a member of the Parliament, but was a lonely voice for indigenous concerns. The war stopped, but the underlying concerns remained. CEPAD was one of the few groups that would help the plight of poor people on the Caribbean Coast as well as the rest of Nicaragua. Rivera deeply respected Parajón's concern for the poor, the indigenous people, and his heart to serve.

Perhaps the most insidious long-term effect of modern war are the land mines. Once planted, they lie buried until triggered by someone stepping on or driving over the mine. These mines can explode with horrific results many years after the conflict is formally over. The De-Mining Commission of the Ministry of Defense invited CEPAD to help collect information about landmine victims, especially in Jinotega and Nueva Guinea, the regions that were both remote and hardest hit during the war. The Organization of American States and non-governmental organizations like Walk in Peace provided victims with prosthetics, treatment, and physical therapy, which is especially difficult in these regions because they were so hard to access. To Gustavo, the landmine victims were not a sad mass of people; they were people he knew. Sue and Simon Plater traveled to a mountainous community where a little girl came up to Gustavo. She was about 9 years old and had only one leg. Earlier, PROVADENIC had helped her get a prosthesis, but now she had grown out of it. Gustavo knew this girl, and she and her family greeted him like a dear friend. Gustavo said, "We have to find a way to get her another prosthesis." As a child grows, they need new, larger artificial limbs. Caring for those maimed by land mines is the work of a lifetime.

A decade after the war ended, there were still conflicts between the government and people who felt marginalized. Many of the promises made in the peace accords were not kept. Some dissatisfied groups approached Gustavo and CEPAD about mediating discussions between them and the government. Gustavo and Gilberto asked the young lawyer on CEPAD staff, Blanca Fonseca, to accompany them. Blanca thought her task was to keep notes, but the notes Dr. Parajón asked her to keep surprised her. He told her to make a list of all those present at the meeting and classify each one as angry or very angry, if he speaks and yells a lot, or if he doesn't speak at all. He also told Blanca to write down if anybody said what their demand was or what the root cause of the problem was. She had no idea why he asked her to do this.

After that meeting, Gustavo and Blanca went over the list and various categorizations. He explained that the angrier the person was, the least likely they were to express a solution to the cause of their anger. That should be taken into account in order to negotiate. He said, "You have to learn what the demand is, the cause, and the possible solution that should come from them. Maybe the person who does not speak at all feels threatened, and yet maybe he has the solution." Blanca continued monitoring each person until they saw changes. The person who always yelled, soon was speaking in civil tones. The person who had been silent was now speaking up, but it was because of the way Dr. Parajón conducted the meetings. If needed, he asked everybody to lower their voices. If he noticed somebody who was not participating, he would ask that person directly about their concerns or thoughts. He made sure everybody spoke, and always kept digging deeper to find the causes for the problems. At the beginning, Blanca was afraid because the room was full of angry men, but Dr. Parajón was always so serene and always prayed with the team before entering the room. Gustavo treated all participants as equals and called them "brother."

Gustavo could also bring creative humor into the tense negotiations. Blanca remembered once when the discussion was very heated, Dr. Parajón got up and raised his hand. He said, "May I ask you something?" When they said, "Yes," he said, "How many would like a cup of coffee and a pastry?" That immediately lowered the tension as everybody was occupied in placing their orders with Gustavo.

After the meetings, Gustavo always taught Blanca lessons as they debriefed. He told her the conflicts are solved around a table, through dialogue. He taught her, "These men can make a difference between living in peace or in conflicts in their communities. We can prevent deaths and crimes by listening to them, by making them speak. It is not an easy road, but we have to first ask the Lord for direction and then treat everybody as equals. Then people switch their anger from people to the real causes, and then we can help them find the solution."[27]

Use of the Bible in Peace Work

How do you train grassroots people in a war-torn land, many of them with little education or who are illiterate, in the methods of peacemaking and reconciliation work? That was the dilemma posed to Gustavo Parajón and the staff of CEPAD as they sought to empower the local peace commissions.

Gustavo always used the Bible in his peacemaking work. Meetings were always begun with a Bible reading and devotional. Whenever he spoke, whether for a

---

27 From interview of Blanca Fonseca by Dámaris Albuquerque.

church, a conference, or an educational setting, he always used a Bible passage or story as the basis for his remarks. So it was second nature for him to turn to the Bible as the foundational witness for the training of peacemakers.

The Organization of American States provided a budget for training the peace commissioners. CEPAD purchased one hundred Bibles in a popular Spanish translation to use as their training text. CEPAD kept the Bibles so they would always be there for the trainings. Gustavo would read passages or invite others to read, even if they had difficulty reading. Gustavo and CEPAD staff showed patience and no judgment toward those who struggled, rather affirmed the right of every person to read holy Scripture and give their own insight into what was read.

Gustavo developed a series of Bible studies for the training sessions that examined various approaches to conflict: Attack, Avoid, Accommodate, Negotiate, and Collaborate. Each approach to conflict was seen in a biblical story. Attack was examined in Acts 15:36-41, where two great early church leaders, Paul and Barnabas, had a sharp conflict over whether to take John Mark on their next missionary journey. The conflict was so intense they split their mission team over it, though years later Paul recognized his mistake and was reconciled with John Mark.

Avoiding was explored in Jesus' conflict with the Pharisees in John 7:1-14. Using Jesus as the center of this study shows that avoiding can be appropriate in certain situations and moments. However, conflict avoidance doesn't ultimately resolve anything, though it may allow you to survive until a better opportunity arises to address the issues. Gustavo's questions helped participants learn the pluses and minuses of each approach to conflict.

Accommodation was explored in the early portion of the story of Joseph and his brothers in Genesis 37:12-28. The story of Joseph was one of Gustavo's favorites to work with. The story has many twists and turns, helping people engage with the complexities of their own lives. Accommodation may allow for survival, but it doesn't address any of the problems underlying the conflict.

Gustavo turned to a woman as the hero in Negotiation. Abigail successfully and creatively negotiated between her family and David in 1 Samuel 25:1-35, preventing a massacre. Gustavo's questions helped developing peacemakers get a sense of how to uncover the needs of the parties to a conflict and what might be able to be yielded by each side for the sake of the benefits that come with peace.

For Collaboration, in the sense of working together to solve a problem, not working in support of an oppressor, Gustavo returned to the climax of the Joseph story in Genesis 45:1-20. Pardon was also practiced in this story. The actions taken to reconcile a family spoke powerfully about how to reconcile a community or a nation.

To conclude the training, Gustavo taught people to practice a skill he exhibited so well: listening. To delve into the practice of listening, he used the story of

Jethro, the father-in-law of Moses, in Exodus 18:1-12. He supplemented the story about listening with the "Ten Commandments to Listen Well" by Keith Davis in *Human Relations at Work*.[28] These simple commandments such as "DO NOT SPEAK" (Commandments 1 and 10!), BE EMPATHETIC, BE PATIENT, and ASK QUESTIONS are able to be grasped by anyone. As Gustavo showed, the work of peace can be done by anyone who has the desire to work on it. He and others at CEPAD trained hundreds, if not thousands, of people in this vital work.

One of Gustavo's favorite stories was that of Jacob and Esau, found in Genesis chapters 25 through 33. The brothers had a nasty conflict in which Jacob cheated Esau. Esau threatened to kill Jacob, so the younger brother fled for his life. Through a long process of spiritual growth and learning, Jacob comes back home to meet his brother Esau, who had also changed. One of Gustavo's favorite verses is when Jacob says to the brother who once wanted him dead, "For to see your face is like seeing the face of God." (Gen. 33:10 NIV) Gustavo longed for his fellow Nicaraguans torn by war to reach the point they could see the face of God in the other. He longed for people in the U.S. to be able to see the face of God in the demonized Sandinistas, and vice versa. Gustavo could lift up this incredible vision because he had seen it in the Bible, and he had seen people who studied these stories transformed as well. Anita Taylor from the east coast was one of those people. She said, "Many times we studied the Jacob and Esau story, and each time we learned something new, something practical to follow that example." What Anita Taylor experienced was multiplied countless times throughout Nicaragua.

Gustavo also used the Bible when working directly with combatants. Years after the war at the Day of the Bible observance, with many church and government leaders present, including President Daniel Ortega, Dr. Parajón recalled using the Jacob and Esau story in the Atlantic Coast work between YATAMA and the Sandinista government with the Moravian Church leaders in the Conciliation Commission. He spoke about having Brooklyn Rivera on his right and Sandinistas on his left. He read the climax of the story in Genesis 33 with the meeting of the two brothers. When Jacob bowed before his brother, he was "expecting a hit from a machete." Gustavo could be very contextual when interpreting the Bible. Instead, Esau hugged and kissed the brother who had defrauded him. As Gustavo concluded: "That made Jacob say 'I have seen God's face on your face,' because in waiting to be killed, he found life. This passage of the holy Scriptures tells us precisely in this version, a group of the Sandinista brothers and of YATAMA brothers could realize that we are all brothers and that the madness of war should end and that we should work together ... and that's how that joint work began."

---

28 Davis, Keith, *Human Relations at Work: The Dynamics of Organizational Behavior,* McGraw Hill, New York, NY, 1962.

In his peace work, Parajón was also careful to conduct denominational peace-making. He chose a Spanish version of the Bible that was used by both evangelical pastors and by the Catholic Delegates of the Word. It was a version that was distributed by the Bible Societies and also had the imprimatur from the Episcopal Conference of Latin America. Even his choice of Bible translation in this work was an act of making peace.

Wars are so devastating and costly. Carlos Mejía, the young man who served in the Nicaraguan army and then later worked with Dr. Parajón on his peace team, felt that cost deeply. He said, "I know what war is. I know what it is to suffer, to see the dead. I never forgot that. War leaves neither winners nor losers. War is tragic, very tragic, and war leaves traumas. I still, old as I am, always remember those images of young people dying, which I would never like to see happen again in Nicaragua, my country that I love so much, or in any other country." He was grateful for the Christian leadership he found in Dr. Parajón, among others, who taught the Nicaraguan people to seek peace. From his time with Dr. Parajón, Carlos speaks of peace as "the most beautiful thing; peace is from God."[29]

Nobody knows how many people died in the war because much of the fighting occurred in remote areas. Estimates about the deaths from the Contra War range from 10,000 to 50,000. Some of the best estimates of the lives lost are in the 30,000 to 35,000 range. That just begins the awful calculus of war. So many more children, women, and men were injured and maimed, especially from the extensive use of land mines by the Contras.

Gustavo, as the medical doctor, put a different perspective on it. He asked, "How much money was spent on the war?" Then he turned the perspective around. What positive things could have been accomplished if those funds were spent on building up the country? What could have been done to improve health care? What could have been done to lift people out of poverty? What could have been done to educate people and provide new opportunities? Instead, millions upon millions of dollars were spent driving the poor deeper into poverty. Millions upon millions of dollars were spent leaving holes in families and communities from those who had died, leaving maimed people to be taken care of for the rest of their lives, leaving broken hope among the casualties. In war, everyone loses. Because of war's horrible result, the work of bringing peace was the profoundly simple work of following Jesus amid a conflict situation. The call to make peace was what Gustavo found in the Bible he read. The call to make peace was the imperative he received from the Lord he followed.

---

29 From interview of Carlos Mejía Ruiz by Dámaris Albuquerque.

Gustavo Parajón and Freddy Solorzano from CEPAD meet with
community members about agricultural issues.

Gustavo Parajón, Roberto Martinez, Dámaris Albuquerque, and
Gilberto Aguirre visit a CEPAD project in 2006.

Gustavo meets with community leaders at a CEPAD project in the village of Siares.

Hurricane damage.

CEPAD staff assesses hurricane damage and needs.

Relief coming for a community devastated by a hurricane.

7

Serving the Poor in Postwar Nicaragua

Ministry in the Postwar Context

Nine years of civil war decimated Nicaragua. Health care, in which Gustavo had invested so much of himself, had seen a dramatic drop in government investment. The percentage spent on health care had increased from 2.3% of GDP in 1978 at the end of the Somoza era to 5.8% in 1987 under the Sandinistas, even during the war. But under the postwar government, health care spending fell to 2.7% in 1992. The gap between people's needs and what the government could do was much greater.

Meanwhile, CEPAD continued its work in the postwar context. The work was more challenging in relation to the government because the Chamorro government didn't know who evangelicals were. CEPAD had worked hard to build awareness and ties with the Sandinista government, but the new government was very close to the Catholic Church power structure. The evangelical community was almost invisible to them. However, CEPAD continued working on their basic tasks of training base community members and pastors, conducting their educational and radio programs, and providing relief and development assistance even as they carried out disarmament and reconciliation work well into the mid-1990s.

Though the grassroots reconciliation efforts required major attention, in the wake of the war both CEPAD and PROVADENIC could bring a fresh focus to their work. There was much to be done. The war had left a large portion of the health infrastructure in a shambles. In 1992, the hospital in Rio Blanco, which served nineteen communities, had no beds. Furthermore, the health center in

Mulukuku, which served twenty-three communities, had no patients. There was a lot of catching up to do as the needs were pressing and urgent. With the national health system in such bad shape, PROVADENIC's work was vital, even after the strains PROVADENIC had been through during the war.

Mission work teams coming from the U.S. took on various service projects to support PROVADENIC. Some groups helped with building projects while the doctors and nurses on the teams carried out medical exams and treatments for patients in the rural clinics.

Mission groups from other countries were a key element of the work rhythms of CEPAD. Some groups would volunteer on different projects. They would also tour various aid projects. Then, of course, came the time to see some of the sights in Nicaragua. Often, teams took boat tours of Lake Nicaragua, including a visit to the Solentiname Islands, made famous by the writings of Ernesto Cardenal, the radical poet priest. They shopped in the markets that sold Nicaraguan art, helping the local economy and beautifying homes around the world. Sometimes, they took trips to scenic volcanic lakes.

Gustavo or Gilberto would always give the orientation talks for these groups. The group would gather outdoors in a circle either at PROVADENIC or CEPAD. Gustavo would begin by saying, "I'd like to answer any questions you might have." He'd go around the circle, hearing each person's question. Then he would answer all the questions in turn. He never wrote anything down at that time; it was just his deep listening and memory that kept straight all the questions that had been raised.

One never knew what the accommodations for mission teams would be. In the early days after the war, CEPAD had yet to build a guesthouse. Many stayed at the Casa San Juan, a local Managua guesthouse, but rolling blackouts made guests aware that this was far from the lap of luxury. Once, however, for a variety of reasons, the CEPAD annual assembly was held at a place with seven swimming pools! On the other hand, folks visiting Matagalpa often stayed at a Catholic retreat center with concrete floors, a tin roof, single light bulbs in the rooms, and abundant rodents as roommates! Where one stayed mattered little, however, because what truly mattered was connecting to the projects with the poor and working alongside those in need. For many who went on such trips, the experience was life-changing. Some continued to work as volunteers with CEPAD or PROVADENIC, or later with AMOS. Some joined the regular donor network, providing support for years to come. Others found new careers for themselves, making a difference in the world inspired by what they had learned and experienced alongside their Nicaraguan sisters and brothers.

CEPAD refined its communications with its support network, which had grown through short-term mission teams, longer-term volunteers, and Gustavo's and Gilberto's speaking trips. In 1992, Bob and Jo Buescher in the United States established CEPAD-USA as a registered nonprofit to facilitate fundraising in the U.S. The earlier informal network to channel funds to CEPAD was now an official organization. Bob was president of CEPAD-USA until his death in 2001, at which time Jo took over. The Bueschers were United Methodists and helped Gustavo connect to that denomination. They secured an invitation for Gustavo to speak at the General Conference of the United Methodist Church. During the war, Paul Jeffrey, a Methodist missionary working for CEPAD, launched the *CEPAD Newsletter*, later upgraded and renamed the *CEPAD Report*. CEPAD-USA helped get the *Report* to donors and mission team members so they could stay closely connected to the latest developments in Nicaragua and the various ministries of CEPAD.

Frustration led to the launching of Radio CEPAD in 1992, just before the 20th anniversary of the founding of the organization. A Christian radio station refused to air pastoral letters from CEPAD, so CEPAD decided to establish a station where they could say whatever they wanted. They aired sermons, news analysis, Nicaraguan singers, and Nicaraguan poets. But as with so much of what CEPAD did, there were multiple purposes. They labored to bring the broadcasts into remote rural areas. They also used the station to train young people, bringing them into management. Having been censored by a Christian station, and having taken a stand against government censorship, Radio CEPAD made a policy not to censor their programs, though, of course, they did promote the broader work of CEPAD.

CEPAD engaged in advocacy at a global level. They mobilized to collect 50,000 signatures to send to G-8 for their June 1999 summit. This signature drive was part of the Jubilee 2000 campaign to call for debt relief from the wealthy countries on behalf of the highly indebted poor countries. A big Jubilee 2000 event was held in Los Angeles, and Gustavo took a delegation there, including young musicians. They were able to play a few songs as well as speak to those gathered.

By the end of the 1990s, international agencies began pulling out of Nicaragua. The United Nations High Commissioner for Refugees (UNHCR) closed their operations in early 1998. UNHCR viewed CEPAD as a capable and competent agency, so they signed an agreement for CEPAD to take over handling undocumented immigrants until they were granted legal status by the Nicaraguan government. Some of those immigrants were on the way to the United States. In one tragedy later in April 1998, a boat with nineteen Ecuadorans tried to enter Nicaragua illegally. The boat wrecked, and all but one person drowned. CEPAD stepped in to assist. To this day, CEPAD is the Nicaraguan agency that works with undocumented immigrants.

When the work with the undocumented immigrants started, the immigrants were held in prison for three months, then deported. Dr. Parajón recruited Blanca Fonseca, a recent law school graduate attending First Baptist Managua, to join the staff at CEPAD to work with these immigrants. She organized the case files, met with people in prison, and studied the current laws. Then Blanca, Gustavo, and Gilberto began a series of meetings with various officials about the situation and to lobby for a new law for how the undocumented people were processed. CEPAD eventually convinced the government to release many undocumented immigrants into their custody while their cases were being processed. Eventually, Dr. Parajón, Ms. Fonseca, and Sixto Ulloa were able to get the National Law on Refugees passed, that allowed the undocumented immigrants to be housed in a noncriminal detention center. They had already created a more humane reality before the law caught up.

The new opportunity presented new challenges. The undocumented people in their care needed shelter, food, and often health care. Many immigrants were from Africa, and some of them were Muslims. Dr. Parajón met with a local sheik to convince him to meet with Blanca. They were able to get Qur'ans for the Muslims and Bibles in English, French, or Spanish for the Christian immigrants. Blanca also visited the Managua mosque and mobilized the Muslim community to help their co-religionists with food and other necessities. Once, Blanca was in her office with a number of Muslim immigrants waiting to be interviewed. The time for midday prayers came, and all the Muslims lined up to pray. Just then, Gustavo entered. Bianca thought he would be upset about Muslims praying in CEPAD, but Gustavo said that even here they remember that God is with them. It didn't matter the name that was used; it was God to whom they prayed.

In 2001, the Nicaraguan government received a $27 million grant from the Inter-American Bank of Development to feed poor children. Because the government had no infrastructure for this work, they contracted with other agencies. CEPAD received the contract to work in Nueva Guinea. Building upon their community networks, they established daycare centers for poor working families and single mothers. Children from birth to 6 years of age received care and nourishing food. CEPAD served over a thousand children at fifteen centers. They also wove health care into the work by utilizing the local health promoters. This allowed CEPAD to address issues of malnutrition with the families.

CEPAD also engaged in education programs to develop leadership in churches and communities. The Secondary Education by Extension Program (ESAD) set up regional education centers in Estelí, Jinotepe, and León. On weekdays, the centers ran educational programs for children in line with the Nicaraguan Ministry of Education's basic norms and guidelines. On Saturdays, classes were provided for pastors and other working adults who had not finished their secondary education. Students could gain their diplomas within five years.

Besides educational needs, CEPAD sought to address some of the psychosocial needs in communities that came from traumas of war and violence, addiction, and sexual abuse. Programs were developed with youth, children, and women experiencing crisis. Many young leaders were trained to work with children, with an aim to build positive family dynamics and act proactively to prevent such problems from developing or reaching crisis points. Sometimes needs overlapped and programs were set up to complement each other. One project developed to build homes for single mothers, some of them dealing with the traumas of losing family members and sources of support during the war.

In all these programs, spiritual development through Bible study applied to the real issues people faced was key. CEPAD kept its Christian religious values front and center, with evangelizing and discipling aspects to all these initiatives.

Organizational Troubles

CEPAD also faced challenges from within. Dr. Parajón had been president since the founding of CEPAD, and Gilberto Aguirre was the long-standing executive director. CEPAD received funds from various international nongovernmental organizations, and sadly this became a temptation to a cluster of evangelical pastors. Some pastors decided to run for election to the board of CEPAD, making promises that funds would be used to feed, clothe, and help house evangelical pastors. They also promised those who voted for the ringleaders that they would obtain jobs with CEPAD. The typical corruption of elections for governments now plagued CEPAD.

Gustavo had thought of stepping down as board president in time for the 1998 CEPAD election, but in the face of this distorted development, someone with his strength and integrity was needed to preserve the organization. As he asked for prayer, Gustavo shared his anguish with a friend: "I hate to see this ministry that has cost so much—including the loss of life of the PROVADENIC health leaders and CEPAD community leaders in the 1980s—thrown by the wayside by unscrupulous people—church leaders, at that."[30]

At the pivotal General Assembly meeting, the voting was conducted by secret ballot, something never done before in CEPAD. The bylaws stipulated that the winner had to receive half the votes plus one. The first and second meetings ended in tie votes. In the third meeting, Dr. Parajón won the majority. The group seeking to take over in order to seize control of CEPAD's resources was defeated. The leadership of CEPAD remained as it was, but the dynamics of the organization were negatively affected.

---

30 From a series of emails from Gustavo Parajón and Gilberto Aguirre to Sue Plater.

In the wake of this divisive election, Octavio Cortés, serving on the Commission of Church Relations for CEPAD's General Assembly, carefully went over the CEPAD denominational membership list. A significant number of denominations were just small groups of tiny churches who banded together. They had been able to access some of the development assistance, but they had not been active in the life and work of CEPAD or participated in the assemblies. The group that had tried to seize control had mobilized folks from these churches with their promises, but these groups had never been constructively engaged. Eighteen of these small denominations, out of seventy-one total members, were voted out of membership by an overwhelming assembly vote, leaving a great sense of relief and peace in the room.

Ever the peacemaker, however, Gustavo was deeply saddened by these developments. He never wanted division. He had worked unsuccessfully to help the Baptists in El Salvador with their divisions (see Chapter 10), and now he felt the same spirit had struck within the organization that he had started and that was so dear to his heart. In the wake of the election turmoil, the vast majority of member denominations stayed committed and true to the vision and work of CEPAD.

Besides the challenges of partners within CEPAD, problems developed with some of their external partners as well. The fall of the Berlin Wall, followed by the collapse of the Soviet Union, marked the beginning of a new era, even the beginning of the 21st century. Many countries that received assistance from the Eastern Bloc found themselves suddenly cut off from key aid. Meanwhile, Eastern Europe became a center of concern for European agencies addressing economic crises. It was a global historic moment unfolding the same time as the wars were winding down in Central America. Some agencies began shifting funds away from Nicaragua, and CEPAD felt the loss financially.

Unspecified allegations from unknown sources accused CEPAD of financial abuses. CEPAD expended a huge amount of energy working with donors over these accusations. The accusations were never supplied in writing, making their source and substance difficult to assess. One European agency brought in PricewaterhouseCoopers (now PWC) to conduct a major external audit. The audit showed nothing to support the allegations. CEPAD diligently worked to improve their financial systems and accountability, including welcoming a volunteer from a mission agency to help bring their financial department up to the latest practices and standards. No corruption was found by either PricewaterhouseCoopers or by a second external audit. Still, some of the agencies involved in these discussions stopped their funding. Some agencies even failed to send funds that had already been pledged for work that had been launched.

Some European agencies that had funded CEPAD during the war because of CEPAD's central involvement in relief development started to reassess their involvement after the war because they did not value the Christian witness in CEPAD. Gustavo had seen another Christian agency that presented all their programs with careful detail, but said nothing about their witness for Christ. The CEPAD board carefully considered this challenge, and decided that they had to stay true to their calling to bear witness to Christ and not become secularized. Gustavo, as CEPAD president, said, "If we become an agency with expertise in two or three fields, but cannot work with our local congregations, we would lose our identity and nature."[31] With all these challenges, the financial base for CEPAD decreased dramatically. This forced significant downsizing, from over 350 employees at the peak to around sixty-five as the millennium turned. They also had to trim their regional offices from fourteen down to six.

There were also huge leadership changes in 2000 and 2001. Gilberto Aguirre stepped down as CEPAD executive director in early 2001 for personal reasons. He was going through a divorce and didn't want his personal concerns to become an impediment with some of the more conservative Pentecostal churches in CEPAD. The board appointed Dámaris Albuquerque as the next executive director beginning April 1, 2001. Dámaris first began her work as a secretary in CEPAD's Masaya office back in 1978. Soon she became director of that regional office. From 1982 to 1995, Gustavo Parajón brought her on as assistant to the president. Then she became assistant to the executive director. Dámaris was a classic example of leadership development in Gustavo's organizations. He saw her potential and called her to take on things she'd never imagined. Even at this point in her career, Dámaris asked Dr. Parajón, "Do you really think I can do this job?" Gustavo replied, "Of course! You have learned so much!" Her years of skillful service showed Dámaris was more than ready to meet the challenge, which was recognized by the entire organization.

At the end of 2000, when his term expired as CEPAD board president, Gustavo stepped down. The board made Dr. Parajón president emeritus, certainly a worthy honor for the founder who had guided the organization to such incredible strength with impactful programs during all kinds of national crises. As president emeritus, he was invited to advise the board and help with international relations if asked by the board president. Such a transition can sometimes be difficult, but Gustavo turned out not to be a meddler, but rather someone who supported the new leadership.

Issues With the Nicaraguan Government

As the war wound down, pastors weren't the only ones to fall prey to the temptation of money. The new Nicaraguan government saw the international funds coming in with the end of the embargo and the promised U.S. aid, and they leapt

---

31 Email from GP to Sue Plater, Jan 26, 2001.

at the opportunity to get a piece of the pie. The government decided to tax all donations coming in that didn't include the word "foundation," a challenging detail since that specific word wasn't in CEPAD's name.

The government added to the intensity of the financial grab by seizing shipments of material aid that came in. Nine shipments were detained by the Ministry of Finance in 1998 alone, as the government refused to sign exonerations from the import fees. Televisions were donated through CEPAD to Habitat for Humanity as part of Habitat's education work in the communities where their projects were located. The televisions were simply seized by the government and auctioned off.

Even with the financial assaults coming from the new government, CEPAD continued its work of advocacy for justice. In 1994, transportation workers launched a four-day strike that was met by government violence against the strikers. Every day Gustavo got on the CEPAD radio station calling for restraint by the police, an end to the violence, and negotiations to settle the dispute.

Eventually, under the Sandinistas, evangelical Christians were treated with more equality, in large part because of the persistent advocacy of Gustavo, Gilberto, and others from CEPAD. Under the new government, the Catholic Church reasserted itself, specifically by inserting the Catholic teaching and practices in public schools, including having masses and students crossing themselves. The required public school textbook had a photo of Cardinal Obando y Bravo on the cover. CEPAD, along with other denominations, including the Baptists, advocated for public education to be "lay education" (nonreligious), as stipulated in the Nicaraguan constitution. After many meetings and appeals, they finally succeeded.

Gustavo was always bothered by government corruption. Political corruption grew in the 1990s, especially 1997–2002 under Arnoldo Alemán. (Alemán was sentenced to twenty years in prison for corruption in 2003, though his conviction was overturned in 2009.) Gustavo explained to an audience in the U.K., "Common ordinary people were very hopeful with the ideals of the Sandinista revolution of the 1980s. The war, the avalanche of the North against the South, the corruption of political leaders from all quarters has greatly disillusioned people. Nicaraguans are very skeptical of politics and politicians."[32]

But even sadder to Gustavo and many others in the CEPAD community was that evangelical Christians proved to be just as corrupt in politics as other politicians. Following the war, many conservative Christian organizations from the U.S., South Korea, Brazil, Mexico, and other places flooded into Nicaragua. Huge stadium events were held, where evangelists preached a prosperity gospel in this desperately poor country. Believe in Jesus, and you will get rich—maybe not put so bluntly, but that's how it came across to people. As many evangelicals got involved

---

32 Gustavo Parajón "AVALANCHE OF THE NORTH AGAINST THE SOUTH," Greenbelt Interview, April 27, 2005.

in politics, they saw the habitual culture of corruption as the way to fulfill that prophecy. Instead of serving the poor, they served themselves. Gustavo mourned this situation. When someone once said that evangelicals are honest, he sadly said, "That's not true anymore."[33]

Some groups asked Gustavo to run for political office, but he always refused to do so. CEPAD was also concerned about its institutional integrity related to the contentious elections. CEPAD had worked with a number of local leaders as peace commissioners, and some of these people wanted to get involved in politics. Meanwhile, the commissioners were still being approached to mediate in some of the local conflicts. So in 1996, CEPAD set a policy that if any of their staff or local commissioners decided to enter politics, they would resign from their role in the organization. CEPAD's executive director Gilberto Aguirre set forth the reasoning based on CEPAD's role to be advocates for the poor and to make sure they were not pushed to the side by any government, no matter the political point of view. He said, "This is how we understand the prophetic role of the church—to orient, demand, and protest where necessary, but always to keep that space open. We lose this force we have the minute we take up a political banner."[34]

More Disasters

Amid all the internal and governmental crises, CEPAD still did what they did best, namely helping people in desperate situations. Earthquakes and hurricanes figured heavily in the story of Gustavo Parajón and CEPAD, and after the war, natural disasters continued the need to call for help to address critical human needs. On the night of September 1, 1992, an earthquake off the Pacific coast of Nicaragua unleashed a massive tsunami. ("Tsunami" was a new word for Nicaraguans in 1992, as they had previously referred to such events as "sea quakes.") Some waves sweeping into the shore were reported as high as 15 meters (49 feet). Homes, boats, cars, and trucks were quickly washed away. As a result, 170 people died, and over 500 were injured. About 13,500 people were left homeless. Over 250 fishing boats were destroyed. Seawater damaged water sources and latrines. The relationship of the tsunami to this particular earthquake was very unusual, prompting extensive study by the scientific community. For those who suffered, science was not their concern. Rather, they asked, "Where are my loved ones; where will I live; what will I eat?"

Within two hours, CEPAD mobilized their staff and local pastors to help people in the community search the ruins for survivors and to organize shelters for those who had lost their homes. As is so often the case, it was the poorest people who had to build their homes in places that were more at risk for disaster, and they

---

33 Interview with Arthur Francis by Daniel Buttry.
34 CEPAD Report, March/April 1996, p. 4.

had the fewest resources to recover. CEPAD set up emergency feeding stations along the coast. They built 116 homes in three communities. They helped fishing cooperatives get new boats and fishing materials. They also worked in reforestation, planting 15,000 trees to create natural buffers between the ocean and people living on the coast. Furthermore, with the growing realization and understanding of trauma, CEPAD brought in therapists to help people cope with what had happened and with all their losses. CEPAD's Children's Ministry Program brought in puppets and play therapy to help the young ones. They also taught teachers and parents skills to help the children be resilient in the face of the tragedy.

In late October 1998, a hurricane formed in the Caribbean and headed toward Central America, particularly Honduras and Nicaragua. Hurricane Mitch was stirred with ideal conditions and developed into a Category 5 storm. Mitch made landfall with devastating winds and rains. Because it was slow moving, the incessant rains led to catastrophic flooding. The heavy rains caused a massive mudslide from Volcan Casitas that buried entire villages and killed thousands of people. Some places were swamped with up to 75 inches (1,900 mm) of rain during the storm. Approximately 7,000 people died in Honduras, and over 3,800 people perished in Nicaragua. Mitch was the second deadliest Atlantic hurricane on record. Furthermore, 2.7 million people were left homeless throughout Central America.

CEPAD got to work, in time going to ninety-five communities throughout the country. They facilitated many short-term mission work teams coming to Nicaragua to help build houses. CEPAD was ready to work, but they struggled with delays because of funding not coming in quickly. Furthermore, the government was very slow in responding to the crisis, taking a long time to provide land for hurricane victims to rebuild homes.

However, whenever Gustavo, Gilberto, Dámaris, and other staff entered into one of the stricken areas, they always began by listening to the people. Gustavo would begin with a short Bible reading, then by listening to the testimonies and concerns of the local residents. One young man told of losing his whole family, and having caring people listen to his anguish was part of the healing. Gustavo taught his staff to listen for details that would show where the need was most acute.

When one highway to the north was finally opened after the rains had washed out or damaged bridges, the vehicles coming into and out of Managua created a huge traffic jam. Gustavo, Gilberto, and some others from CEPAD were stuck in the traffic, so they decided to turn aside and visit one of the former PROVADENIC local health providers who lived not far from the traffic jam. Sulay Madriz was so moved to see these familiar caring faces after the trauma of the hurricane that she just cried and cried with sorrow and relief.

With all the experience CEPAD had in disaster relief, and knowing how severely Honduras had been hit by Mitch, Gustavo sought to bring encouragement to the folks across the border. Gustavo, Gilberto, and Dámaris hopped on a Mission Aviation Fellowship flight and met with the Christian Commission for Development. As always, they read the Bible together and prayed, then they listened to those coping with the emergency. Whatever wisdom their Honduran friends needed was shared.

A long string of volcanoes is the spine running through Central America, and Nicaragua has its share of these beautiful yet deadly mountains. Cerro Negro is the youngest of the Central American volcanoes, born in a series of eruptions in 1850. A cone of black basalt cinders rose out of the surrounding forest, thus its name in Spanish, "Black Hill." Fortunately, the volcano is in a sparsely populated region with no major town at risk for lava or pyroclastic flows, though ash has often reached León.

Cerro Negro erupted three times in the 1990s. The first eruption was in 1992, leaving a few people dead and about 20,000 displaced. A smaller eruption took place in 1995. Then on August 4, 1999, Cerro Negro erupted again. Although it only erupted for two days, the volcanic earthquakes and aftershocks destroyed and damaged many homes. Thousands of people were evacuated into schools and churches in León and nearby communities. CEPAD immediately began to deliver aid to the displaced people. They brought first aid kits, baby care kits, blankets, mattresses, plastic tarps, and hammocks. Basic food and sanitation items were provided: corn and beans, milk, soap, washboards, candles, and matches. They even brought coloring books for the children crowded into the schools and churches with their families. New houses cost about $2,000 each to build. With the help of funds from Baptists and Methodists, CEPAD was able to construct nineteen houses for families who had lost everything.

However, politics rather than volcanic activity provided unnecessary drama. Nicaraguan President Arnoldo Alemán refused to meet with León Mayor Rigoberto Sampson to discuss and coordinate relief. Sampson was in the affected community, but Sampson was also in a rival party. Since politics was eclipsing human suffering, CEPAD brought prophetic challenge as well as material assistance. CEPAD called for national unity and nonpartisan cooperation related to the crisis.

PRESTANIC

In 1991, CEPAD launched a small microfinance program. Microfinance and microcredit had become a growing concern in the Two-Thirds World, with the inspiration and model of Muhammad Yunus from Bangladesh. Yunus received the Nobel Peace Prize for his work financing small cooperatives for women through his Grameen Bank. With their close contact with people in poor communities, CEPAD could see the needs for financial assistance and the benefits of the microfinance model. Furthermore, as funds were drying up from international donor agencies, the leadership of CEPAD was looking for initiatives that were self-sustaining and that might even become a source of sustainable income for the organization.

PRESTANIC took off as CEPAD's microfinance program. PRESTANIC was the acronym for a long name in Spanish that people promptly forgot! Armando Gutiérrez was named executive director. As the project grew, many people were helped to develop small businesses or farms from the low-interest loans they could get through this program. A larger percentage of the borrowers were women, and they were more reliable in repayment than the men.

Sylvia Zeledón was the wife of a pastor of a small poor congregation that paid him a negligible salary. To support the family income, she decided to convert part of their home into a restaurant. No bank would give her a loan, so she asked CEPAD for help. Through the credit program, CEPAD loaned Zeledón $800 USD to get a refrigerator, cooking utensils, and tables for the front room of their home. She opened her new business in June 1992 and, thanks to a steady clientele, paid off the loan in less than a year.

Eventually, however, an inner contradiction began to emerge within CEPAD between their microfinance program and the rest of CEPAD's programs. On the one hand, CEPAD was giving gifts to people in emergency relief and development assistance, but on the other, PRESTANIC sometimes played the role of the debt collector. These two roles didn't sit comfortably together.

Gustavo and others decided to approach the CEPAD General Assembly about spinning off PRESTANIC as a separate organization. Many did not want to let go of a possible source of funds for CEPAD's core work. Gustavo and Armando decided that a deeper understanding of the work of microfinance was needed. They invited some people who had received loans to speak to the CEPAD assembly. These borrowers shared how credit had helped them to improve the economy and life conditions for them and their families. They put the center of the discussion on the people being helped, rather than CEPAD's finances.

Perhaps a deeper issue was whether an independent finance organization would stray from CEPAD's core principles about empowering the poor. The solution was worked out in the bylaws to establish PRESTANIC's organizational assembly with three members of CEPAD's board, plus the executive director and the five founding members of PRESTANIC (Gustavo, Gilberto, Armando, Evenor Jerez, and Pastor Bildad Blandón). That would keep the organizational links strong, particularly with the central vision of empowering the poor. The extra time spent on helping the General Assembly see the vision and work through the concerns led to a positive vote to spin off PRESTANIC. Gustavo Parajón was then selected as first president of the board of directors for PRESTANIC.

Some of Gustavo's friends in the U.S. tried to get churches to put some of their endowment funds in PRESTANIC. Endowed funds could then be part of a church's mission engagement while still yielding a 5% or 6% return to the churches. There was even discussion about partnership with U.S. denominations. Events in Nicaragua derailed these plans.

In 2007, Daniel Ortega was reelected as president of Nicaragua. The next year, Ortega made a statement that people took as government support for people not paying off their loans. A group known informally as "No Pago" (No Payment) had protested high interest rates from microfinance institutions. When they protested in front of the presidential office building, Ortega directed them toward the microfinance offices. One office was burned and others shut down, though none were related to PRESTANIC. Many borrowers just stopped paying on their loans. PRESTANIC's assets plunged from around $20 million ($5 million equity) to around $5 million ($1 million equity) as many people simply considered their loans canceled. Financial support for initiatives among the poor withered, and financial chaos swirled in the country because basic trust in agreements had evaporated.

When Dr. Parajón died, PRESTANIC was still in difficult shape. Gilberto Aguirre became president of the board until his own death. Dámaris Albuquerque was then elected as PRESTANIC's board president. Through these leadership changes, PRESTANIC was revamped to be smaller and more focused. They stopped funding farmers and centered their work on women and women's cooperatives. The faithfulness of women to pay off their debts helped PRESTANIC to regain its stability.

Though he had passed away, the Bible study Dr. Parajón used to establish the vision of PRESTANIC continued to inspire. He led many devotionals on 2 Kings 4:1-7, in which Elisha helped a poor widow and her sons get out of poverty by investing miraculously and enabling her to sell olive oil. Giving poor women the help they need to become self-sufficient and escape poverty continues to be the guiding light for PRESTANIC.

The Parajón family gathered for Gustavo and Joan's 50th anniversary.

The Parajón family, December 1984.

Joan Parajón playing her flute.

The Parajón-Domínguez Choir at First Baptist Church, 2010.

Joan Parajón directs the Parajón-Domínguez Choir.

The Parajón-Domínguez Choir on tour in the Dominican Republic in 2010 (Gustavo in white).

The Parajón-Domínguez Choir in First Baptist Church's sanctuary built after the earthquake.

Children from Sunday School participating in worship at First Baptist Managua.

8

Pastor:

Doctor of the Church

First Baptist Managua

So far in this book, we have focused on Gustavo Parajón's work as a public health doctor and as a peacemaker. The core of his ministry identity, however, may have been being a pastor. He was ultimately driven by his love of Jesus, and that drove him into serving people, whether rural folks with no health care or those suffering in a war-torn country. His work in health and in peacemaking always had a pastoral focus. He would begin meetings with Bible readings, often with a short devotional, and prayer. He would teach, train, and speak of reconciliation based on stories in the Bible. He loved the Scriptures, read them daily, and thought deeply about them. Then he wove what he learned in the Bible into everything else he did.

Gustavo was the son of a pastor. His father took him on mission trips into the campo, the rural areas, traveling by mule. That awakened his heart to the plight of people living at the margins of society. After losing his parents as a young teenager, members of the church, as well as the Wyse family, supported and reared him. After his return to Nicaragua in 1968 with his family, on several occasions he served as interim pastor when the pastor had to travel for an extended period of time or when the church was between pastors. Gustavo was always recognized as a spiritual leader in the church, so during the early years of the war, when he was appointed co-pastor of First Baptist Church of Managua, it was no surprise. A year later, in 1984, he became the senior pastor.

One practice Gustavo picked up from his father was the desire to learn a person's full name, then he would always use the person's name when meeting them.

In Baptist churches, many people are related to each other, so Gustavo also asked about their relatives. He remembered what he learned and would inquire how loved ones were doing. He liked to listen to people's stories, and people in turn felt valued and cared for by their pastor and their doctor, in whatever role he was in.

Baptists can be a rather contentious lot, particularly since they have no authoritative hierarchical church structure like Catholics and Anglicans have. Instead, there is support for freedom of conscience as each believer engages with the Word of God. The result can be a wide range of opinions, so what holds such a congregation together? First Baptist Managua's differences included the political differences that had torn the country apart in war. On the one hand were church members who supported the Sandinistas, including Sixto Ulloa, who had served in the National Assembly representing the Sandinistas. On the other hand were strong supporters of the earlier Somoza government and, later, of Violeta Chamorro's UNO party, the opposition that upset Daniel Ortega in the February 1990 election. The missionary and liberation theologian George Pixley (Jorge Pixley in Central American circles) was an active member. There was also a large church-planting ministry with an evangelical fervor. These folks were all members of Gustavo's congregation, brothers and sisters gathered around one communion table. How did he manage to keep such a politically divided flock together?

As in the rest of his ministry, Gustavo's pastoring was based on his continual and practical use of the Bible. He called people to simply follow Jesus, bringing forth their best. Just as he had met with people on both sides of the war in his reconciliation efforts, he met and listened to people in his congregation, from those like Sixto, who worked closely with him in so many projects, to those who criticized him. He treated them all as brothers and sisters. Whoever someone was, he would visit with them, talk as equals, and eat with them around their tables.

The construction of the first building for Primera Iglesia Bautista de Managua began during the pastorate of the Rev. Dr. Arturo Parajón, Gustavo's father. Don Arturo died in February 1954, before construction was finished. The building was dedicated in 1957. The lovely building suffered irreparable structural damage during the 1972 earthquake and had to be demolished. The congregation started meeting on a temporary basis in a little wooden building constructed over the basketball court in the parking lot of the Baptist Hospital. That "temporary" sanctuary was the church home for 25 years.

Under Gustavo's pastorate, the congregation grew so much that it was spilling out of the facility. In 2000, a beautiful new building with a large sanctuary was built and dedicated. The partnership between the Parajón family and the First Baptist Church of Cleveland proved foundational. The Cleveland congregation gave a loan to finance the construction. Dr. William Cumming, who had been on many mission trips to work with PROVADENIC, put his own home up as collateral for the loan. Acoustics were especially important, given how central the choir was to the worship and programming of the church. Many more people could be seated in the new sanctuary, including up in the balcony. The higher ceiling opened everything up so that the sound of praise could fill the sacred space.

Gustavo developed communication methods that reached not only church members, but that went far beyond into the larger community. With both CEPAD and First Baptist, he set up a radio program where he and others could speak to various matters from the Bible. He produced a daily devotional, "Cada Día con Cristo," "Every Day with Christ." He worked on the devotional with a shepherding team from the church. "Cada Día con Cristo" was produced for decades. One of Gustavo's main missions in life was to encourage everyone, especially the youth he mentored, to read the Bible. Every opportunity he had, he would quote from the Bible, and the radio programs and devotional provided a daily discipline for listeners to get into the Bible in a meaningful way.

A natural teacher, Gustavo mentored many generations of youth during his years as pastor of the church, and even in the years before. He formed many church leaders through example, always insisting on the importance of having goals and objectives and, above all, a plan. He taught planning and evaluation skills, and the need to organize all areas of life. After stepping down from the pastorate, many of those he had mentored became leaders in the church.

In 2003, Gustavo and Joan Parajón retired as American Baptist missionaries with International Ministries, which helped his life to be less complicated as other responsibilities shifted, too. Then, in 2010, Gustavo retired as pastor of First Baptist, having served for over twenty-five years.

Music and Joan's Leadership

First Baptist Managua has long been known for its music. The choir was formed in 1922 and directed by Gustavo's parents, the Rev. Arturo Parajón and Beatriz Domínguez, shortly after they returned from seminary in Saltillo, Mexico. Years later when they died, the choir members decided to name the choir after them: The Parajón-Dominguez Choir (Coro Parajón-Domínguez). It is worth noting that the choir was directed for long periods of time by Professor Gustavo Wilson, a Nicaraguan from the Caribbean Coast of Nicaragua. The Parajón-Dominguez Choir is the oldest and largest active choir in Nicaragua, well-known across Central America for its excellence.

With her outstanding musical training and experience in Chicago, Cleveland, and Boston, Joan arrived in Managua ready to give her all in music, within the church, but also in the larger community. She said, "I felt that the Lord really had a place for me, and through the music that I had grown to love so much, I knew

I could witness effectively."[35] She began organizing a youth choir in 1969, which grew under her leadership and Gustavo's support. The young people worked hard with the aid of music recorded on 7-inch magnetic tape reels, then later cassettes, so they could learn to sing in parts. They were thrilled to develop new musical skills. The youth choir gave a Christmas concert at another Baptist church on December 22, 1972. It was the last time they sang together as a choir. Hours later, the earthquake devastated Managua, and many of the choir members moved out of the shattered city to other communities in Nicaragua.

The choir sang sporadically following the earthquake and with all the challenges of establishing a viable worship space. After the birth of Rebecca Parajón in 1975, two members of the choir asked Joan if she would take over the Parajón-Dominguez Choir. She accepted and continued as director until 2019, except for a few years around 2013–2016, when Jorge Bojorge directed the choir. The choir sang every Sunday as part of the worship service at First Baptist. It grew to a maximum of sixty-six members, though usually the choir numbered from forty-five to fifty active members. The Parajón-Dominguez Choir had an age range from 15 to 75, a rich intergenerational group.

The dynamic music program at First Baptist became a place for young people to discover their gifts and blossom. Some became professionals in various musical careers. Also in the late 1980s, Janyce Pixley formed a children's choir, and later a youth choir to provide a place for adolescents to sing. The children's choir was later directed for many years by Marta Parajón when Janyce left Nicaragua. Joan started a bell choir after receiving a set of bells as a donation. Some of the members of the Parajón-Dominguez Choir learned how to play the bells, and the bell choir became a regular part of their concerts and worship services.

Gustavo loved music as well. He was in the choir from the very beginning, singing in the front row of the tenor section. In a society known for its machismo spirit among men, people noticed how their pastor submitted himself to his wife's leadership in the choir. Gustavo never said anything about this, but it was noticed. Gustavo also took his love of music into his health ministry. When he began meetings of the PROVADENIC staff or local health committees with devotions, he would frequently include singing with the Bible reflections. Gustavo loved to lead the Mennonites who oversaw the work of four PROVADENIC health clinics in the hymn, "God of Grace and God of Glory."

Joan took her music ministry beyond the church. For many years she directed a prison choir. The prison work started when Canadian missionary Georgia Rendle, working in the Tipitapa Prison in Managua in 1994, asked Joan for help in directing the men's choir she had formed. Together they developed a unique choir, Coro Libertad, which sang together for many years. In a delightful surprise, they were

---

35 IM Pen Sketch, International Ministries, 1974.

allowed to take the choir out of the prison to sing in the National Theater for many years as part of the Parajón-Domínguez Choir's Christmas concert. For Joan, it sometimes was a bittersweet experience. As a Christian, she always rejoiced to see someone go free, but as director, she was sad to lose a choir member. But her love and simple humanness stood out with healing power to go along with the transformative power of the music. After they were released, many ex-prisoners would call her, appreciative of the impact she and the message in the music made in their lives.

Joan also entered the more prestigious places for music in the country. In her early years in Nicaragua, she played flute and taught classes in the Nicaraguan Conservatory of Music. She remembers being the only Protestant there. She entered the Parajón-Dominguez Choir into the annual choral festival at the National Theater. As their popularity grew, the choir began to give an annual Christmas concert there. When they added songs from Handel's "Messiah" to their repertoire, they were accompanied by an orchestra. This concert was highly anticipated by the public every Christmas season. The choir was invited to sing in many churches in Nicaragua, including Catholic churches. This breakthrough welcoming of a Baptist choir into a Catholic church was noteworthy in the predominantly Catholic country. The priests in the churches where the choir sang were very warm and receptive to them, one saying it was the most beautiful music ever sung in his church.

Joan covered a wide range of musical expressions with the choir, as well as the congregation. She had picked up and translated into Spanish the music of many Christian musicians such as Ken Medema, Joel Raney, Craig Curry, Leslie Gomez, Jim and Jean Strathdee, and others. When Ken Medema, as well as other composers, visited Nicaragua, they were delightfully surprised to learn how much their music was known and appreciated there. They also sang a lot of music by Joel Sierra, who became pastor for a couple of years. Joan was especially interested in collecting new songs and hymns written by Nicaraguans and other musicians from Latin America. She loved to bring contemporary and Latin American music into First Baptist.

The music program became a major channel for developing the gifts of young people. Carlos Martinez was attending the Baptist Conservatory where Joy Crocker was the piano teacher. Joy also played piano for the church and choir at First Baptist for a number of years, and she invited the 12-year-old student to the Sunday service. As Carlos practiced on Saturdays and Sundays with the choir, Joy told him that if he played well, he could fill in. When the choir toured in Puerto Rico, Joy thought the 13-year-old Carlos was ready to accompany one of the songs in the concert, which he did beautifully. She also taught Carlos to depend on himself rather than on the sheet music, "You have to be ready if the wind blows your papers away." It was Joy who blew away when she returned to live in the U.S.

As a teenager, Carlos became the regular pianist for the choir. Carlos went on to become a professional musician, composer, and teacher.

Gustavo was an anchor for the tenor section, but it was clear Joan was the director. However, for congregational singing, Pastor Parajón could be a little more difficult. When he was sitting in the pastor's chair, he was just behind the congregational song leader. He had a powerful booming voice, which he didn't tone down during the hymns. If the song leader was going too slow for him, Gustavo would sing faster, with a pounding rhythm, a challenge especially for a young person still learning to use their leadership gifts. This story was told with a smile of fond remembrance.

During the war in Nicaragua in the 1980s, with all the displacement and turmoil, the choir shrunk to thirty or forty members. After the war ended, the choir grew again, reaching up to sixty-six members. Through Joan's leadership, the Parajón-Dominguez Choir also expanded its ministry reach beyond Nicaragua. In 1992, the choir traveled to Puerto Rico to participate in a music festival of choirs from Latin America. While there, Joan met the Dominican composer Rafael Grullón, beginning a creative relationship. Grullón sent Joan some of his compositions for the choir to sing at the annual choral festival at the National Theater in August 2009. The composer came to Nicaragua with his son-in-law, Moisés Almonte, for the special event. Afterward, Grullón invited the choir to tour in the Dominican Republic, which they did a year later. The Parajón-Dominguez Choir was also invited to sing in churches in El Salvador and Costa Rica.

Family Life

The Parajón family life was heavily affected by Gustavo's ministries. Marta and David were born in the U.S. and were old enough (4 years and 2 years, respectively) to remember the two-month journey by jeep through the U.S., Mexico, and other Central American countries to their new home in Nicaragua. They remembered the earthquake in December 1972, when CEPAD was born. That not only shook their home, but it shook their home life. Gustavo became far busier. His journeys beyond Managua increased over his already heavy travels with PROVADENIC around the country. He took frequent trips as a member of the Christian Medical Commission, based in Geneva, and trips to speak in churches in the U.S., leaving less time at home and with the children. On January 28, 1975, Rebecca Olivia was born, about ten years younger than the other two children and with a far busier father for those formative years. By the time of the revolution in 1979, Marta and David were teenagers, enjoying their independence. In Becky's early teen years, Gustavo was deep into the peace and reconciliation efforts.

There were many happy memories. Before becoming pastor, Gustavo liked to take an occasional weekend away from the church to take Joan and the children to a beach on the Pacific Ocean. But on Sundays, before getting in the water, he would lead the family in the Sunday school lesson. Then they could go play in the water! He also liked to take the children in the Jeep and go exploring. They would turn into dirt roads just to see where they went. Gustavo would do this with the grandchildren as well when they got old enough. "I want to see where this takes us," he would say as he made the turn. At bedtime, Joan or Gustavo would usually put the children down and read them stories. When Gustavo was there, he would sing songs in Spanish that his mother had sung to him.

As the counterrevolution was developing, First Baptist Managua asked Gustavo to be their pastor "in his spare time," but he didn't have any spare time between his work with PROVADENIC and CEPAD, especially with all the travel those roles involved. He had to meet with international guests and mission teams as they showed up, especially in the growing concern for solidarity with Nicaragua as it stood up to U.S. might. Then there were all the trips out of the country, the times to speak and inspire others. Truly the load was a superhuman one. The good doctor was far too busy to do it all, and as a result, he was frequently absent from home.

Then the peace work was added on top of the relief and development work, on top of the pastoral work, on top of the health care work. Joan once asked, "Are you sure that you need to do all these things? We have a family. We're here waiting for you to come home." Gustavo responded, "Yes, I know. I'm glad you are here taking care of the children, but I need to do these things. I feel I am doing the Lord's will. I'm glad you're here." On the one hand, Dad became the kids' hero, but on the other, he was sorely missed.

On top of those roles, Gustavo was also pastor and mentor to church youth and had an open home policy, just as his father had done. This meant Gustavo often brought the youth home for dinner and Bible study, and sometimes slumber parties. This meant large pots of food in the kitchen, meals elbow to elbow at the table, guitars and singing late into the night, and lots of loud laughing and fellowship.

Though Gustavo was very personable and engaged deeply with many people, he had a deep introverted side. Getting away from work became his alone time, often resulting in more shallow interactions with his family. His family sometimes got him as he was shutting down to recuperate and restore himself. At times, he would come home in the evening, simply collapse in his chair, and fall fast asleep. Costly as his aloneness at home was for the family, all the children loved him and took on the deep love for others Gustavo exercised in his ministry and hospitality. They saw his faith in Jesus and how it was lived out in kindness and love to others. In their unique ways, each of the children embraced what they saw modeled in their father.

Joan was sustained through Gustavo's frequent absences by her faith, testifying that God gave her strength to meet the challenges she faced. She also had a circle of dear friends to talk to, including some from the days at First Baptist Cleveland. Those relationships stayed strong as mission teams came regularly, with some of the friends staying for extra time. Nancy Wheaton, who first met the Parajóns when she brought a vehicle from Cleveland to Managua after the earthquake, became a part of the family, with the children feeling very close to her as well. Nancy visited almost every year. She also received Marta, David, and Rebecca into her home in Cleveland during some of the most difficult days in Nicaragua or when Gustavo's and Joan's travel schedules were too complex.

Often in his travels, Gustavo went into dangerous regions, so his family back at home didn't know if he really would come back. Land mines were a serious concern, blowing up vehicles, adding to the death toll and leaving many people without arms and legs. Even the soldiers at the periodic checkpoints warned Gustavo, "You are on your own. Proceed at your own risk." The Parajón family knew that risk as they sent him on his way. They anxiously wondered: Is this the last time to say goodbye? When Gustavo left Joan and the children, he would say he loved them. He told them not to worry and to trust in God. However, in a way, it is far easier for the one who goes into danger than for the loved ones left behind.

Early in the war, David left Nicaragua for school, following in his father's footsteps, first at Denison, then at Case Western in Cleveland for medical school. He inherited neither the family's musical genes nor his grandfather's and father's pastoral calling. However, he had appreciated the medical work from his childhood days, when he helped out with the vaccination campaigns. Inspired in large part by his father and Dr. William S. Cumming, David had a love for science, all the sciences: chemistry, physics, and biology. In his father, he saw how science could be put toward the good purpose of helping people in need with their illnesses. He had traveled with his dad into rural communities, and heard his father preach as well as carry out the public health mission. David planned to step into that medical and public health work.

In 1982, Marta married Edwin Gutiérrez, who was a good friend of Gustavo's and his assistant in PROVADENIC and CEPAD. On January 25, 1984, their first daughter, Cynthia, was born. When Cynthia was just 2 ½ months old, tragedy struck. Many families were at a Sunday school outing for the church at Xiloá, a volcanic crater lake not far from Managua. Nobody was sure how it happened, but Edwin drowned. At first, nobody could find him, but he was finally located and pulled onto shore. Gustavo desperately performed CPR and mouth-to-mouth resuscitation to try to save his son-in-law, but to no avail. They took Edwin to the nearest hospital, where he was pronounced dead. Gustavo was devastated by what happened and brought Marta back from the hospital.

After Edwin's death, Marta wanted to move back home with her parents, but Gustavo said, "No, stay in your house. This is your daughter's home." However, to provide her support in her time of grief, Gustavo stayed in Marta and Cynthia's home for two weeks. Looking back, Marta was grateful for the wisdom of her father in getting her to face the reality of living without her husband.

In 1988, Marta married Denis Cuéllar, an orthopedic surgeon at the Baptist Hospital. He had been a member of the choir and youth group at church and had spent many hours in the Parajón home as a young person. Gustavo presided over the wedding of his daughter and his younger colleague. Marta and Denis had three daughters: Debbi, Raquel, and Annie. When each of Marta's daughters was born, Dr. Parajón was right there in the operating room. Marta had her dad holding one hand and her husband holding the other, Edwin with Cynthia and Denis with the other three. Joan wasn't allowed in because she wasn't a doctor!

As the war dragged on in 1989, the stress of work, travel, and danger took a toll on Gustavo's health. He had a hypertensive heart crisis while Joan was in the U.S. with Becky. Marta and Denis spent time at the hospital tending to Gustavo and fielding the stream of concerned visitors. One of the young men from the church also took shifts through the days and nights until Gustavo could return home.

To get further treatment for his heart, Marta traveled with her father to the Cleveland Clinic, where a member of First Baptist Church served on the staff. Marta's relationship with her father blossomed as she became his caregiver, checking labels on everything to monitor his sodium levels. Their conversations moved to deeper levels, more like those of friends rather than father-daughter.

Becky, the youngest, grew up with Gustavo at his busiest, creating a lot of empty space in her life. However, her dad encouraged her to dream. She wanted to learn French and live in France someday. Gustavo supported her in those studies and in studying in Paris for a semester. He also took Becky with him in 1987 to the Greenbelt Festival in the United Kingdom (see Chapter 10).

In June 1995, David married Laura Chanchien in a wedding ceremony in Managua. They were commissioned as missionaries with the American Baptist Churches and moved to Nicaragua in September 2001. Soon, they were deeply involved in the health care ministries in Nicaragua, taking over Gustavo´s work with PROVADENIC. They had three children: Cristina, Scotty, and David.

In June 2005, Rebecca married Brian Clark in Virginia Beach, Virginia, where they continue to live as of this writing. They had two children: Lauren and Preston.

Hospitality was a major part of the household rhythms for the Parajóns. Gustavo served as a mentor for generations of young people from church and many of them visited the Parajón home and often stayed overnight, which led to lively dinners and breakfasts. Many people remember that Gustavo loved spicy food and hot peppers, which he had with almost every meal, probably a culinary expression of his Mexican roots. A young missionary couple, Ray and Adalia Schellinger-Gutiérrez, lived nearby. Adalia was the daughter of Gustavo's childhood friend Rolando. They shared dinner around the Parajón table at least once a week, sometimes more. So many international visitors spoke warmly of their time in the Parajón home.

Breaking out of the cultural model for men, Gustavo would help serve dinner at the table and bring dishes out from the kitchen. Sometimes he helped to cook, then after dinner he joined in cleaning the dishes. The young men from the church noticed this different example of what a Nicaraguan man looked like exercising Christian servanthood in the home.

Having so many guests in the house brought a lot of energy to the Parajón home, which could be exciting for the kids at times. For the children, however, so much hospitality also meant that their home and lives were constantly on display. Privacy was minimal, sometimes a need that was achingly felt. On the other hand, they were exposed to so many people from different cultures that they all grew up with a deep appreciation of diversity.

Grandchildren

Gustavo was stepping out of many of his roles, or at least winding them down, as the grandchildren started arriving in the family. He had more time for the grandchildren than he had given his children. He was very creative as a grandparent, doing different things in different ways with each child. Each one felt a special connection to him. Annie was the youngest of Marta's children. Gustavo noticed that her Spanish wasn't as strong as it should be because she mostly spoke English with her friends. So Gustavo spoke exclusively to her in Spanish.

Joan and Gustavo would invite the grandchildren to spend the night with them, just one at a time. In the evening was story time, but never from a book. Gustavo would make up the story as he went, making the grandchild the main character in the fantasy adventure. Then it was a song, followed by bedtime. In the morning, they would make breakfast, sometimes hotdogs filled with cheese and bacon, sometimes cheesy scrambled eggs. The real treat for the grandchildren was talking with their grandparents, who conversed with them like they were adults. Gustavo would ask good questions, causing the young ones to think and go deeper. Joan would sing with them, teaching them to appreciate music at an early age.

Saturdays would be the family lunch, with everyone gathered at the big table, Gustavo at the head. Gustavo had a special closet with his "own toys." In order to avoid arguments over the toys, he would tell the children, "You want to play with my toys? I'll share with you." Grandpa also loved sweets and often had a treat waiting in the pocket of his shirt, the ever-present Nicaraguan dress shirt, a *guayabera*. Or they would raid the freezer for frozen *pupusas* (tortillas with cheese—Gustavo loved cheese!). Sometimes there was a balloon in the guayabera pocket that Gustavo would blow up so they could play balloon volleyball.

Gustavo and Joan took separate vehicles to church because of their different schedules. Driving home with Grandpa was always a special treat, sitting in the front seat and singing or talking. The musical grandfather loved singing songs with the grandkids. Gustavo would sing with different voices for the different characters in the children's songs.

The Parajóns had a property on a Pacific Ocean beach. It was a cheap, undeveloped mess of cacti and brambles when they got it, but they could camp and have fun in a beautiful spot. The family and youth from church helped clear the land in order to make space to build a small hut and later a roof for shade. Raquel would get up early with her grandpa for a walk on the beach. They would look at rocks and have lively discussions. Gustavo had his "beach outfit"—shorts, bright purple water shoes, and a faded red Lands' End polo shirt with a blue collar. He often had those persistent questions: "Do you want to go to the waves or the tidal pool?" Being with him was an interactive experience.

Hanging out with their grandparents brought the grandchildren into contact with so many different people who enjoyed the hospitality of the Parajón household. The kids learned to talk to grown-ups earlier than their friends. They learned many lessons from some of the amazing guests they met. Some guests became friends after repeated visits. One highlight for the grandkids was when Nancy Wheaton had her ears pierced by Gustavo! They saw the respect guests accorded to their grandparents, and that brought pride to the young ones.

The grandchildren often joined with the mission teams that poured into Nicaragua to work at CEPAD, PROVADENIC, and later, AMOS. Gustavo wanted the children to witness life and ministry among the rural communities even as he had with his father. He got them involved. When Debbi was 8 years old, she was translating for some mission teams, especially for the folks from Cleveland, who felt like family anyway. Going to the rural communities with the mission teams didn't feel like a chore because the kids could be with Gustavo, see his life and what he had built. This was something Gustavo wanted the grandchildren to experience firsthand.

The guests weren't the only ones honored by the Parajóns. There was a guard at First Baptist named Bergman. Gustavo taught the children to see beyond the class divisions that could be so strong in Nicaragua. He never acted like he was Bergman's boss, rather, he greeted him by name. He told the kids, "You always say 'Hi' to Bergman."

In the church, the grandchildren heard Gustavo preach. They listened to the "long, beautiful sermons on love and understanding," as one remembered. They learned from him about how broad and forgiving God's grace was and not to judge anyone. These were more than words as they saw the teachings of Christ lived out in how their grandfather acted. He welcomed their discussions of theology with him even in their preteen years. He wouldn't give answers to their questions, but helped them go through their own thought processes to come to their own answers.

Occasionally, there was a need for discipline, as a child would act out. Gustavo's typical discipline was not loud, but rather a simple question, "Is this the correct way?" He could be stern, but made sure the child was thinking about and internalizing what was right and wrong.

Like the children, the grandchildren picked up from Gustavo about being caring and empathetic toward other people. They saw both his strong religious beliefs and that he didn't bulldoze over people. When faced with a challenge, Gustavo would always choose kindness, and the grandchildren noticed. They followed him, each seeking in their own way to put as much good into the world as they could.

Joan modeled similar values to the grandchildren as well. She had lived a life of resiliency and faith. She left her middle-class background to move to Nicaragua. She had survived an earthquake, a revolution, and a war, making do with her husband often gone. She had learned the Spanish of the country well and embraced the culture as her own.

Rebecca's children, as Gustavo and Joan's youngest child, don't have the memories of Marta's and David's kids. Lauren was 4 years old when her grandfather died, and Rebecca was pregnant with Preston at the time. Gustavo did know that Rebecca was pregnant. Rebecca and her family were living in Virginia, unable to just drop into the old family home. Their heritage from their grandfather will have to be passed down by stories.

Technology

For someone who seemed to always have the latest techno gadget, Gustavo's interest started by being totally unaware. His son-in-law Edwin Gutiérrez, in the early 1980s, challenged him to look into computers that were then coming into the country for the first time. Gustavo said he didn't need one. His DAY-TIMER pocket agenda was sufficient for him, as he had everything written in it. "Everything I need is in this little notebook," he said. When Gustavo discovered email, however, he became a self-taught computer whiz.

Soon he had his PalmPilot to go with his computers. He visited Great Britain and introduced his English friends Sue Plater and Garth Hewitt to computers. He introduced Sue to email and set up her email address, but for a while she could only email Gustavo, because nobody else she knew had email! When Gustavo visited England or the U.S., he took apart the telephones in his hotel rooms so he could hook up the wires to his computer and get a dial tone in the days of dial-up internet.

Pastor Parajón was an evangelist about technology. When the Platers and Hewitts worshiped at First Baptist, they noticed many of the congregants singing the hymns by taking the words off their PalmPilots! Gustavo also introduced a young Roberto Martinez to email to stay in touch with his brother Carlos who had gone to the U.S. to study at Ottawa University.

The Platers and Hewitts accompanied Gustavo and Gilberto Aguirre up the Río Escondido ("Hidden River") in eastern Nicaragua. However, in that small open boat, both Gustavo and Gilberto set up their small computers on their laps to do word processing.

One of the ironies for this computer whiz is that Joan was the one who handled the technological needs at home and got everything fixed. Joan's father had been an electrical engineer, and he taught his daughter how to understand and fix gadgets. If what needed fixing was beyond her skill, Joan was the one to engage the repair service, not Gustavo.

International Ministries held an annual World Mission Conference at the American Baptist Assembly in Green Lake, Wisconsin. The WMC was preceded by a gathering of all the missionaries who were back in the U.S. or Puerto Rico for "home assignment." When Gustavo was there, he would hook up with Stan Slade, a missionary from El Salvador who was later on IM central staff. The two were the early techies, hanging out together writing bootleg email while others were off enjoying the lake, the woods, the golf course, or taking a nice nap. Stan was always impressed that Gustavo had the latest in technology and the smallest and most efficient versions. Early on, Gustavo came with alligator clips to connect his small portable computer (SCION) directly into the outlet wires after taking off the switch covers. Gustavo was the first person Stan knew to talk about Linux, how much faster and more efficient it was. The older missionary, as Stan noted, was "right there with the gadgets!"

Gustavo with young men from
First Baptist Managua.

Roberto Martinez with Gustavo Parajón.

Gustavo doing Bible study in a small group during a CEPAD Assembly.

9

Spiritual Formation

We have covered so much about the life and activity of Gustavo Parajón. He was involved in the major fields of public health, peacemaking, and pastoring. In almost every interview for this book, the conversation turned at some point to the deep spiritual reality that both inspired and shaped the way Gustavo engaged in his ministry. His spiritual rootedness drove the way he related to people. How was he formed spiritually? It's a question we can't answer in full since he is no longer with us, but we have many clues and stories that can provide an adequate picture.

Many of the people interviewed for this book also talked about how Gustavo influenced them. The conversations about careers and life direction will be covered in the legacy chapter. Here, we will look at how, for many people, Gustavo shaped their spiritual journey, their way of being in Christ, and their way of following Christ in a hurting world. Some of this was through intentional mentoring and discipleship, but some was just by people watching him live out his faith and being shaped by his example.

The Shaping of a Servant of God

Gustavo was shaped for a lifetime through two habits from his father. One was a love for the Bible. The other was visiting the rural communities of Nicaragua to minister to people there. There he saw a oneness in evangelical witness and care for the needs of people as they faced systemic injustice and poverty. He remembered going with his father on horseback to take supplies to rural areas: "We were taught as children to believe the gospel has a component of social justice."

Along the way, it also clicked for him as a young person that he could be personally connected to this loving God who was interested both in him and in the people around him. As he said, "There came a moment in my life when I was face-to-face with Him, and I had to make a choice: Christ and His Love or the glorification of myself and my desires. I chose to accept Him as Master and Lord of my life."[36] At the age of 9, Gustavo was baptized by his father. His relationship with Christ and the Holy Spirit was dynamic. God helped him deal with what he struggled with, as he expressed once: "I have felt in a powerful way the Holy Spirit unraveling some of the coiled areas in my life."[37] In 1954, a team came to First Baptist Managua to conduct special revival services that stirred many of the young people, including Gustavo. In that setting, the call to be a missionary crystalized, specifically to be a medical missionary after having seen all the desperate health needs while traveling with his father in the rural communities.

As Gustavo engaged in his daily study of Scriptures, he developed simple questions to help open his mind and heart to the message in those pages: What was the passage about? What does it teach us about God, Jesus, the Holy Spirit, and humankind? What does it teach about me? For Gustavo, our behavior, and specifically his behavior, should be shaped by the Bible. In order to do that, we need to know the Bible better. Gustavo and his childhood friends Rolando and Roger all studied together and underlined their Bibles to highlight what they were hearing from God.

Many people, however, read the Bible regularly, talk about a personal relationship with Christ, and end up at a very different place in terms of issues of justice, peace, and service to those at the margins of society. What were the scriptural keys that unlocked his interpretation of the Bible's overall teaching? The central point from which all else flowed in his understanding was the person and work of Jesus. He often quoted Mark 10:45: "For even the Son of Man did not come to be served, but to serve, and to give his life as a ransom for many." (NIV) Service was central to Jesus, seen in how he healed the sick, fed the hungry, and related to outcasts.

As a teen and young man, this message was colored by the marginalization of Baptists and other Protestants by an often dominant and repressive Catholic majority. Faith could be expressed in a defensive tenacity that was compassionate with a narrow focus of making people "like us." He came onto the campus at Denison with such a mindset, but by the time he was launching his health care ministry in Nicaragua, he was far more open. How did that change take place? Part of it may have been being around other Christians, especially in Cleveland,

---

36 IM Pen Sketch, International Ministries, 1974.
37 "Meet a National Leader," Baptist Council on World Mission, Newsletter, Oct. 1975.

who held his same core beliefs but with more openness both to the diversity of the human community and of the Christian community.

As he wrestled with Scripture, he saw the servant Jesus approach people without bias or prejudice. He reflected during a radio interview, "How did people find out about Jesus? Through what He did: Healing the sick, stopping to talk to people who society considered marginalized and not worth stopping to talk to, like the blind man who was there begging on the road to Jericho. There Jesus stopped, and his disciples, the apostles, were not very happy. 'Shut up!' they told him, but the man screamed more, and Jesus stopped. How interesting. I was very impressed by that story in Luke that the Lord did not ask him: 'Well, are you from my church? Are you from my denomination? Or are you a Marxist? A Roman Catholic?' He said, 'What do you need?' The blind man said to him: 'My sight!' And the Lord granted it."[38]

Gustavo was also taken with the story from John 4 about the Samaritan woman who met Jesus at the well outside her city. This story led Gustavo into a need-centered ministry that didn't worry about people's labels. As he told it in that same interview, "The Samaritan woman, who obviously in the first place, was from a marginalized people, totally despised by the Jews. Second, a woman, and then her profession. And Jesus stopped for that woman, and that woman changed. She was transformed. That was the way Jesus did his ministry, and so when the church serves that way, there is a unity in service that is amazing. That is what we have been able to see through the years in CEPAD, how from the Anglican Church at one end to the Apostolic churches at the other, however, as a single person in Christ, we have been able to serve the rest of Nicaragua." Christians found their ultimate unity in following the ways of Jesus in the Bible, and that brought powerful unity as they engaged in Christ-like ministry in their own context.

Part of Gustavo's own spiritual formation regarding openness to the Christian expressions of other denominations came into the intimacy of his daily devotions. He began to use the Anglican Lectionary using the daily readings and the collects for various occasions. Whenever he would go to the U.K., he would get the latest edition, or when Garth Hewitt would visit Nicaragua, he would bring the most recent version for Gustavo.

Gustavo's walk with Jesus shaped him into a person known far and wide for his humility. Tomás Téllez, general secretary of the Baptist Convention of Nicaragua during the Contra War years, testified about Gustavo: "I believe that his greatest gift was that of humility, which multiplied into a great gift for people. He was a very brilliant man, trained in one of the best universities in the United States, and he could have settled there and had a great medical career and earned prestige and a lot of money. But he preferred to return to Nicaragua and work for the poor,

---

38 CEPAD anniversary interview with Gilberto Aguirre.

collaborating with Jesus Christ to bring abundant life (John 10:10). He always related to peasant people, with little or no education, with very limited financial resources, and he treated them with sympathy, with respect, and on equal terms. That built bridges with all people and allowed him to do a great job in these fields of health, education, and development for the benefit of thousands of children, women, peasants, youth, and the population in general—a work of great social benefit in the Name of Jesus and for the building of His kingdom on this earth."[39]

Along with his humility was a powerful sense of the presence of God within and deeper than this one man. Gustavo's devotional life was not an intellectual or academic exercise, but was for the sole purpose of getting closer to Christ. Gustavo's missionary colleague Stan Slade captured the godly presence reported by so many who knew him: "Gustavo had a calm that was the opposite of withdrawal—engagement. How do you be a channel of a loving God to this person he was interacting with even if they were hostile towards him? By radiating the love of God. A tremendous confidence and trust came through him. The source was a deep engagement to and commitment to the Lord. He was continually being transformed by the Lord. There are a lot of folks who can speak in great insights, but with Gustavo one felt the substance and reality. There was almost a tangible presence of God at work in and through this amazing brother. I felt I encountered the fruit of the Spirit in Gustavo."[40]

The Spirituality of Ministry

Gustavo took the saying of Jesus in John 10:10 that he came that we might have abundant life, life in all its fullness and turned it into the clarion call at places of need. Life was being robbed by no access to health services and conditions that made treatable illnesses deadly. So he followed Jesus to bring abundant life through community-centered health care. Life was being robbed by structural poverty or disasters that stripped so much from people. So Gustavo followed Jesus to bring abundant life through emergency relief and the empowerment of long-term development. Life was being robbed by war that left devastated families and communities. So Gustavo followed Jesus to bring abundant life through making peace and forging reconciliation. Through it all, he sought to introduce people to the Jesus he knew and who motivated him by reading stories from the Bible and praying with a specificity that invited others into his prayers.

Gustavo's good friend and colleague Octavio Cortés remembers what Dr. Parajón taught him: "Service and serving the poor, he used to say, is the flip side of the Gospel. It is not something additional." Gustavo expressed this spirit of service drawing upon Isaiah 53: "The methodology of Jesus is the methodology

39 Interview of Tomás Téllez by Daniel Buttry.
40 Interview of Stan Slade by Daniel Buttry.

of the Suffering Servant, of the poems that we see in Isaiah. It then becomes very clear that violence is not redeeming in any way, that violence only engenders more violence. God loves all people and has given us Jesus as a wonderful gift that has shown us that violence has no part in the plan that God has for the world."[41]

The vision in a simple phrase from the Lord's Prayer also compelled him to action: "Your kingdom come, your will be done on earth as it is in heaven." (Matt. 6:10 NIV) In Gustavo's eyes, we don't passively and patiently wait for "heaven" to arrive. Rather, we are to live out the ways of heaven here and now on earth. Isaiah 65:17-25 fleshed that vision out in great detail: Children wouldn't die in infancy, and old people would live full lives. People would be able to build houses and enjoy them, plant their crops and harvest them. "The wolf and the lamb will feed together, and the lion will eat straw like an ox, and dust will be the serpent's food. They will neither harm nor destroy on all my holy mountain." (Is. 65:25 NIV) Between his work in community-based health care, relief and development, and peace and reconciliation, Gustavo was engaged in the nitty-gritty substance of living out that prophetic vision.

One of the deep spiritual challenges Gustavo faced was the vicious criticism aimed at him from Christians in the U.S. and in Nicaragua. As he expressed it poignantly: "The frustrating and difficult to understand elements in these crises are that some of the persons involved are leaders, of the churches, denominations, where we have been ministering all our lives. We all know and serve—we say—the same Lord. Why, then, these conflicts?"[42]

Gustavo's response to these attacks was shaped by the Bible, not engaging in counterattacks, but seeking God's grace for the inner strength, patience, and compassion to endure. He turned to 1 Peter 1:6, 7: "In this (living hope and an imperishable inheritance) you rejoice even if now for a little while you have had to suffer various trials, so that the genuineness of your faith—being more precious than gold that, though perishable, is tested by fire—may be found to result in praise and glory and honor when Jesus Christ is revealed." (NRSV) In the story of Shadrach, Meshach, and Abednego being thrown by King Nebuchadnezzar into the fiery furnace, Gustavo was comforted by the report of a fourth person in the furnace with them. (Daniel 3:25) He wrote a friend, "In the labyrinth of the conflicting emotions that surge within us, in the unexpected and shocking surprise, in the severe disillusionment and oftentimes depression, we have been accompanied by the fourth ... And that indeed, is cause for rejoicing. The presence and comfort of the Spirit, the source of that living hope and reassurance of the inheritance is a joy."

---

41 From the film "God Loves Justice", https://www.youtube.com/watch?v=dx7YAyF0wmo.
42 Email to Sue Plater, 4 Nov. 1997.

He also drew strength from Paul's testimony in 2 Corinthians 4.7-18, especially verses 8 and 9: "We are pressed on every side by troubles, but we are not crushed. We are perplexed, but not driven to despair. We are hunted down, but never abandoned by God. We get knocked down, but we are not destroyed." In the fiery furnace of criticism, Gustavo let the Spirit shape him into a person of grace and humility. He looked at how Jesus lived under pressure and sought to show the same attitudes. Joyce Hollyday of *Sojourners* wrote about the ugliness of the IRD's attacks, but she saw firsthand what had taken shape in Gustavo: "To look into the eyes of Gustavo Parajón is to see compassion and integrity."[43]

Ministry of Mentoring

Having been deeply shaped by his walk with God and daily reading of the Bible, Gustavo was intentional about helping others discover the power of the living Christ and God's Word. He gave much of his time to develop and support small groups, often of young people, to grow as disciples of Christ. He also mentored people in leadership, shaping the leaders for generations to come. He mentored in one-on-one relationships, seeing leadership and abilities in others and calling them out.

Anita Taylor thought of herself as being one of Gustavo's "adoptive kids." There were so many folks there like her, young people mentored and shaped by him who went on to become key leaders. Anita said, "He was always supporting us, finding out strong points and bringing out the best of us. We were important."

Gustavo began his work at First Baptist with the youth group, and young people continued to be one of his great passions. He engaged them in Bible study. He could do the deep exegesis and interpretation, but always in a way to lift people up in their walk of faith. He constantly used questions: "What do you think of this passage?" He taught young people not just to parrot correct answers but to enter into dialog with the Scriptures, a dialog that could last a lifetime as he modeled in himself. Gustavo loved to dig into the theological richness of the Scriptures and mine the truth that was there, however, he always would show grace both in the Word itself and in how he taught it.

Part of mentoring the young people in the church was teaching engagement in mission. Just as his father took him to the rural areas, Gustavo took youth groups out to the different communities in Chinandega in which PROVADENIC worked. The youth helped build latrines, worked on clinic buildings, taught health education, and tutored in literacy. So many young people built a solid foundation for lifetime Christian service through these experiences.

Gustavo could be firm and fair in how he handled discipline with the young people. When a Regional Youth Congress was held in Panama, the church young

---

43 Hollyday, Joyce, "Usual Operating Procedures," *Sojourners*, March, 1987.

people wanted to go. They raised funds for the trip by washing cars. One young man wanted to go to Panama but refused to join in washing the cars. He went to Dr. Parajón and told him, "The Lord told me you are going to give me my ticket." Gustavo replied, "Well, let's wait until the Lord tells me, too." The young man wasn't allowed to join the group on the trip to Panama.

In the late 1990s, a young Roberto Martinez was in the youth group. Gustavo would ask him to take responsibilities that he hadn't thought of before. Soon, Roberto was president of the youth group. Gustavo trained the youth leaders how to make yearlong plans, how to organize who would lead meetings, setting up plans for retreats and mission trips. Roberto learned how to handle logistics. For one mission trip to a PROVADENIC clinic, no chaperone was lined up. Gustavo told them, "I trust you all. Who do you need?" The youth stepped positively into that trust until Marta and Denis showed up a couple days later. Gustavo's trust was an inspiration for young people to step into excellence, and they did again and again.

Later, Roberto became the secretary for the board of First Baptist Managua. Again, Gustavo trained him how to take minutes: Use good descriptions, but not too long; put a little box next to action items so people can quickly see them. He sat next to Gustavo, watching him lead the meetings. Eventually, Roberto would become a medical doctor and the chair of the board for AMOS Health and Hope, and it was those skills he learned from Gustavo as a young person in church that allowed him to shine in those roles.

Gustavo was called to Mexico to receive an award from the Baptist World Alliance, and all the main church leadership traveled with him in support. So Gustavo told Roberto he was in charge of the church while he was gone. Roberto had preached before, so that wasn't so bad. But when the mother of Octavio Cortés died, Roberto had to plan the memorial service and go to the cemetery. He preached at the memorial service and presided at the graveside service. He was 24 years old at the time. Gustavo could see what young leaders had in themselves and could do, often way beyond their own imaginings. Roberto did just fine in a serious time of family crisis.

Gustavo and Joan went so far as to bring young people into their home when necessary. Carlos Martinez, Roberto's older brother, had been a rising star as a teen, playing piano for the choir. He went to college in the U.S., then dropped out for personal reasons. The Parajóns took him into their home for two years. Rather than turning away from him in disappointment, they encouraged him. Besides Carlos, his whole family was affected by the grace experienced from Gustavo and Joan.

In 1995, Gustavo took Carlos to the Greenbelt Festival in the U.K. (see Chapter 10). Afterward, he took Carlos to Boosey and Hawkes, a major music store in London. Gustavo was always investing in the education of young people, so he opened up this feast for an aspiring young musician. Gustavo bought him a book on tonal harmony and the score to Rachmaninoff's Piano Concerto No. 2. He also purchased 11" x 17" manuscript paper to encourage Carlos' composition. Gustavo's investment in young people's lives was always focused on the person's heart, their dreams, and the opportunities ahead.

In his administrative leadership in PROVADENIC, CEPAD, AMOS, and the church, Gustavo was always teaching. He showed how to be a good leader and how to relate to people, as well as how to handle the nuts and bolts of getting tasks done efficiently. Milton Argüello started with CEPAD and eventually went into the business world. The ministry setting of CEPAD under Dr. Parajón was where he learned to focus on data, on the facts. Gustavo taught Milton to be disciplined in what he did and to handle matters in an executive manner, to get to the point and not waste precious time. Milton said, "The doctor had a method called Curry; and in private companies they have exactly the same, but they don't apply it as well as the doctor applied it." Parajón learned this administrative methodology from a seminar by David Curry in the early years of CEPAD. The approach centered on questions to help identify a problem, what it was and what it wasn't, and then how to proceed to correct it. Gustavo was rigorous in his assessment and planning and taught those skills to the younger leaders working with him. Gabriel Gaitán referred to his time on staff with CEPAD as a school because he learned so much that applied to every area of his life: "I really appreciated and learned from him his way of analyzing problems and situations. His ability to prevent risks or consequences of the decisions made was really amazing as well as his firmness to make decisions."

Though Gabriel was learning how to handle business well, Gustavo took him and others deeper into specifically Christian discipleship: "Every discussion and decision was made under the light of Jesus' teachings and of his apostles', always focused on those with least opportunities, always promoting quality and empathy in everything we did. I personally believe that both him and Gilberto Aguirre could say as Paul: 'Imitate me, just as I imitate Christ.'" (1 Cor. 11:1)

Carlos Mejía Ruiz spoke about how he was shaped as a person in his thirty years at CEPAD, especially by Dr. Parajón: "I officially started (in CEPAD) in 1973. I was like 16 or 17 years old ... CEPAD for me has been a school, a university. It trained me because I was a young man who smoked marijuana, drank liquor, was a disorderly young man. And when I came to CEPAD, CEPAD taught me what a young man should be. A young man must have a commitment to God first and to his country. We learned that from Dr. Parajón. He said titles are not worth anything; what is worth something is your commitment, your love for those who have nothing, the dispossessed. CEPAD was my school ... The men who formed it are men of God, men who never made a profit, men who always sought the welfare of the people, men of courage, men who loved my country."[44]

Even in leading devotions for the staff at PROVADENIC, CEPAD, or AMOS, Gustavo modeled a way of engaging with the Bible. He didn't just lead another short devotional. Evenor Jerez was one of those whose lives were shaped by Gustavo's spiritual disciplines at work: "He used a methodology to scrutinize the Bible that contributed to the biblical and theological formation of the participants in different meetings or devotions."

The modeling by Gustavo and learning by the staff continued as they traveled to various communities, whether for relief and development work or reconciliation. Juan Carlos Palma was with Gustavo in Jinotega in the reconciliation process. He learned from Gustavo: "He was a teacher. He was very calm. He always approached every situation with wisdom, using a Bible passage. I remember clearly the books of the Kings, Amos, and the Proverbs being used by him."

Gustavo turned simple communications for consolation into deeper sharing that profoundly impacted people. His communications went to a deeper level because of his wise and direct application of the Bible that he knew so well and applied so precisely. He sent an email to a family whose son went through difficult surgery. He began by sharing from his own walk in the Scriptures: "Speaking on tiredness, fatigue, and frustration, I found Isaiah 40:1-11, the passage we have in our lectionary for today, very refreshing." He then quoted the whole passage, highlighting special parts in italics. The family passed the message on to the son, who printed it and put it on his wall. To another family who lost a family member, he wrote, "Amidst our pain and tears, we are comforted by the words of Jesus and Scripture." What he shared was read at the funeral.

"You can do this," was one of Gustavo's most common phrases. Again and again he put a challenge before someone, assigned them a task beyond anything they had ever done, then said, "You can do this." More often than not they did and would look back on that moment as a breakthrough in their growth as a leader.

"You can do this," he said to Joan as they headed back to Nicaragua. "You could put a choir together and direct it," he said. Joan responded, "I don't know if I can do that!" "Yes, you can," rang in her ears. Joan's choir became one of the great legacies, not only in First Baptist Church Managua, but also across the country and even to other countries.

"You can do this," Gustavo said to Ray Schellinger when a mission team came from Oregon to put on a roof for an island church an hour boat ride into Lake Nicaragua. Ray was a new missionary and had never hosted a team or handled the logistics for such a construction endeavor. The challenges were a rude awakening

---

44 Interview of Carlos Mejía Ruiz by Dámaris Albuquerque.

for him, but over the years in Nicaragua, and later Mexico, he would facilitate countless teams.

"You can do this and represent Nicaragua," Gustavo said to Dr. Adalia Ruth Gutiérrez Lee, a young medical missionary he sent in his place to a global conference in Switzerland. Pharmaceutical companies and medical nonprofits were gathering to discuss responses to the HIV/AIDS crisis. It was her first of many international meetings. He taught Adalia how to run a nonprofit and to relate to government officials. Later, she and her husband, Ray Schellinger, launched Deborah's House in Tijuana, Mexico, a ministry she couldn't have undertaken without the mentoring she received from Gustavo.

"You can do this," Gustavo said to 24-year-old Dámaris Albuquerque when he needed to send someone to India to help the Nicaraguan government see how community-centered health care operates. He had taught her how to book his flights, work with travel agents, arrange for two hours for flight transfers, and develop an itinerary for all his trips. Now she would be the one going; the flights were for her. She and nurse Lilliam Escobar went representing PROVADENIC, along with two Sandinista health officials to learn from Indian public health practitioners what the Sandinistas wouldn't recognize in their own nation. The trip was a success. Dámaris came back home tired and worn out from all the challenges, including flight disruptions. However, she did it, the first of many international trips in her growing leadership.

"We can do this," he said to his daughter-in-law, Dr. Laura Parajón. They were looking at the collapse of PROVADENIC and launching AMOS (see Chapter 11). After all she had been through, the new challenges seemed overwhelming. Gustavo encouraged Laura's leadership and showed up with advice, connections, and hard work just when it was most needed.

So many people were affected in so many ways by Gustavo Parajón. He shaped their faith. He shaped their understanding of the Bible. He shaped how they thought about other people, especially people at the margins of society or one's critics. He shaped how they handled administrative tasks and the responsibilities of leadership. He shaped how they embraced their own capabilities to take on the challenges and opportunities before them. He shaped how they in turn would shape the lives of those they could mentor. The man God shaped Gustavo to be became one of the special instruments used by God to dramatically shape the lives of countless people in Nicaragua and around the world.

Daniel Buttry greets Daniel Ortega with Gustavo Parajón at the 1992 International Baptist Peace Conference in La Boquita, Nicaragua.

Bruce Cockburn talks about his experiences in Nicaragua at the 1987 Greenbelt Festival.

Platers and Hewitts with Gustavo at the 1992 Greenbelt Festival.

Album Cover for Cabaret Nicaragua from the 1987 Greenbelt Festival.

Garth Hewitt singing at CEPAD.

The Scottish Christian Friends of Nicaragua busking to raise money for Nicaraguan medical relief.

Dr. Parajón receives the Human Rights Award from the
Baptist World Alliance in Mexico, 2006.

Gustavo speaking at a conference on conflict resolution
held in Chiang Mai, Thailand in 1996.

10

Global Reach

Dr. Parajón was a citizen of the world as well as of Nicaragua. He followed the news, but in time he became a news-maker. He was particularly interested in where the poor were suffering even more because of war, politics, or natural disasters and climate events. He didn't seek publicity for himself, but he engaged in ground-breaking work in public health and peacemaking that had an impact far beyond his immediate work. He participated in global organizations and committees that put him in dialogue with people from other countries facing similar concerns and struggles. As his work became more well known, he was sought after as a speaker. He spoke with a quiet, slow-paced calm, but what he said was so pertinent and profound that people were gripped by his presentations.

Public Health Visionary

Dr. Parajón's first area of ministry was health care, beginning with the vaccination campaign and eventually growing into PROVADENIC with a large chain of local health clinics staffed by local health promoters. The Christian Medical Commission (CMC) was established in 1968 to assist the World Council of Churches in its evaluation and support of church-related medical programs in the developing world. Gustavo joined the CMC in its formative days.

Through their studies, the CMC found that facility-based (hospital-centered) health care didn't reach those who needed health care the most, especially the poor. The poor suffered the worst outcomes. Most church and Christian mission health work was centered on hospitals and curative work. However, half of hospital admissions were for preventable diseases. Furthermore, church-sponsored hospitals were becoming financially nonviable. So the CMC, with Gustavo involved in shaping the effort, promoted community-based health care that was just, equitable, and available to the poorest people in their own communities.

The CMC also noted the vast difference in health care in the richer countries compared to the poor ones. Distributive justice needs to be part of how primary health care is shaped, making sure that care is brought to poor communities. Poor communities also have more exposure to compounding problems for health, such as poor water and sanitation facilities. In health care planning, Christian organizations need to take into account the dynamics of injustice and bring effective strategies to bear to deliver primary and preventative health care to those with the least access to health resources.

The CMC became a voice for advocacy about these issues within the World Health Organization. The WHO had taken a top-down approach in a global campaign against malaria. The campaign failed for the most part because it was unable to get to remote communities with the greatest need. The CMC was one of the key advocates for shifting the WHO's top-down health care paradigm to the bottom-up vision of community-based care.

The paradigm shift happened in September 1978, when the World Health Organization sponsored a global conference on primary health care in Alma-Ata (now called Almaty) in Kazakhstan in what was then the Soviet Union. Representatives from governments and nongovernmental organizations gathered from 130 countries. Dr. Gustavo Parajón was among them, representing PROVADENIC and the Christian Medical Commission. Dr. Raj and Dr. Mabelle Arole in India and the "barefoot doctors" in China were other pioneering visionaries with this model of health care.

The concepts worked out in the programs of PROVADENIC and in the studies and commitment of CMC. They showed the value of community-based primary health care utilizing trained local folks as the first line of health care providers. These concepts were incorporated into the Alma-Ata Declaration for Primary Health Care, sometimes presented with the slogan "Health for All." Health was defined in a holistic way, "a state of complete physical, mental, and social well-being, and not merely the absence of disease or infirmity." Health was called "a fundamental human right." The declaration addressed the "gross inequality" in the health status of people, both between the "developed and developing countries" as well as within countries. It stated, "The people have a right and a duty to participate individually and collectively in the planning and implementation of their health care." The declaration lifted up the importance of bringing primary health care closest to the communities of need: "It is the first level of contact of individuals, the family, and community with the national health system bringing health care as close as possible to where people live and work, and constitutes the first elements of a continuing health care process." The elements in the declaration were not academic concerns in Nicaragua but were lived out in the way PROVADENIC functioned through the local committees and health promoters.

The Alma-Ata Declaration became a guiding light for the development of such programs around the world. Studies by the WHO showed that this emphasis of primary health care closest to the people and communities in need led to better health outcomes, lower costs, and greater user satisfaction. To this day, many faith-based organizations like AMOS, other non-profits, and even some government agencies promote just and equitable primary health care centered in poor communities as their driving model. Many refinements have been made since, such as focusing on particular diseases or health conditions that can be easily addressed with maximum impact. None of these have changed the basic paradigm that was shaped by Gustavo and other practitioners at Alma-Ata. Rather, they have built upon, expanded, and refined that paradigm. In Alma-Ata, Dr. Parajón and his colleagues laid a foundation for a revolution in the delivery of health care that is still spreading around the world.

Between the public health work of PROVADENIC and the relief and development work of CEPAD, many people and organizations around the world were intrigued and excited about the vision for their work and the empowering way they went about serving alongside those who were most vulnerable. Some European organizations had given to relief efforts following the 1972 earthquake, but were distressed to find the funds that they had given had not been spent as intended. Finding Nicaraguan partners with fiscal integrity in PROVADENIC and CEPAD brought renewed excitement and commitment to assist in Nicaragua. Many European agencies especially stepped forward during the 1980s and the U.S. embargo against Nicaragua. Assistance came from church-related and ecumenical agencies in Germany, the Netherlands, Sweden, Finland, Norway, Denmark, Switzerland, and the U.K. A Christian organization from New Zealand joined in following publicity about CEPAD in the World Council of Churches bulletin. Various denominations and ecumenical agencies in Canada and the U.S. were regular donors.

Often, involvement went far beyond giving funds in the various currencies. Many groups sent short-term teams of volunteers to assist PROVADENIC and CEPAD projects. Some volunteers came for longer stints. People from Germany, England, Scotland, and the U.S. might encounter each other serving in a rural community in Nicaragua or receiving a shared briefing from Gustavo in the Managua offices. From Anglicans and Lutherans to Baptists and Mennonites as well as Presbyterians, Methodists, Disciples, and folks from the Reformed churches and

United Church of Canada, almost the full spectrum of the Protestant expressions joined in the work in Nicaragua. All these folks returned home to tell their stories and strengthen the relational bonds beneath the financial support.

Gustavo was the best known face for PROVADENIC, CEPAD, and even for Nicaragua itself for many of these Christian organizations. He was often invited to speak across Europe and in North America. During a speaking trip in Germany and Switzerland, he was especially delighted when his Christian hosts opened up opportunities to speak to nonreligious NGOs about the needs of the poor in Nicaragua. The Peacemaking Program of the Presbyterian Church (U.S.A.) invited Gustavo for a six-week tour to talk about the war in Nicaragua and his peacemaking efforts. He was a major speaker at conferences, such as Chautauqua in New York state. He spoke at United Methodist assemblies and mission conferences and national gatherings of his own American Baptist churches. Following Dr. Parajón's presentations, the United Methodists issued a powerful letter to the U.S. government opposing its policies against Nicaragua. After coming for the Greenbelt Festival (see below), Gustavo was invited on speaking tours in England and Scotland. He met with the grassroots activists who raised funds for Nicaraguan aid, with high level church leaders, and with dear friends who had visited his country and given of their time and love in volunteer service. Gustavo sometimes brought a Nicaraguan colleague with him, or even sent a woman or man in leadership to represent him, CEPAD, PROVADENIC or, in a way, all of Nicaragua. Gustavo and his colleagues wove together the lives and actions of people from around the world with the people engaged in service in their Nicaraguan homeland.

Central America

In October 1986, amid the wars in both El Salvador and Nicaragua, a major earthquake devastated the area around the capital city of San Salvador. Over 1,000 people died, 10,000 were injured, and 200,000 were left homeless. Even though the nations had mirror opposite conflicts in terms of politics, CEPAD mobilized to help their brothers and sisters to the north. CEPAD sent two teams to bring advice, counsel, and material aid for the work of the Baptist Association of El Salvador (ABES), initially Gustavo and Gilberto, followed by Darwin López and Paul Jeffrey. They brought food, water, and medical care to some of the hardest hit neighborhoods. The Nicaraguan church community also raised $5,000 USD to help their Salvadoran neighbors with relief needs.

In January 2001, another earthquake struck El Salvador, just south of San Salvador. The earthquake triggered a massive landslide that claimed 585 lives. Almost 1,000 people died in total. CEPAD again stepped in to help their neighbors. Gustavo, Gilberto, and Dámaris went to visit, listen, and pray. There was a lot of conflict in the convention, but the Salvadoran Baptist women were united in their concern to meet the needs around them. Gustavo encouraged them to keep working from that unity. Based on what the team encountered, CEPAD sent two staff to provide training in psychosocial work and emotional relief. No other organizations existed in the region exactly like CEPAD, so they could be of immense assistance, not just in the aid itself but also in their knowledge for how to respond quickly and efficiently in a crisis.

Gustavo was also asked to help in his peacemaking capacity, not between governments but between conflicted Christians. José Norat, the area director at International Ministries (IM) responsible for Latin America, asked Gustavo to help in negotiations between IM and the Baptists in El Salvador (ABES). The new leadership in ABES following the war turned against the IM missionaries serving in El Salvador. They were asked to leave, and ABES wanted to sever its ties with IM. José thought Gustavo's gift to artfully get into the truth might be helpful in this delicate relationship.

The negotiations were very difficult. At one point, Gustavo asked a Salvadoran Baptist leader if he had denounced an IM missionary to the police. The leader replied, "Yes. I would do it again." Though Gustavo's diplomatic style and skills were helpful, the relationship was beyond repair. ABES broke its ties with IM. A few years later, however, new leadership came into control at ABES. One of the first things they did was send a plaque of appreciation to José Norat for his work, a first step in restoring the relationship between the two bodies.

Gustavo was a go-to person for IM when delicate negotiations were involved. He helped José mediate in a conflict between another Latin American Baptist convention and IM missionaries. That process was more successful with tensions transformed and the relationship between that convention and IM able to continue even stronger.

In the early 2000s, the violence in Chiapas, Mexico burst into world attention. CEPAD sent a team of people who had been active in Nicaragua's peace efforts, including the local peace commissions, to engage with peacemakers in Chiapas. They shared about the conflicts each group had gone through and explored the successes and challenges of on-the-ground peacemaking efforts.

Greenbelt Festival

The Greenbelt Festival is an annual celebration of the arts, faith, and justice. Beginning in 1974 with mostly evangelical Christians and a crowd of about 1,500, Greenbelt grew every year. The festival hit its attendance peak in 1983, with around 30,000 festival-goers. Music is always a huge draw with both new and established artists. Some of the musicians featured have been Cliff Richard, Bruce Cockburn, Moby, BeBe and CeCe Winans, Mavis Staples, Deacon Blue, The

Proclaimers, Amy Grant, Randy Stonehill, Noel Paul Stookey, Steeleye Span, and Goldie. People gathered for Greenbelt at several different locations over the years. They come from across the U.K. and other countries for four days of camping out and catching all kinds of music on the various stages.

Besides the music, comedy, and the arts, a major part of Greenbelt is listening to presentations from the cutting edges of faith and world issues. Two areas of special attention in the 1980s and 1990s were South Africa in the struggle against apartheid and Nicaragua. This passion for justice and peace made Bruce Cockburn feel that Greenbelt was very different from festivals in the U.S. The Christianity in the U.K. as found at Greenbelt had a more dynamic energy in its mainstream expressions than American Christianity, in his experience.

Gustavo Parajón became a regular guest, later bringing in other Nicaraguan resource people as well as building relationships that connected back to the work in Nicaragua. In his talks at Greenbelt, Gustavo always used a story from the Bible, sometimes surprising people with stories they'd never seen connected to current issues in such a way. His way of speaking was always calm and quiet, yet his stories could be incredibly dramatic and riveting.

Gustavo was first invited to be a speaker at the 1987 Greenbelt Festival. He came with Joan and Becky. The Scottish Christians for Nicaragua held an event in the biggest tent at Greenbelt and renamed the space Cabaret Nicaragua to raise money for medical aid to Nicaragua. The artists included those who had been to Nicaragua to see what was happening for themselves. The Scots had their busking group and were joined by Bruce Cockburn, among others. Cockburn played his powerful song "Nicaragua." Gustavo told the crowd what was going on with the war as well as the situation of the ordinary Nicaraguans. An album was later produced called "Cabaret Nicaragua" with cuts from the various artists and even a clip from Gustavo's talk. Proceeds from the album sales supported aid projects in Nicaragua.

When Bono from U2 found out that Gustavo would be there, he wanted to come with his wife, Ali, to see him. They had visited the Parajóns in Nicaragua, and Bono was deeply moved by Gustavo's Christian faith in action in a place of deep conflict. For the Greenbelt folks, however, Bono's desire to come created a logistical nightmare, especially at a festival where 20,000 U2 fans would be present. The solution was to bring Bono to meet Gustavo in disguise. Bono put on the yellow reflective jacket and cap of a parking attendant—nobody really looks at them, just at the jacket! He enjoyed the music, Gustavo's presentation, and then joined a small group for extended conversation with Gustavo. Though 12-year-old Becky didn't know much about U2 at the time, she was interested in seeing someone in a Christian rock band. She soon took off to see what else was happening around the festival while the others talked more deeply.

Garth Hewitt is an Anglican priest and singer-songwriter willing to take on contemporary issues with fire and passion. Garth and his wife, Gill, first met Gustavo in person at Cabaret Nicaragua, though Garth was chair of the speaking committee that invited Gustavo to Greenbelt. Garth was taken by how Gustavo exhibited an integrated spirituality by bringing together the Bible with a commitment to the poor and to peace. Garth had begun an organization called Amos Trust to engage with and support various initiatives in places of need, such as street children and Palestine. As he and his wife, Gill, got to know Gustavo, Garth wanted to connect Amos Trust with Gustavo's work in Nicaragua.

Sue and Simon Plater—Sue was chair of the Greenbelt board—went to Nicaragua and El Salvador with Martin and Meg Wroe in 1989 to see what was going on for themselves. In 1993, the Platers returned to Nicaragua, this time with Garth and Gill Hewitt, concentrating on visiting CEPAD projects. This trip strengthened the bonds between CEPAD and Amos Trust. Personal relationships were also forged between the Platers and the Hewitts, and Gustavo and Joan that grew stronger and deeper over the years and extended to all their families. When the Hewitts' youngest son, Joe, became seriously ill, Gustavo spent a day with him. After that, Gustavo always inquired about how Joe was doing. Then, when the Hewitts' son Benjamin got married, Gustavo spoke at the service at St. Boltoph's Bishopsgate in London. These relationships provided the structure that brought Gustavo back repeatedly to Greenbelt and to other connected visits around England and Scotland. Many other people from England and Scotland visited Nicaragua over the years because of Gustavo's connections to Greenbelt, Scottish Christians for Nicaragua, and Amos Trust.

Gustavo worked many of his colleagues into the rotation at Greenbelt so there was always a Nicaraguan presence and presentation. Sometimes a family member or a younger person from the church accompanied him to help with some of the physical challenges at the festival, especially after Gustavo's heart crisis in 1989. David came in 1992. Gilberto Aguirre went to the festival, establishing deep ties with the Platers. El Profe also visited Amos Trust, building a connection between that organization and CEPAD, which had a long-lasting impact. Every year, the tent for Nicaragua was holding larger and larger crowds. Carlos Martinez accompanied Gustavo in 1995. Carlos played the piano while Gustavo talked intensely about Nicaragua. Later they traveled around England. Carlos remembers that all the time Gustavo was teaching, such as helping him to read the London tube maps. Roberto Martinez accompanied Gustavo to Greenbelt in 2003, then came on his own in 2006 to connect with Amos Trust.

One spinoff from Gustavo's Greenbelt visits was a visit to Leadership '89, a more heavily evangelical spring event. The music was all worship and praise music. Sue Plater was connected with the main committees for both events and lined up Gustavo to speak there. He made a solid connection through his strong Bible presentations, but also stretched them with the social implications of following Jesus. One friendship that resulted from Leadership '89 was with the Rev. Philip Mohabir, who led the African and Caribbean Evangelical Alliance. His wife, Muriel, had a cousin on Corn Island in Nicaragua, adding a special "it's a small world" connection.

Gustavo's last visit to Greenbelt was in 2010. Garth produced a short film of Gustavo sharing his biblical vision, "God Loves Justice." Gustavo spoke about the vision of living for God in Micah 6:8 and in Jesus as the Suffering Servant. Following Gustavo's death, Garth appended at the end of the film: "He made the Gospel visible to us because he walked so closely in the footsteps of Jesus and showed love and justice in action."[45]

The Things That Make for Peace

In 1992, beside a beautiful Nicaraguan Pacific beach at La Boquita, the second International Baptist Peace Conference was held. Tomás Téllez and Róger Velásquez did most of the logistical work, but Gustavo Parajón was a major plenary speaker. One of the themes of the conference was the involvement of religious leaders in major efforts to resolve civil wars and other major conflict situations with presenters from El Salvador, Burma (now called Myanmar), Sri Lanka, Zaire (now called Democratic Republic of Congo), and South Africa. Inspired by these practitioners, including Gustavo, a dream was born at La Boquita, which led to the establishment of the Gavel Memorial Peace Fund for the Baptist Peace Fellowship of North America. That fund provided financial support and training for indigenous peacemakers around the world, much like John Paul Lederach and the Mennonites provided support and funds for the Caribbean Coast peace initiative in Nicaragua. Later, International Ministries of the American Baptist Churches called Daniel Buttry, who was at La Boquita, to be their Global Consultant for Peace and Justice. He worked as a partner in mediation and training in many countries around the world. Gustavo Parajón was the visionary stone plunged into the pool of world affairs that sent ripples far beyond his direct involvement, inspired by his example.

At the fourth Global Baptist Peace Conference held in Rome, Italy in February 2009, one of the most memorable moments involved Dr. Parajón. He was a plenary speaker, sharing about the ongoing peace and reconciliation work in the wake of the long and brutal Contra War. After his presentation, there was a question and answer period. One person who rose was the Rev. Sini Ngindu Bindanda, a Baptist pastor originally from D.R. Congo serving an immigrant church in Milan. He made a long complex statement about the war in Congo. The moderator (from

45 YouTube: https://www.youtube.com/watch?v=dx7YAyF0wmo&t=3s

the U.S.) kept asking him if he had a question for Dr. Parajón. As Pastor Bindanda continued to make his statement and the moderator kept trying to cut him off, Bindanda finally demanded in a loud voice, "Let me speak!" The moderator gave up and let Bindanda finish his comment.

Then Gustavo responded with the wisdom that transformed the entire experience. He spoke about how being able to have a voice is so difficult and so critical for people coming from small countries, not in terms of geographic size or population but of power on the world stage. Gustavo spoke about the war in Congo as the bloodiest on the planet since World War II, yet it received very little attention. Gustavo said that Bindanda's voice was speaking for the millions of voiceless people coming from one of the places in the world with the greatest suffering. He gave voice to their unheard cries for justice and for peace. Dr. Parajón didn't relate to this Congolese pastor from his position as a big global peace figure who was a plenary speaker with important things to say. Instead, Gustavo, drawing upon his own experience coming from a small country being battered by a larger power, graciously made the space for another marginalized voice to be heard. He also sensitized the ears of those in more mainstream positions to hear that voice. People remember his response to the Congolese pastor more than his plenary presentation, illustrating how spiritually sensitive Gustavo was to the true teaching moment when it arose.

Gustavo was a plenary speaker and workshop leader at the Conflict Resolution Training Conference, November 1996, sponsored by the Asian Baptist Federation in Chiang Mai, Thailand. He was joined by Saboi Jum from Burma. Saboi was a Baptist minister who had led mediation efforts between ethnic insurgent groups and the military government, much like Gustavo had done in Nicaragua. Saboi was also at the conference in La Boquita in 1992. Gustavo and Saboi's example and sharing inspired a late night gathering in a hotel room of church leaders from Nagaland in northeast India. They launched a peace and reconciliation initiative among conflicted Naga political factions and the government of India that in the years to come would bring an end to fighting that had gone on since 1955.

Following their close work together on the Caribbean Coast conciliation process, Gustavo and John Paul Lederach traveled together to teach and inspire other peacemakers. Lederach wrote in his books about the relationship in peace teams between the Insider/Partial and the Outsider/Impartial. The Insider/Partial was someone from within the conflict who had an identity wrapped up in the conflicted relationships. Gustavo and the Moravian leaders were the Insider/Partials in Nicaragua. Though they were all Nicaraguan citizens, Gustavo came from the Spanish-speaking dominant population with connections to the Sandinista government while the Moravians were indigenous people closely linked to the indigenous resistance groups. They all knew the key people involved and had lived with the history of the conflict. They had status in their communities that gave them relational authority for the peace process. Gustavo and the Moravian leaders would have to live with whatever results or failures came from the process.

John Paul Lederach was the Outsider/Impartial. He wasn't Nicaraguan, and when the time came, he could go back home, outside of the conflict. However, because he was outside, he could be viewed as a more neutral presence in the team. He also brought skills in conflict transformation and financial resources through his mission agency, Mennonite Conciliation Service. As a teaching team, Parajón and Lederach could model how these dynamics worked.

Gustavo and John Paul went to the Philippines, where there was a lot of interest in the idea of the Insider/Partial and Outsider/Impartial teams. They met with various groups from the left-middle to the center of the political spectrum. They shared the stories about how mediation could take place without a power mediator such as a diplomat from an outside superpower or an organization like the United Nations. In the process of their travels, the two peacemakers became good friends.

Gustavo's peacemaking work, along with that of the Moravian Church leaders and John Paul Lederach, was featured in a number of books. Lederach wrote about the peace initiative on the Caribbean Coast of Nicaragua in many of his writings, but especially in his book *The Journey Toward Reconciliation*. Daniel Buttry wrote about it in *Christian Peacemaking: From Heritage to Hope*. However, Lederach and Buttry primarily worked and wrote in Christian contexts. A groundbreaking book came out of a Washington foreign policy think tank and lifted up the role of nongovernment leaders, especially religious leaders, in bringing about ends to complex conflicts, including civil wars. Douglas Johnston and Cynthia Sampson edited *Religion, the Missing Dimension of Statecraft*. Bruce Nichols wrote a chapter titled "Religious Conciliation between the Sandinistas and the East Coast Indians of Nicaragua." Nichols explored all that Parajón, Shogreen, Lederach, and others accomplished. Jimmy Carter wrote the foreword referencing what happened in Nicaragua as an example of the impact religious leaders could make amid a major violent conflict.[46]

Just as Gustavo helped shape a new global paradigm for health care, through example he has been a forerunner in the growing awareness of a new paradigm in peacemaking. This paradigm recognizes the creative role religious people can and often do play to end violent conflicts. Johnston and Sampson's book countered the arrogance of international diplomats that they can handle everything just fine. Instead, Parajón, Shogreen, Lederach, CEPAD, and the Moravian leaders were showing that they could lead to the breakthroughs the diplomats failed to achieve. After the end of the war, Gustavo, working with local conciliation commissions,

---

46 Douglas Johnston and Cynthia Sampson edited *Religion, the Missing Dimension of Statecraft*, Oxford University Press, New York, NY, 1994.

was able to secure the surrender of arms from military groups in a situation where government and trans-government officials did not have the trust to successfully play that role.

Many other countries around the world have seen religious leaders play strategic roles in bringing peace, including providing mediation to end armed conflicts. What had once been scorned by top-level government leaders has now been seen as a potential major resource to bring peace to hot conflicts. Professional mediators, diplomats, and scholars have even given a formal name to the type of work that the Nicaraguan church leaders carried out in partnership with Lederach: Track II Diplomacy. Track I is the efforts for peace made by governmental and international diplomats. Track II is the action taken by "non-state actors," nongovernmental organizations, often led by religious leaders.

Awards and Recognitions

Gustavo Parajón received numerous awards and honors for his work in health care and peacemaking. The American Baptist churches gave him the Dahlberg Peace Award in 1981, an award first given to Martin Luther King Jr. The award was for his peace and development work, both prior to the Contra War and for the peace efforts to end that war. That same year, his alma mater, Denison University, granted him a Doctor of Humane Letters degree. Denison also established a scholarship to be awarded each year to a student from a traditionally underrepresented population who has excelled academically and has demonstrated leadership and service in the community. Given Gustavo's deep personal investment in students, this scholarship likely meant more to him than the honors focused on him. Following the peace initiatives that helped end the Contra War, Parajón was nominated by former President Jimmy Carter for the Nobel Peace Prize. In 2002, at the commemoration of the 150th anniversary of the founding of Managua, Dr. Parajón was awarded the Sesquicentennial Medallion as an Outstanding Citizen of Managua.

In July 2006, Gustavo was given the Human Rights Award by the Baptist World Alliance in Mexico City. In his speech, he tied together his concerns for poverty and war, seeing the former as the driving force toward the latter. He said, "Poverty is the number one problem in Nicaragua. Poverty always brings about an increase of violence, especially against women and children." Parajón went on to say he worked with "humble men and women, poor in the material sense but rich in the spiritual sense that felt peace was the norm that was what Jesus Christ was asking us to have."[47]

Perhaps the most meaningful award was presented on October 17, 2006 by the Central American Parliament (PARLACEN). They awarded Dr. Parajón the

---

47 EthicDaily.com, "Nicaragua Baptist to Receive Human Rights Award" by Robert Parham.

Francisco Morazán medallion for his work for peace and reconciliation related to the war between the Nicaraguan revolutionary government and the Contra insurgents. The ceremony was held at the First Baptist Church of Managua, a historic occasion. No session for PARLACEN had ever been convened in a Protestant church in this heavily Catholic region. Such was the respect accorded to Dr. Parajón across Central America.

Among the participants was a large delegation from Nueva Guinea, including many who had served on that local peace commission. One of the Contra leaders in the region, Comandante Gallo, came for the occasion to honor this peacemaker. The church was filled with many diplomats, officials, and people from across Nicaragua connected with Dr. Parajón's life and work. Usually at such a momentous event, the Nicaraguan national anthem would be sung by the Nicaraguan military choir, but this time everyone was led by the Parajón-Domínguez Choir of First Baptist Church, directed by Joan Parajón. Gustavo Parajón wasn't the only one honored. The entire Protestant community out of which he came and that had worked with and through him in such a transformative way in Nicaragua was recognized.

Dr. Gustavo walking in rural communities in PROVADENIC era.

Dr. Gustavo singing songs during devotional with AMOS health promoters.

Dr. Gustavo teaching AMOS health promoters about the Bible.

AMOS health promoters with Dr. Gustavo Parajón (center front)
and Dr. David Parajón (back right).

From PROVADENIC to AMOS

Dr. Parajón observed a major difference between health needs in the U.S. and in Nicaragua and other poor countries. In the U.S., major causes of health problems are overeating, lack of exercise, and anxiety. In Nicaragua, health problems are primarily related to poverty: polluted water, malnutrition, lack of prenatal care for pregnant women, and lack of simple immunization programs for children. Some of these same problems may be found in poor communities in the U.S., but with poverty rates so much higher in Nicaragua, the health effects of poverty are massive and endemic.

Health care was the centerpiece for Gustavo's mission work when he and Joan first came to Nicaragua in 1968. PROVADENIC was the vehicle for his vision of community-based health care to take shape and reach so many of the rural areas that had received no care at all. Forty years later, however, Gustavo's dreams were going to crumble and then be raised up again in a strong, renewed way. At the center of this new chapter of health care ministry, Gustavo's son, David, and his wife, Laura, would be pivotal leaders.

When David Parajón met Laura Chanchien, the key to going on their first date was that Laura could speak Spanish and knew who Paulo Freire was! David had participated in a literacy program in Nicaragua at age 15, teaching adults to read and write using Paulo Freire's participatory methods. Laura had used Freirian methods in teaching English as a second language to immigrants in Rhode Island when she was in college at Brown. After their relationship began to grow, Laura met Gustavo and learned about his work.

Laura and David were married during their training in medical residencies at the University of New Mexico in 1995. In 1999, they visited Nicaragua after Hurricane Mitch devastated the country and region and were deeply moved by the destruction they saw. They were also deeply inspired by the resilience of the people and the great work done by the health promoters of PROVADENIC. They witnessed up close the relief and reconstruction work that Gustavo was coordinating that involved people not only from Nicaragua, but also from many U.S. churches sending mission teams to rural Nicaragua to help rebuild communities.

Two years later, after David's and Laura's medical and public health training was done and they felt called to overseas missions, they connected with International Ministries. Initially, International Ministries planned to assign them to Rwanda, but the situation there changed. Instead, they were assigned to go to Nicaragua to help PROVADENIC and the ongoing reconstruction process that involved many churches. Laura loved the vision of primary care and community health she had seen in Gustavo's work and, along with David, agreed to a five-year term, which became much longer! David and Laura were commissioned as International Ministries missionaries to Nicaragua at the 2001 World Mission Conference in Green Lake, Wisconsin, when their children were almost 1, 3 and 5 years old.

Problems with PROVADENIC

When David and Laura arrived in Managua, they joined Gustavo at PROVADENIC. After a couple of years of working alongside Gustavo, getting to work with all of the health promoters, helping to strengthen the medical aspects of the program and working alongside mission teams, Gustavo retired. Laura became the medical director of PROVADENIC, working under a board appointed by the Baptist Convention of Nicaragua. Laura had learned on the job, including dramatically upgrading her Spanish skills. As a physician and public health professional coming from the U.S., navigating the landscape of working in Nicaragua was extremely challenging for Laura when she started. She said about that period, "Gustavo had an ability to know when you needed help, and when you just needed a little nudge."

Soon, a crisis forced them to reconfigure their work. The Baptist Hospital was in terrible financial shape, so David was brought in by the Baptist Convention board as the new medical director with a team of professionals to try to pull the hospital through the crisis, because collapse was on the horizon. David had earned a master's in public health from Johns Hopkins University that included training and administrative experience in the U.S., prompting the invitation to join the team to work on the hospital. During the three years he was at the Baptist Hospital, David earned a master's in business administration at INCAE and was appointed general director for the hospital. David and the team of professionals who worked to rescue the hospital secured funds to remodel critical areas of the hospital, they stabilized the finances, and helped to identify and form new young leaders. One of those young leaders later became general director of the Hospital Bautista, Dr. Juan Carlos Solís.

Though Laura had been trained in public health and family medicine in the U.S., nothing had prepared her for the intricacies of being the medical director managing a church-based nonprofit in Latin America. Gustavo helped her learn how to work in such an organization and to gain needed skills. She learned on the job how to work with a board, how to read a balance sheet so as to organize finances, and how to address human resources issues. Gustavo connected Laura to Sandy Strachan from the Strachan Foundation. Sandy became her mentor for organizational development and coached her in leadership skills, such as aligning staff and supporters in their mission and vision, and organizing finances at the intersection of the church world and good business. Gustavo also connected Laura with the many churches that had been supporting and visiting the rural communities as partners in the work.

Over the next few years, PROVADENIC became more successful and expanded its reach to remote communities. Its budget showed steady annual growth. However, a turning point came when all of the members of the board were replaced by new members who were not familiar with the work. It became clear to both Gustavo and Laura that the new board of PROVADENIC was not interested in the original mission of community-based primary health care in remote rural areas. The coming of the new board coincided with the end of David and Laura's five-year missionary cycle. Frustrated by this situation and the complexity of working in another country, Laura resigned from PROVADENIC and was ready to go back to New Mexico. Gustavo challenged her: "Then who is going to fight the good fight?" "I don't know; not me!" Laura responded. Gustavo listened to her frustration, but then he lifted up all the babies, all the mothers, and all the clinics that were affected. There were also many other communities in dire need of health care in other areas of the country that had already heard about the work of PROVADENIC. These new communities were ready to get started. Laura couldn't leave them. He told Laura that she had "earned a doctorate in life and public health" in Nicaragua and could start all over and do it better with all the lessons they had learned at PROVADENIC. He said, "The best social justice thing you can do right now is not leave. But if you stay and build back better, you have done the social justice thing for the poor." He encouraged her to be patient and look for the prize to serve God and the poorest people.

Gustavo backed up his caring words with caring action. Laura was far from her family back in the U.S., so Gustavo gave her extra support and care. He would bring little corn tortillas for her, doing small acts of kindness to let her know he cared. With Gustavo's encouragement, Laura and David provided the leadership that built a dynamic new ministry for public health.

Together with other Nicaraguan leaders, and through CEPAD, the Parajóns started afresh by looking at another region of the country, Boaco, where the communities had been on a waiting list because of huge needs for health care. With the community needs in mind, they began to imagine how to carry forward the mission and vision of PROVADENIC, the mission of working alongside communities in their journey to build health, doing WITH communities, not doing FOR, nor doing TO, but with participatory methods and local leadership building at the core. Through the vision and work of Gustavo, now carried forward by a new generation, a new organization was born, called AMOS Health and Hope, or simply AMOS. The method they chose to implement their mission was using an empowerment and partnership model to align community, government, churches, and universities at the national and international level to build a movement for community-based primary health care.

Gustavo, David and Laura's network of friends and donors assembled quickly. José Norat from International Ministries pledged moral support if the churches would provide missionary support to David and Laura. Many churches stepped forward and pledged moral, prayer, and financial support for David and Laura's missionary support, as well as for helping new communities in need and expanding to unreached areas. Charitable organizations like the Strachan Foundation pledged support and made a major grant. Sandy Strachan continued to coach Laura about building a better board and developing sound organizational structures. Garth Hewitt boosted morale by writing a song about the new work. Many mission teams came to Nicaragua and went to the rural areas to share and work alongside the people, enduring the hardships of rural Nicaragua. Most importantly, many people in churches far and near, from many denominations, promised to provide support, and followed through.

A founding meeting was held in Muskegon, Michigan in the U.S. to launch the new health organization. As always, Gustavo was deeply embedded in the Scriptures in his thinking. He shared the story in Genesis 13 about the conflict between Abraham (Abram) and Lot. Sparked by a conflict between their shepherds, Abraham took his nephew to a high point to look out over the land. Abraham gave Lot the first choice of where to go, saying he would go the other way. PROVADENIC was the organization Gustavo had built and given so much of himself to its work, but now others were leading with a different vision. Following the example of Abraham, Gustavo was not willing to put up a nasty fight to try to control PROVADENIC. There were enough communities needing health care that they could go another way. As Gustavo said, "We will start something new."

The group engaged in brainstorming about how to move forward. They formed a board for the new organization, with Gustavo as the founding president, made up of Gilberto Aguirre, Dámaris Albuquerque, Octavio Cortés, Sixto Ulloa, Dr. Bill Cumming, Dr. Kevin Lake, Dr. Bob McElroy, the Rev. Tim Spring, and Royce Jones, soon to be joined by medical professionals and key donors and friends from the U.S. and Nicaragua.

Sadly, without the leadership of the Parajóns, PROVADENIC floundered and closed within two years. When Gustavo was asked if he felt sad to see PROVADENIC's work of forty years come to an end, he replied that he had much to celebrate! He cited Luke 4:18-19, saying that through all those who came to do this work, the good news had been proclaimed to the poor, as the communities empowered themselves through the health promoters, the community members, the mission teams, and all who had been involved throughout the years to help bring health and life to so many children and women in communities.

Launching of AMOS

In 2006, AMOS Health and Hope was officially founded as a Christian non-profit to continue the development of a comprehensive model of health care for poor and marginalized communities. It kept to the vision of community-based primary health care embodied in PROVADENIC and expressed in the Alma-Ata document that Gustavo had helped create. The Alma-Ata Declaration of 1978 (the World Health Organization's International Conference on Primary Health Care, see Chapter 10) emerged as a major milestone of the 20th century in the field of public health, and it identified primary health care as the key to the attainment of the goal of "Health for All." With a new generation of health professionals and decades of experience, AMOS refined the model while retaining the foundation expressed at Alma-Ata. The key was still training local leaders in the villages to be health workers.

They came up with the acronym of AMOS: A Ministry Of Sharing. Amos was a biblical prophet who stood for the poor and social justice. Gustavo did have one concern about the name, as it was so close to that of CEPAD's dear partner in the U.K.: Amos Trust. After consulting Garth Hewitt, they all decided it was okay because the mission and visions of both AMOS organizations were centered on justice, and the way the justice work was implemented in the organizations were different and yet complimentary. Garth gave his full blessing to the new ministry. The Rev. Tim Spring from North Hills Community Baptist Church in Pennsylvania came up with the idea that AMOS Health and Hope also stood for A Ministry Of Sharing Health and Hope, an idea that everyone liked and kept.

They had a pressing need for a place from which to operate. AMOS began working out of a warehouse of CEPAD, setting up a small office. CEPAD had the building on the outskirts of Managua on the edge of a volcanic crater called Nejapa. The run-down building had broken windows. There was an old swimming pool full of leaves and debris. As David looked at the property, he felt there were lots of possibilities. Tim Spring, a pastor from Pennsylvania who became the AMOS treasurer, was with David as they looked over the site and said, "David, you are a man of faith!"

All along the way, Gustavo kept encouraging Laura, "You need to do this, too, because God wants you to!" David and Laura recruited new people to the work team, one of whom was medical student Roberto Martinez, the one-time First Baptist youth leader who had gone on to medical school at the Nicaraguan National University, and was highly recommended by Gustavo. "Toño," as he was called, served at AMOS as coordinator of rural health work and eventually became chair of the board of AMOS.

The old PROVADENIC clinics and health promoters had been left stranded by the collapse of that ministry. The community leaders developed and trained over the years did not sit passively after their organizational support dissolved. Quickly, they began to look for support from other organizations. Upon hearing of the establishment of AMOS, many of the former PROVADENIC clinics and health promoters made contact. Many of them joined AMOS as resources to support them became available. It was inspiring to see that even with the lack of organizational support and few material resources, the health promoters had continued to care for their communities with what they had at hand. They had continued to implement the low-cost preventive strategies they had learned, such as home visitations to check on newborn babies and their mothers. These local health providers showed AMOS that the most important resource of the ministry was committed people who had it in their hearts to serve those in need in their communities, a biblical principle, which was the foundation of both PROVADENIC and AMOS.

The needs were still urgent, measured in human suffering. While child mortality rates had greatly decreased in the past fifty years, inequities still persisted in Nicaragua in access to health care, mortality, and health outcomes. A poor child in Nicaragua was still 3.3 times more likely to die than a child who was not poor. According to the World Bank, the poorest people in Nicaragua still had the least access to health facilities. Though PROVADENIC had done great work over the years, there were still so many people in desperate need, especially in the poor rural communities. In communities unreached by PROVADENIC and then later by AMOS, many children were still dying from preventable and easily treated diseases. Too many pregnant women were dying from postpartum hemorrhaging.

As with PROVADENIC, communities in partnership with AMOS would identify their priority needs. One community identified the need for an elementary school, so AMOS helped build the school that was then used also as the center for the work of the community health workers. Some communities had severe water problems because of dust or being fouled by animals. Water filters were brought in, resulting in better health and lives saved.

Mission teams continued to be a vital part of the ministry of AMOS as they had for PROVADENIC. Churches would send teams to AMOS with a specific community-identified project in mind. The mission teams often included different kinds of professionals, often health related, making it possible to do several different types of activities simultaneously while in the rural communities. They labored alongside community members in the blazing hot sun or in the rain and mud. They used flashlights to go to the outhouses at night, slept on cots or hammocks, bathed in insect repellent, took bucket baths, and ate Nicaraguan food like gallo pinto, a traditional beans and rice dish. Teams would bring tools and funds to build. They often brought materials for children: books to read, toys, coloring books, and crayons. Most important was the message of love incarnated in their presence. With these friends coming to work alongside them, people living in remote villages felt they were not forgotten and that they mattered.

Public Health Ministry Continues to Grow

AMOS utilized the community-based primary health care (CBPHC) model. In their words, "CBPHC is a comprehensive health intervention that links existing health systems with community health workers at the local level who can implement simple, lifesaving interventions in their communities to address the challenge of achieving 'Health for All.'" Laura, David, and Gustavo secured five years of funding through the Strachan Foundation. They built up support from many churches, other foundations, and concerned individuals, allowing AMOS to get off to a strong start.

Building on the CBPHC model was the development of public health research consistent with the model. Community-based participatory research involved community leaders and health care workers in shaping and conducting the research that could ultimately inform and impact health care in their context. Through use of elicitive questions, following the educational model of Paulo Freire, local people became active participants in the research. AMOS became a dynamic learning organization as its staff learned more about their community partners and their experience and could thus shift what they were doing to be more effective. AMOS continues to grow today, putting forth a powerful vision for health for all people, grounded in the biblical values that Gustavo and the whole AMOS team placed at the heart of the ministry.

Gustavo's favorite place at AMOS was the circle of rocking chairs near the entrance. For him, the circle was a symbol of everyone being equal. He would sit and chat with guests and visitors, asking about their story and what their lives were about. Gustavo never imposed his views on others, rather he mostly listened and learned from them. He helped mission teams build their community as they discussed together. Throughout these rocking chair discussions, he lived out his belief in the ability of all people to make a difference in this world. He had seen so much division, from wars in the nations to wars in the churches. His aim was to bring people of all faiths, beliefs, and politics together to help build a future of mercy and justice. Sitting and talking together in rocking chairs was one small communal action toward that future.

Cardinal Obando y Bravo sitting next to Marta Parajón in First Baptist Church of Managua at a Memorial Service for Dr. Gustavo Parajón.

Gustavo Parajón's casket carried into First Baptist Church Managua.

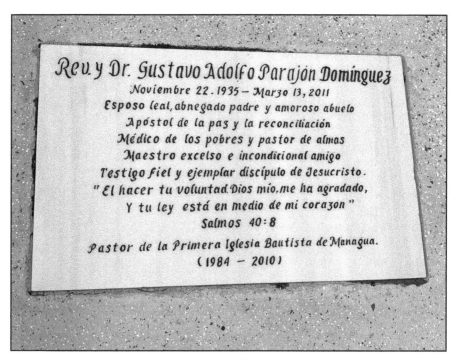

Gravestone for Gustavo Adolfo Parajón Domínguez.

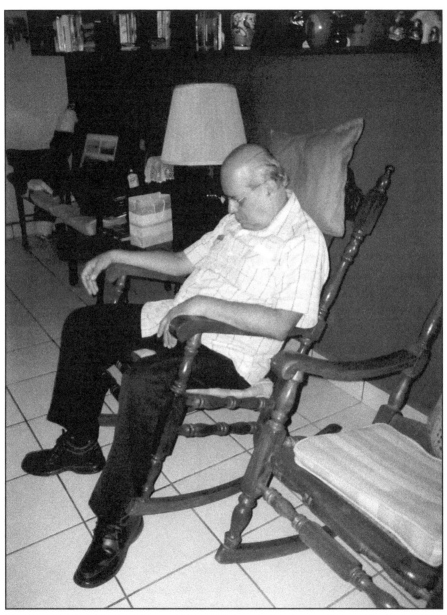

Gustavo catching a nap in a rocking chair at Marta's house the day before he died.

Joan and Gustavo.

Death and Legacy

Last Days

On June 8, 2009, Gustavo and Joan Parajón celebrated their 50th wedding anniversary. The celebration was held at First Baptist Managua, the church that had been such a special community for their ministries and their life together. The church was also the extended family that took Gustavo in when both his parents died. For all the ups and downs, First Baptist had been a healing community for Gustavo and a place where Joan flourished.

Less than two years later on March 13, 2011, Gustavo Parajón died. As friends shared their stories together, many at CEPAD and the church recalled conversations with him that previous week in which he showed special care to them. After choir rehearsal Saturday evening, Gustavo said goodbye and hugged many of the folks. Normally, Gustavo would head home early to give pastoral space for Joel Sierra. However, this time he lingered even though he wasn't feeling so well. Looking back, many thought that Gustavo was saying goodbye to people, at least subconsciously.

Early Sunday morning, Marta was awakened by a call from Joan: "Papi is lying on the floor in the kitchen! He's not breathing!" Marta and Denis leaped out of bed and rushed over. Denis performed mouth-to-mouth resuscitation. Marta did CPR on his chest. Nothing worked. Marta called David, who was out camping with Laura and the kids. David raced over to the house. Though his body was still warm, Gustavo was gone.

Joan tried to contact her dear friends at First Baptist Church in Cleveland. She reached the church office and said, "I need to talk to Martin (Rolfs-Massaglia, the pastor)." The person on the phone said Martin was teaching in a class. Joan urged, "I need to talk to Martin NOW!" Martin was interrupted and came to the phone to hear from Joan that Gus had passed away. Nancy Wheaton was traveling. After many phone calls, it was decided that Martin and Jim Knauf would represent the church at the funeral. Nancy came later to provide support for Joan and the family after all the activity around the funeral had quieted down. She spent three hard and precious weeks with Joan.

By the time the news reached the U.K., it was too late to get to Nicaragua for the funeral. Garth and Gill Hewitt's daughter Abi was in Los Angeles, so she caught a flight to represent all the dear friends in Greenbelt and Amos Trust. Both organizations later held memorial services for Gustavo.

This may have been the way Gustavo had wanted to die. A few months earlier, his dear cousin Guillermo Parajón-Fletes died slowly, not eating and just wasting away. Gustavo told his family, "May God deliver me from a long death, suffering and making you all suffer." He didn't want to be a burden for his family. The doctor didn't want to be hooked up to tubes. He gave a directive not to resuscitate. He made Marta promise to do all to keep him alive; but if nothing could be done, let him go. Marta was thankful she didn't have to make that decision to disconnect or not. Grace was experienced along with the sorrow.

Funeral

There were many funeral and memorial services held for Gustavo Parajón. Five services were held at First Baptist Church, and each one filled the church with different people. After learning about Gustavo's death, Pastor Joel Sierra reworked the plans for the main Sunday service, as everyone's mind was filled with thoughts about their long-standing pastor. Sixto Ulloa took care of the funeral arrangements for the family. Gustavo's body had been taken from the Parajón home to the Baptist Hospital, from where he was transferred to the funeral home. By mid-afternoon, they had brought his body back to First Baptist for a first memorial service. The church was so packed that another service was held later in the evening, with time for many people to share about how Gustavo had made an impact in their lives.

Two more services were held on Monday, again with long lines of people sharing how Dr. Parajón had been a father, a friend, a mentor, or a confidant to them. People from across Nicaraguan society participated: intellectuals, politicians, musicians, health workers, directors of various organizations, church members young and old, and ordinary Nicaraguans whose lives had been valued and touched by this man of God. People shared story after story about how the good doctor had helped them.

The main funeral service was held on Tuesday. First Baptist Church was beyond capacity, with seven or eight hundred people jammed in and people even overflowing into the parking lot. Music filled the church, as it had meant so much to Gustavo. Gustavo's granddaughter Cristina, in the ninth grade at that time, read her poem "Las Guayaberas de Mi Abuelito," "My Grandpa's Guayaberas." The final number from the Parajón-Domínguez Choir was Handel's "Hallelujah Chorus." At the end of the service, in a very emotional moment, the granddaughters accompanied Marta to sing a lullaby Gustavo used to sing to them, "El Arenero" ("The Sandman") with the final words: "close your eyes and go to sleep." As his coffin was carried out of the church on the shoulders of dear friends and colleagues, the crowd spontaneously stood up, applause breaking out in appreciation for the one who had been their shepherd for thirty years. Those present remember that moment as profound, special, and full of love.

Following the funeral at First Baptist, Gustavo's body was taken to the Casa de los Pueblos, the Presidential Palace, for a state funeral. The event was broadcast throughout the country. The Nicaraguan flag was placed upon his coffin. President Daniel Ortega gave Joan Parajón the Cultural Independence Order Rubén Darío in recognition of the valuable contribution made by her husband to attain peace in Nicaragua after a long, bitter war. After President Ortega and his wife spoke, Marta spontaneously spoke about her father's great love to serve God all his life and how that motivated his special love for the poor. Then Joan recited a moving and powerful poem by the Nicaraguan poet Rubén Darío about social justice, "Hemos de Ser Justos" ("We Must Be Just").

At the conclusion of the state funeral, a huge procession left the Presidential Palace to lay Dr. Gustavo Adolfo Parajón Domínguez to rest in the Parajón-Domínguez family gravesite in the Cementerio Occidental de Managua. His grandchildren assisted the church youth in holding the ropes to lower his casket into the grave. The coffin was blanketed in a Nicaraguan flag, and the choir sang E.M. Bartlett's "Ya Tengo La Victoria, Victory in Christ." At the graveside, there were more prayers, readings from the Bible, and songs. Many seemed reluctant to let go of this beloved man, so it was getting dark when the service ended. Cathy Strachan Lindenberg captured the feelings of so many in a message she sent to those who couldn't be there: "I think we left the cemetery about 7 p.m., everyone exhausted, but with great gratitude in our hearts for having the privilege of our lives touched by such an extraordinary gentle, loving, compassionate man, who listened well without judgment, and who encouraged and believed in those he ministered to, always concerned about greater social and economic equality and justice for all. I was so grateful to have been one of these persons."

The day after the funerals, CEPAD's staff and the General Assembly held a memorial service at their facility. The family wasn't present, but this was a more intimate time of sorrow and celebration for the man who brought the organization into being. Those who had worked alongside him and had been mentored and trained by him had their own special time of remembrance together.

The following Sunday, the Roman Catholic Cardinal Miguel Obando y Bravo attended the morning worship at First Baptist Church. He had been out of the country when Dr. Parajón died. The cardinal came in his clerical garb and spoke in honor of Gustavo Parajón, who had served with him on the National Reconciliation Commission.

Cardinal Obando y Bravo's presence marked a historic event in Nicaragua because it was the first time that a Roman Catholic cardinal visited a Protestant church. Marta was asked to give some words on behalf of the family. She thanked the cardinal for coming and spoke of the meaning of his visit, which showed the great respect he had for her dad. She mentioned that her dad always promoted ecumenism in the country, especially since historically there had been a great divide. She related the experiences her dad had shared when he would travel out of Managua to visit churches with his father. Once, when Gustavo was a child, they had to close all the windows and doors of the small Baptist church building because the local Catholic priest was leading a group of people from the town armed with sticks and stones to attack the church. Marta said that they had come a long way in learning to live together and share their faith that united them. Proof of that relatively new unity was the presence of the cardinal in the Baptist church. It was a historic moment.

First Baptist had another service later in the month to celebrate the life of Gustavo Parajón. There were special testimonies by close associates, dear friends, and people he had mentored. Gustavo's closest friend, El Profe Gilberto Aguirre, delivered the message. The Parajón-Domínguez Choir sang throughout the service, and Joan read a poem.

During the disarmament efforts that Dr. Parajón led following the end of the war in Nicaragua in 1990, 1,115 decommissioned weapons were buried in the central park of Nueva Guinea. A monument for peace was erected where the destroyed weapons were buried. The Zonal Peace Commission held a special commemoration at the park and the peace memorial on the same day as the funerals in Managua. Those gathered decided to dedicate that monument to the memory of this peacemaker. Later, a plaque was placed on the monument that read: Monument for Peace, Gustavo Adolfo Parajón Domínguez. "Blessed are the peacemakers, for they will be called sons of God." (Matthew 5:9)

For those gathered in Nueva Guinea, it was a recognition not only for Dr. Parajón's work for peace, but also for his dedication to the region, action that went back to the years when he first traveled to bring health to the scattered communities in Nueva Guinea. The Zonal Peace Commission members continue to uphold the motto they learned from Gustavo and used during those hard days of conciliation and disarmament: "Seek the prosperity of the city where I have sent you, and pray to the Lord on its behalf. In its peace you will have peace." (Jer. 29:7)[48]

Carrying On the Legacy: Institutions

Of all the institutions Gustavo Parajón had led, First Baptist Church of Managua had the most difficult time after his death. Dr. Parajón retired from the pastorate of First Baptist in June 2010. Gustavo thought that the Mexican musician and seminary graduate Joel Sierra would be a perfect fit for the church as the next pastor. Joan had first met Joel at a music conference in Costa Rica in 1986. Joan invited him to come to Nicaragua. Joel and his wife, Evita, moved and worked there for almost a year, from 1989 to 1990. Joel's main project during the time they were in Nicaragua was to put together a hymnal of some of the favorite songs used by Baptists around the world. After Joel and Evita left, Gustavo and Joan stayed in close touch with them.

As the time approached for his retirement, Gustavo worked to build up support to bring Joel Sierra to be pastor, including raising the money for the salary Joel requested. Gustavo was willing to leave the church to not cause problems for the new pastor. However, the Parajón family insisted that they would stay at First Baptist Managua, since it was their long-standing home church. Joel also insisted that Gustavo stay. Everything seemed on track for a good transition.

But within months, it was all unraveling. Whereas First Baptist had developed lay leadership that was well trained and engaged in many aspects of the church's administration and participation in the worship services, Joel's style was to not delegate and make most of the decisions, as well as leading the worship, hymns, and preaching. Since that was so different from Gustavo and how the church had functioned, a clash developed between Joel and most of the church leadership. He also sought to implement many significant changes, but too quickly and without the necessary congregational support. Historically, the church had internal conflicts that Gustavo had managed to constructively resolve through his peacemaking skills and personal engagement. He always encouraged dialogue and allowed everyone a fair chance to speak, including his own critics. Once Gustavo died, the glue that held the church together in relative peace was gone. Conflict erupted, and Joel found himself in a very difficult situation. One group found their champion in Joel, resulting in a huge and deep rift in the congregation. Under these circumstances, it was impossible to implement the changes he wanted to

---

48 Gran Águila, by Dr. Rolando Escobar-Doña, published by CEPAD, 2012.

make in the church, and he formally resigned in April 2012. He left in June to return to Mexico, less than two years after he had arrived to be pastor.

Even after Joel Sierra's departure, the arguments continued, leading to a formal split of the church in February 2013. Those supporting Joel left to form another church. They stayed in contact with Pastor Sierra, even having him preach at times via Zoom.

The church leadership, along with approximately two-thirds of the congregation, remained in the sanctuary. The choir shrank to thirty-two members after some went with the split-off congregation. Joan Parajón continued to direct the choir. The choir became inactive for the first time during the COVID-19 pandemic from 2020 to 2022.

The deacons led the congregation until six years later, when Marta Parajón was called by the congregation to be the pastor. She had never spoken much in public, but the moment her father died, she felt a transfer of his spirit, similar to what had happened to Elisha when Elijah was taken up into heaven (2 Kings 2). Marta discovered she had words to say. Earlier she could only envision herself leading songs, or working with the youth, but anything else in front of the congregation was beyond her imagination, especially preaching. After her father's death and the split of the congregation, she felt deeply that God was calling her, so she stepped into the new role. Her father was so large in her awareness that Marta couldn't imagine having become a pastor while he was still alive. Yet as her ministry grew, she sometimes ached with the desire to talk to him as a mentor in ministry with whom she could consult. She imagines, "When I preach, I can feel my dad smiling down!"

Before Gustavo died, he had seen the demise of PROVADENIC, but this heartache was countered by the launching of AMOS under the leadership of Laura and David. AMOS thrived and grew beyond what PROVADENIC had been and reached areas where CEPAD had not been working either. Though AMOS started as a venture of Baptists, it quickly became ecumenical, with many churches, denominations, foundations, and even universities involved. Besides providing the community-based primary health care so central to their vision, they also participated in providing service and learning opportunities for medical, nursing, and public health students. AMOS coordinated global health courses for these students. AMOS also provided opportunities and utilized short-term and long-term volunteers and short-term mission teams who immersed themselves into the AMOS work.

The Nicaraguan government health department increasingly recognized the importance of the AMOS model as it was explained to them and as the results of the work of the health promoters was brought to their attention. Health promoters saved the lives of women and children in the rural areas, sometimes by referring patients to the government health clinics or hospitals kilometers away in a timely way. They also assisted in making sure all of the children in their communities got vaccinated during national vaccination campaigns. The health promoters made sure that pregnant women in remote rural communities went to the city for pre-natal checkups by physicians, coordinating well in these ways with government health workers.

Shortly after Gustavo's death, AMOS received a major donation of a new facil-ity in 2012 that had been used for medical work by a Southern Baptist missionary couple, Dr. Nour and Carolina Sirker. When Carolina became ill with advanced ovarian cancer, Dr. Sirker decided to take care of her full time. Sadly, her cancer did not respond to the various therapies, and her death devastated Dr. Sirker, lead-ing him to retire. Meanwhile, the AMOS board had decided to find and purchase a new property because they had outgrown the property that had once been a CEPAD warehouse. AMOS was growing by leaps and bounds, with increasing numbers of students, volunteers, and mission teams coming to visit. It became normal to have many tables, chairs, and even cots for sleeping at night out under the mango trees in the yard because there was simply no more room in the AMOS compound.

After exhausting all real estate options, the board of AMOS asked David and others to keep looking. In what was undoubtedly a "God-incidence," David remembered Dr. Sirker from the days of his work at the Hospital Bautista and called him to ask if he had any suggestions. The call reached Dr. Sirker just as he was in Ft. Lauderdale visiting his home church to discuss the future of the property. They were looking for another ministry to which to transfer the property so that it could be used for the Kingdom. The timing was perfect. The board of Dr. Sirker's ministry and the board of AMOS got together, and the property was transferred for use by AMOS. It became the new AMOS headquarters and a training center, as well as the first urban clinic that AMOS managed. Thanks to the generosity of donors, the property was developed under the leadership of Laura and David Parajón, with the expansion of existing structures and addition of several buildings, including a conference and training center and dorms for the many mission teams passing through.

In 2018, Laura stepped down as medical director of AMOS to take a part-time job at the University of New Mexico. She began to travel back and forth between the U.S. and Nicaragua before going full time at the University of New Mexico in 2020. Meanwhile, David continued as executive director of AMOS for another year and a half, having been trapped in Nicaragua due to the COVID pandemic and the closing of international travel. In late 2020, he moved to New Mexico to rejoin Laura. Dr. Gabriella Woo then became executive director. Dr. Woo had worked closely with Laura in AMOS for nine years, working her way up before stepping into this new role. Dr. Roberto Martinez is the president of the board as of this writing. The new leadership of AMOS has grown from within the organization and knows their health ministry paradigm thoroughly, a testimony to the careful design and development of Gustavo, David, and Laura Parajón.

When the COVID pandemic hit, AMOS was struck particularly hard. Not only was it a health crisis, as AMOS had experienced with other diseases such as Zika, but it was also a crisis that shut off the flow of mission teams. Mission teams provided much volunteer labor, but they also provided funding for AMOS through funds for the community projects as well as covering their accommodations and food. Many of those teams and the churches they came from provided additional donations beyond the time of the trips themselves, often becoming regular donors after seeing the work firsthand. When the pandemic hit, AMOS had to deal with financial cuts and some staff cuts. As of this writing, AMOS is recovering and stabilizing.

CEPAD had gone through multiple leadership transitions while Gustavo was still alive. In early 2001, he stepped down as the president of the board. In April 2001, Dámaris Albuquerque became the executive director. Gustavo was named president emeritus of the board. He attended every meeting, but no longer presided. He let the new leadership lead without him questioning everything. When he died, the CEPAD staff and board were able to continue without missing a beat because they had been working in leading roles for ten years. Dámaris lost her personal advisor and mentor when Gustavo died, but she continued carrying on with the ministry, being assisted by her husband, Gilberto Aguirre. In June 2020, Gilberto died, and by December, Dámaris resigned. She continued to serve as an advisor to the new director Emily Reyes, making sure that the vision and mission of the initial founders was not forgotten. After almost fifty years of dynamic service, new generations of leaders are stepping forth. As with AMOS, the leadership transitions at CEPAD were a sign of the vibrant leadership models and leadership development practiced by Gustavo, Gilberto, Dámaris, and many others over the years.

Dr. Parajón had practiced rigorous administrative analysis and planning, and he taught those skills to the younger leaders growing up within the organization. CEPAD still uses what he taught in their training of new staff. The result is an organization with administrative focus and clarity along with a disciplined approach to solving problems.

From 2001 to the present, CEPAD has been working on five-year cycles with a number of communities in community development initiatives. The core programs under community development are: Community Leadership Formation, Agricultural and Environmental Promotion, Women's Empowerment, and Strengthening Pastoral Leadership. These programs have been working in over forty communities in six regions of the country for each five-year cycle. When Gustavo died, CEPAD had worked through two cycles involving forty-two communities in each cycle.

In 2021, CEPAD started another cycle, adding a new region and six more communities. So CEPAD now works in forty-seven communities in seven regions with their community development programs. Besides these core programs, CEPAD is strong in other activities and its administrative core. There is the Attention to Refugees Program, the International Relations Department, Radio CEPAD, a high school in León, the Planning, Monitoring and Evaluation Department, and the Financial and Administration Department. A total of seventy staff people work at CEPAD. It continues as a strong, vibrant ecumenical organization making a positive impact among poor communities throughout the country as a vital expression of their Christian witness.

Carrying on the Legacy: People

Though Gustavo Parajón founded institutions that have had a massive impact in Nicaragua and even across Central America, the richest legacy he left was in the lives of people he helped shape. Some people spent years under his mentorship. Others just encountered him for a short time that opened new horizons in their thinking and possibilities.

In his family, Gustavo's impact shaped calling and ways of being. In mid-life, Marta became the pastor of First Baptist, following in her father's footsteps in a way she never imagined. Marta, along with the help and support of her husband, Denis, has had the responsibility of leading the church during difficult moments of political unrest in Nicaragua and the COVID-19 pandemic, as well as healing after the events that led up to the church split. David became a missionary medical doctor, inspired by his father's example. Along with his wife, Laura, they navigated the shift from PROVADENIC to AMOS, carrying on the community-based primary health care for which Gustavo had been a visionary. Rebecca's way of reflecting her father is succinctly captured in how she signs her emails: "Live simply. Love generously. Care deeply. Speak kindly."

Gustavo's legacy ripples out and influences the lives of his younger surviving family. His grandchildren and great-grandchildren, both those who were raised with Gustavo and Joan and those who were raised on the stories of them, can draw from the lesson plan of their lives to find inspiration and guidance in how to live a life of compassion and service to others.

Many of the grandchildren show his influence directly and indirectly. As of this writing, Cristina Shannin Parajón is working with the homeless in Albuquerque, New Mexico, having finished college and after working in New York for a couple of years with a management firm. She learned from her grandfather about building bridges to people, navigating bureaucracies, and bringing stakeholders together, skills she utilizes all the time in her efforts with the marginalized in her city.

Davey and Scotty worked in homeless shelters in New Mexico during the COVID crisis. Scotty studies computer science, but rather than cash in for the big dollars in Silicon Valley, he is looking for ways to assist underserved communities. He developed a map to manage isolation and quarantine in the biggest shelter in Albuquerque. He developed a Zika education tool and related computer system that is still being used in Nicaragua to fight the virus. Together, Davey and Scotty developed a similar tool for the state of New Mexico to fight vaccine hesitancy in Hispanic/Latinx communities. They both plan to be involved in medical or public service work for their careers, inspired by their parents and grandfather, and giving their careers twists of their own.

Cynthia Gutiérrez, Gustavo's oldest granddaughter, is the executive director of Cancer Hope Network, based in New Jersey. After majoring in psychology and obtaining a master's in social work, Cynthia has moved up in the organization, which provides help and advice to those diagnosed with cancer and their families. Cynthia uses her skills to work with people as well as showing the compassion she saw modeled by her grandfather.

Debbi's love for teaching is inspired by both Joan's and Gustavo's passion for education and devotion to helping others connect and learn about the world around them. Debbi continues to work as a high school English teacher, where she uses her grandfather's mentorship example as inspiration. She has turned her classroom into a safe space where students are not afraid to share their opinions as they find their voice. Debbi also serves as the director of the Sunday school program at First Baptist Managua, creating fun and interactive spaces for kids to learn about the Bible.

For Raquel and Annie, Gustavo's lessons translated into a passion for accessibility. Raquel completed her undergraduate studies in psychology in order to establish a foundation for a master's in early childhood education. While pursuing her undergraduate degree, she also began teaching herself Nicaraguan sign language in order to be able to further engage with and learn from the deaf community in Nicaragua. Upon completing her studies, Raquel plans to work in public education in Nicaragua to create robust and accessible programs for all children. Annie also studied undergraduate psychology to gain the tools to translate her grandfather's lessons in compassion into action. During the height of the COVID-19 pandemic, she worked with people experiencing homelessness in Bennington County, Vermont, assisting in accessing resources and advocating for individuals and families. She now works in human resources to further her experience in connecting people to each other and to opportunities and resources.

One of Gustavo's major concerns was supporting young Nicaraguans in their quest for quality education. Lidya Ruth Zamora graduated from the Baptist Hospital School of Nursing in Managua in 1971. To further her studies, Dr. Parajón used his Ohio connections to help her get a scholarship through the Ohio Baptist Convention to study for a bachelor's degree in nursing science at Alderson-Broaddus College in West Virginia (now Alderson-Broaddus University). He continued to support her educational development by helping her get scholarships for a master's degree and then later a doctorate in nursing. Zamora then became the first ever female director of the School of Nursing at the Polytechnic University of Nicaragua (UPOLI). Dr. Parajón's support enabled Dr. Zamora to become a major figure in health education in Nicaragua.

As Lidya grew, she realized how her sponsor had taken a special care to nurture and empower young people who were so often overlooked, namely those who were poor. She said, "Now, I recognize that there were some socioeconomic boundaries not talked about in the Baptist churches that he trespassed for the sake of giving people an opportunity to succeed and become leaders who could serve our brothers and sisters in Christ." Gustavo made connections between young people with leadership potential, colleges that could educate them, and scholarship funds to turn what was once impossible into degrees and careers.

Denis Cuéllar was one of the many young leaders from First Baptist that Gustavo took under his wing. Denis mentioned he would like to study medicine in order to help people in need have access to quality health care, but he didn't have the financial means to go to medical school. Congruent with his vision of encouraging young people to obtain an education, Gustavo approached two Baptist churches in Ohio to ask them to sponsor Denis' education as well as that of Ricardo Rodríguez, another young person from the church. The churches generously responded to Gustavo's request. Denis graduated from medical school in León, Nicaragua and went on to specialize in orthopedic surgery and practice in the Baptist Hospital, caring for countless people in need. Denis and Marta married and he is now the president of the board of deacons of First Baptist Managua and head of the finance committee. He preaches on some Sundays and leads Bible studies with a passion, continuing Gustavo's legacy in the church.

Milton Argüello experienced two turning points in his life in a vehicle with Dr. Parajón. The first was when he was a young man hitchhiking with his friend Denis Cuéllar. Gustavo drove by and picked them up, and from that point on Milton became part of the young people at First Baptist. He moved to the U.S. to follow a girlfriend and ended up driving a truck distributing seafood. When Gustavo came to that city, Milton picked him up at the airport. In a truck full of fish, Gustavo asked if he was happy and if he wanted to continue his education. Milton said he did want to go to college. Gustavo got to work with his friends and secured a scholarship for Milton to go to Denison University. Milton graduated and returned to Nicaragua to work for many years at CEPAD and PROVADENIC with his mentor before moving into the business world.

Gustavo's granddaughter Debbi Cuéllar returned to Nicaragua after Gustavo's death to be with her grandmother. Fresh out of college, Debbi was drifting a bit, trying to figure out what direction to take her sociology and anthropology major with a religion minor and how to make it into a career. She got a job with a cell phone company, where Milton Argüello was the director of human resources and also Debbi's boss. She was struck by how like her grandfather Milton was, his tone of voice and how he treated people. Just like Gustavo had encouraged Milton in his growth, Milton encouraged Debbi to get her master's in English education, launching her teaching career. What Gustavo had been to Milton, Milton became to Debbi, a beautiful circle supporting the development of young lives.

Carlos Martínez was extensively mentored by both Gustavo and Joan Parajón. His amazing potential as a musician was developed in part by Carlos' hard work but also by the guidance received by many people known to Gustavo. Carlos was able to study piano in college in Kansas thanks to Gustavo's contacts. He returned to Nicaragua for some years and was a vital addition to the choir at First Baptist. He performed with them everywhere they went, whether at the National Theater or on tour inside and outside the country. When Nicaragua convulsed in a year of violence in 2018, Carlos left to establish himself in Kentucky. He established a successful school of music which he has been operating full time to help others achieve their potential in music, helping and mentoring them even as he had been helped and mentored by Gustavo and others.

Gustavo had mentored Carlos' younger brother Roberto Martínez from his years in the youth group and choir. Pastor Parajón gave the young man advice and direction, often alongside perceptive questions that helped Roberto shift from engineering to medicine. Later, as PROVADENIC was imploding and AMOS was being born, Gustavo shared all that was happening with the young man. Roberto wasn't a decision-maker at that point; but Gustavo shared extensively because he could see that Roberto would be a key leader in the future, and Gustavo wanted to help equip him for the serious challenges of leadership. Following his schooling, Dr. Martínez went on to join the staff of AMOS, then later become chair of the board. Roberto directed AMOS when Laura and David were on U.S. assignment for a year. Roberto went to Syracuse University for a master's in public health, after which he attended Case Western Reserve for his doctorate in public health. Roberto has continued on a medical career that ministers to those at the margins, as his mentor did.

In small group leadership settings, Dr. Parajón sometimes raised the question about how to decide what you want to do with your life. He shared the story about refusing Somoza's request for him to testify before Congress that there were no human rights abuses in Nicaragua. He also turned down an offer to be the Nicaraguan minister of health under Somoza. He could have taken that governmental position to try to make a difference in health care, but did not because he knew that the Somoza government was not really interested in either the rural poor or those who were marginalized. Gustavo challenged people to remain true to what God wants you to be in your work. That thinking prompted many young people to make career choices away from lucrative jobs into serving more directly among the poor, wherever they might be.

Blanca Fonseca called Gustavo Parajón her spiritual father. As a young law school intern, she had just finished working in the Penal Justice Office of Nicaragua's Supreme Court of Justice. She was active at First Baptist in Managua, and her pastor counseled her in a way that kept driving her deeper into her relationship with Christ even while seeking her calling. After finding out she had completed her internship, he asked Blanca if she would like to work for a Christian organization that helped the most vulnerable in different aspects. Blanca replied that she had two other job options, but if he wanted, she could go for an interview. Pastor Parajón said, "No, not if I want you to; it's if YOU want to work for people who cannot defend themselves. It is not a big salary, but you can go to the interview if you want." Blanca expressed that she did not know if she was competent enough since she had recently graduated. Dr. Parajón said, "If you work for the Lord, He will help you."

Blanca Fonseca eventually became CEPAD's staff lawyer helping undocumented immigrants (see Chapter 7). But Dr. Parajón helped her grasp the biblical vision that inspired what she was doing. He shared with her the text from Matthew 25 that what we do for the least we do for the Lord along with the many passages that urged us not to forget the orphans, the widows, and the "aliens" or strangers in our land. Gustavo said the immigrants were the most vulnerable ones because they did not have anything: no country, no home, and often in the case of those in Nicaragua, no families. They had abandoned everything in their desperate journey. That was Blanca's first lesson from Dr. Parajón, and she still shares that lesson when she leads workshops. She adds, with the echo from her mentor, "Jesus himself was persecuted and had to flee."

Gustavo's vision and work impacted people from the U.S. who had come to serve in Nicaragua. Ann Hershberger was a young Mennonite woman who went to Nicaragua straight out of college, trained in health care in a typical hospital-centered model. She served under the auspices of Rosedale Mennonite Missions, joining in the work of four PROVADENIC clinics that the Mennonites managed. As Ann experienced the model of community-based public health work Dr. Parajón used to shape PROVADENIC, Ann says she was ruined for hospitals. She learned deeply from Gustavo about how to get health care directly to the communities most in need. After her time in Nicaragua, Ann taught at Eastern Mennonite University in public health for thirty years. She testifies that Gustavo shaped her understanding of health care, and through her Gustavo's impact shaped hundreds of EMU health students. Ann Hershberger is now the executive director of the Mennonite Central Committee U.S., and she brings the ideas and paradigms she learned from Gustavo Parajón into how she leads that agency in its public health ministries across the world.

"Gustavo was the father of my career," is what Deirdre Strachan said. She was one of the "INCAE wives" mobilized by Gustavo to be an early PROVADENIC volunteer team. Her husband, Harry Strachan, was an old family friend and neighbor of Gustavo and president of the training center in organizational and business management. Along with other wives of faculty and staff at INCAE, Deirdre learned about what Gustavo was doing in rural health care and was inspired to get involved. What she experienced and the skills she learned then led her to get her master's, followed by a doctorate in public health at Harvard University. Driven by the encounters in Nicaragua with poor women having multiple pregnancies, she launched her career in reproductive health.

Another "INCAE wife" was Fran Korten. She worked with Gustavo in those early days of PROVADENIC, but the next twenty-five years of her career flowed from what she experienced. As the INCAE women engaged with mothers and pregnant women in the rural communities, they started asking questions about family planning. Gustavo enthusiastically supported them in their initiatives. Later Fran helped develop the Family Planning Program for Central America. Then she and her husband, Dave, edited a book of case studies related to family planning management. They connected to the Ford Foundation, which funded much of their family planning and population control. Fran was then brought into management with the Ford Foundation in Asia. Without her experiences in PROVADENIC and Gustavo's belief in her capabilities and support for her passion to help the women, none of this would have happened.

Cathy Strachan Lindenberg went to Nicaragua to serve in rural public health from 1968 to 1969. Her father and Gustavo were the two people who most influenced her life and direction. Gustavo wrote letters to recommend her for nursing school and public health school. She wrote her master's thesis on PROVADENIC, specifically on a nutritional study of ninety children and beliefs and practices in family planning and nutrition in rural Chinandega. In her late 20s, she joined the staff of the World Health Organization with Dr. Parajón's recommendation. Her basic approach to build from the grassroots up and make health care sustainable came from what she learned from him as her mentor.

Jerry Eve from Scottish Christians for Nicaragua was working at a bank when he met Gustavo. He was struggling with what his vocation should be as he grew in his concern about issues of justice. In hosting Gustavo around the Greenbelt Festival and then in Glasgow, he saw a Christian who had a social conscience. Gustavo got under his skin in a good way, stirring his vision for what he could be. When they parted once at the end of Greenbelt, Jerry felt like a lost soul. Gustavo gave him a hug that connected to Jerry's lostness with love. "Thank you for looking after me," he said, words that were part of the way Gustavo became an anchor in his life. Jerry decided to train for ministry in the Church of Scotland, in which he was ordained in 1995. Jerry's conversations with Gustavo, listening to him speak, and just watching his demeanor was instrumental in igniting the new vision for what his life work might be.

The stories could go on and on, both in Nicaragua and in countries from which people came to visit or where Gustavo traveled. This is just a sampling of those who shared their stories in the process of producing this book.

In Latin America, there is a tradition of acknowledging those who have died as still being present with those who live on. Sometimes this ritual is done as part of a worship service, for communion or the mass. Sometimes it is done in a public vigil or protest. Candles are often lit. The names of the dead are called out, and after each name is spoken those gathered cry out: "Presente!"

Gustavo knew well the biblical image that resonates with this ritual. Hebrews 11 recites the stories of the great figures of faith in the Hebrew Scriptures. Then Hebrews 12 turns to the present moment: "Therefore, since we are surrounded by such a great cloud of witnesses, let us throw off everything that hinders and the sin that so easily entangles. And let us run with perseverance the race marked out for us, fixing our eyes on Jesus, the pioneer and perfecter of faith." (Heb. 12:1-2a NIV) We who continue to live have our leg of the race to run, but we are encouraged and inspired by those who have gone on, that great "cloud of witnesses."

This amazing Nicaraguan doctor, pastor, health care visionary, disaster and development leader, prophetic voice, and peacemaker has gone on. His legacy continues in the organizations he started but most importantly in the people whose lives he shaped. Together we lift up his name: "Gustavo Parajón!" Together we cry out: "Presente!"

Gustavo Parajón in one of his guayaberas.

Epilogue

Two of Gustavo Parajón's grandchildren wrote eloquent poems, one of which was read at one of the memorial services. You, dear reader, have joined us for a long journey in the life of this man. Whether or not you personally knew Gustavo Parajón, you can now feel what is expressed so simply and eloquently in these love poems to a dear grandfather.

My Grandfather

By Scotty Parajón

My grandfather
He was a great man
Who fought for
Peace
Justice
Freedom
And love
He worked with many people
Such as
Jimmy C.
Garth H.
And many more
He sought the good
In every man

He loved
And treated everyone
As brothers,
Sisters,
Sons,
And daughters
And when he spoke
He spoke of how being
Kind
And loving
Was as important as
Anything else
But now he has joined the Lord
And will rest in eternal peace
But he will live on
In our hearts

Las Guayaberas de Mi Abuelito

By Cristina Parajón

Mi abuelito, como muchos conocen,
Le gustaba andar de guayabera.
Y como saben las guayaberas

Pues tienen muchos bolsillos

Y a mi abuelito le encantaban
esos bolsillos en que ponía
tantas cosas agradecidas

De ellas sacaba
Llaves para el carro
Globos para niños
Lapiceros para dibujar
y esos lapiceros multicolor
Un pañuelo para soplar
Cuando tristes, queríamos llorar

Pero creo la razón
Que a mi abuelito

Le gustaban tantos los bolsillos
Era que, en su corazón
Él tenía muchos bolsillos también

Y colocaba a cada persona
En un bolsillo en su corazón

Y por su ejemplo tan amoroso

Le fui a preguntar

Como podría yo
hacer bolsillos en mi corazón.
Leyendo la Biblia—contestó—
Escuchando a Dios,
Tratando de entender a los demás.

Y así nos enseñó
como hacer bolsillos
en el corazón

Y muchos pusieron a mi abuelito
En un bolsillo todo suyo
Y cuando viajó al paraíso
Muy triste nos sentimos
Que ese bolsillo quedó vacío

Pero ahora ya entiendo
Que los bolsillos
Nunca se vacían
Y mi abuelito,
El que me hacía papas en la mañana,
El que me cantó Pio Pio,
El que me enseñó a tener paz,
Y el que me enseñó a hacer bolsillos
Nunca se irá de la guayabera de mi corazón, Jamás.

My Grandpa's Guayaberas

By Cristina Parajón

My grandfather, as many know,
liked to wear guayaberas.
And as you know guayaberas
have many pockets
And my grandpa loved these
pockets in which he put
so many things for which he
was grateful.
From these pockets he would take out
Car keys
Balloons for kids
Pens for drawing
and those multicolored pencils
A handkerchief to use
When sad and we wanted to cry
But I believe the reason
That my grandfather
liked the pockets so much
was that, in his heart
He had a lot of pockets too
And placed each person
In a pocket in his heart

And for his loving example
I went to ask him
How could I
make pockets in my heart.
Reading the Bible—he answered—
Listening to God
Trying to understand others.
And so he taught us
how to make pockets
in the heart

And many put my grandfather
In a pocket all their own
And when he traveled to paradise
We felt very sad
That that pocket was empty
But now I understand
That the pockets are
Never empty
And my grandfather,
The one who made me potatoes in the morning,
The one that sang Pio Pio to me,
The one who taught me to have peace,
And the one who taught me to make pockets
He will never leave the guayabera of my heart, never.

Gustavo sang this lullaby to his grandchildren. At his funeral they sang the lullaby, in turn, to him.

El Arenero

Muy despacito por aquí pasa un arenero que trae un costal.
Saca arena de él y lo echa en los ojitos.
"A dormir niñito/a, a dormir así"
Repite el arenero que pasa por aquí.
"A dormir niñito/a," repite el arenero.
Cierre los ojitos, a dormir así.

The Sandman

So very slowly, a sandman passes by carrying a sack.
He takes out some sand and puts it on the eyes.
"Go to sleep little child, go to sleep like this,"
The sandman repeats as he passes by.
"Go to sleep little child," the sandman repeats.
"Close your little eyes, go to sleep like this."

Acknowledgements

This book has been produced as a work of love by a diverse group of people. Initially the Parajón family and the leaders of CEPAD and AMOS came together to envision the project. Gustavo Parajón had started to write his autobiography or memoirs, but very little had been actually put together by the time he died. CEPAD produced a biography of more limited scope immediately following his death, *Gran Águila*, by Rolando Escobar-Doña. In the years that followed the desire grew among many people for a more thorough work of the doctor's amazing life and ministry.

A team was assembled to work on the project: Dr. Roberto Martinez from AMOS, Dámaris Albuquerque from CEPAD, and Sue Plater from Greenbelt in the United Kingdom. Their work was sometimes augmented by Joan and Marta Parajón and by Dr. Gabriela Woo and Christine Lafferty from AMOS. They asked Daniel Buttry to join the project as author, to which he readily agreed.

As the project continued it became clear that Dámaris was doing much of the heavy lifting in the work at the Nicaragua end. She was planning, doing research, and conducting and translating interviews. Dan asked that she become a co-author because she was already sharing so much of the work. Dámaris agreed, and together she and Dan have become the team within the team doing most of the writing, editing, fact checking, and polishing.

The team is also greatly appreciative of the Parajón family. These family members were interviewed: Joan Parajón, Marta Parajón and Denis Cuéllar, David and Laura Parajón, Rebecca Parajón Clark, Raquel Cuéllar-Parajón, Debbi Cuéllar, Annie Cuéllar-Parajón, and Cristina Shannin Parajón. Furthermore, Joan, Marta,

David, and Laura helped immensely after the first draft of the manuscript was completed. They helped refine much of what was said, added stories and rich details, and from their first-hand experience helped make the story both more accurate and more satisfying. Thanks also to Annie Cuéllar-Parajón for finding tapes of Gustavo Parajón from when he addressed a Chautauqua conference in a series of Bible studies on peace and reconciliation.

So many friends and colleagues of Dr. Parajón gave extensively of their time to be interviewed. These folks added so much color and richness to the book through sharing their experiences with Gustavo and the stories of their shared journeys. We deeply appreciate them all: Jerry and Judy Aaker, Gilbert Andino, Milton Argüello, Carlos Arosman Barahona, David Batstone, Bildad Blandón, Juan de Dios Blandón, Jo Buescher, Bruce Cockburn, Octavio Cortéz, Paul Duke, Carlos and Lilliam Escobar, Blanca Fonseca, Arthur and Marlene Francis, Gabriel Gaitán, Ed Griffin-Nolan, Adalia Ruth Gutiérrez Lee, Armando Gutiérrez, Jim and Ann Hershberger, Garth and Gill Hewitt, Joyce Hollyday, George Jackson, Vernon Jantzi, Paul Jeffrey, Evenor Jerez, Fran Korten, John Paul Lederach, David McLachlan, Carlos Mejía Ruiz, Marion Wyse Metz, Ian Milligan, Cathy Strachan Lindenberg, Carlos Martinez, Roberto Martinez, Ken Medema, Don Mosley, José Norat Rodríguez, Deborah Norton, Juan Carlos Palma, Ketly Pierre, Randy Quintana, Brooklyn Rivera, Carlos Sánchez, Gerald Schlabach, Andy Shogreen, Stan Slade, Jonathan Sledge, Douglas Small, Craig and Rachel Smillie, Tim Spring, Deirdre Strachan, Harry Strachan, Anita Taylor, Tomás Téllez, Róger Velásquez-Valle, Jim Wallis, Mary Weaver, Nancy Wheaton, Martin Wroe, Arthur Wyse, Paul Wyse, Philip Wyse, and Lidya Ruth Zamora.

Some of those interviewed also shared written resources and photos with us. From their love and respect for Dr. Parajón they eagerly contributed more to the project. We give special thanks to Paul Jeffrey and Jo Buescher for sharing years' worth of "CEPAD Reports" with the close-to-the-moment stories.

Some friends helped with additional research. We appreciate Ruth Rosell from Central Baptist Theological Seminary who dug out *Sojourners* magazine articles. Thanks to Doug Small of Scottish Christians for Nicaragua for providing recordings from the Cabaret Nicaragua album produced out of the Greenbelt Festival. Gracias to Tomás Téllez for help with the Baptist Convention of Nicaragua files and sharing many of the historical details. Thanks to Bernice Rogers for her careful research through International Ministries' archives.

Polishing up the manuscript has also been a team effort. We appreciated the help with editing by Sue Plater, Roberto Martínez, Joan Parajón, Marta Parajón, David Parajón, Laura Parajón, and Christine Lafferty.

We brainstormed many titles for the book. One of our favorites was "The Best of What We Are: The Life of Gustavo Parajón." That title comes from the lyrics of

Bruce Cockburn's song, "Nicaragua." We appreciate Bruce's generosity in allowing us to use his words for our title even though we ended up choosing a different title. Bruce's words captured how so many of us feel about Gustavo.

The book publishing business has had to face financial challenges. The business model of a couple decades ago does not work in the current economic context. We discussed a number of options with various publishers, but chose an option where we had to up-front money for publication. We could not have produced this book without the generosity of AMOS Health and Hope and some special donors to AMOS who made the project possible.

Our final partner along the way has been publisher Front Edge Publishing of Read the Spirit. We especially appreciated our first encounter with Co-Founder David Crumm. David helped orient us to the complex publishing issues we would face. He was not just trying to sell his services (or drive us off!). He graciously sought to empower us on the team to make wise decisions for the sake of the book. Director of Production Dmitri Barvinok and copyeditor Celeste Dykas worked on the editing process, coaching us along the way. Marketing Director Susan Stitt has helped us find multiple channels to get out the word about our book. It has been fun and energizing to work with the Read the Spirit folks!

Finally, as Gustavo would have reminded us repeatedly, none of this could have happened without the gracious and sometimes mysterious working of God. More than once we have sensed the moving of the Holy Spirit through our efforts. Gustavo's life was dedicated to God and became fruitful because of how God moved through him to touch so many lives in such a variety of ways. Our prayer is that God will use our work in this book to continue that divine gracious touch through the stories of this man who lived so passionately for his Lord and Savior, Jesus the Christ.

About the Author:
Daniel L. Buttry

Rev. Dr. Daniel L. Buttry recently retired as the Global Consultant for Peace and Justice with International Ministries of the American Baptist Churches. He pastored two churches in the United States and for nine years directed the Peace Program for the ABC. From 2003 to 2020 he served helping Christians around the world to be more effective peacemakers, including in inter-religious conflicts. He has conducted conflict transformation trainings around the world, and in a few situations has been part of mediation teams between armed groups. He has written a number of books on topics such as church renewal, preaching and peacemaking, including *Blessed Are the Peacemakers* and *Peace Warrior: A Memoir from the Front*, and most recently *We Are the Socks*. His wife Sharon Buttry also served with International Ministries as the Global Consultant for Community Transformation. Together they wrote *Daughters of Rizpah: Nonviolence and the Transformation of Trauma*, released in 2020. Dan and Sharon live in Hamtramck, Michigan (Detroit), and have three adult children. For more about Dan and his ministry, visit www.globalpeacewarriors.org.

About the Author:
Dámaris Albuquerque-Espinoza

Dámaris Albuquerque-Espinoza is a Nicaraguan, born into a Baptist family. Trained as a software engineer with studies in Business Administration and Finances, she made her career in the ministries founded by Dr. Gustavo Parajón. At Provadenic, the Vaccination Project of Nicaragua, she worked as a secretary and at CEPAD she worked in various positions. She retired from her last position, Executive Director, in December, 2020.

She served on different boards, both national and international, including as Vice Moderator of the ACT Alliance (Action by Churches Together) in 2014-2018 and President of Prestanic, a Nicaraguan microfinance institution from 2020 to the present.

Dámaris Albuquerque-Espinoza is a member of the Filadelfia Baptist Church in Masaya. She was the wife of Gilberto Aguirre until his death in 2020, is a mother of two and a grandmother of two.

CPSIA information can be obtained
at www.ICGtesting.com
Printed in the USA
BVHW032042200123
656722BV00002B/72